D1356834

MARY CONTINI, together with her husband Philip and daughter Francesca, are the directors of Valvona & Crolla Ltd, Scotland's oldest delicatessen and Italian wine merchant, and one of Europe's original specialist food shops. Founded in 1934, the business grew from humble beginnings, serving the fledgling immigrant Italian community in old Edinburgh and now lists food products and wines from around the world as well as supplying the rest of the UK via a speedy on-line delivery service. In 1996 they opened VinCaffè, a wine bar, restaurant and shop in Edinburgh's city centre, and 2008 saw the start of a joint venture with House of Fraser with openings in the Jenners stores in Edinburgh and Lomond Shores.

The shop has received countless accolades, including over 19 awards for Scottish Wine Merchant of the Year and Italian Wine Specialist of the Year from International Wine Challenge, *Which? Wine Guide* and *Wine Magazine*. *Observer Food Monthly* has described it as one of the top five independent food shops in the UK. The Caffè Bar and VinCaffè have also won numerous awards.

Mary Contini's previous books include *Dear Francesca* (Ebury Press, 2002) and *Dear Olivia* (Canongate Books, 2006), and with Pru Irvine: *Easy Peasy* (Ebury Press, 1999), *Easy Peasy All the Time* (Ebury Press, 2001) and *Easy Peasy Baking* (Ebury Press, 2008).

ORTOSARDA
CARCIOFI SARDEGNA
€ 1,95
CADAUNO

Valvona & Crolla

A year at an Italian table

Mary Contini

EBURY
PRESS

This book is dedicated to all the skilled and enthusiastic colleagues and members of our family who have worked in Valvona & Crolla over the past 75 years, and who helped make it what it is today.

1 3 5 7 9 10 8 6 4 2

Published in 2009 by Ebury Press, an imprint of Ebury Publishing

A Random House Group Company

The Random House Group Limited Reg. No. 954009

Addresses for companies within the Random House Group can be found at
www.randomhouse.co.uk
A CIP catalogue record for this book is available from the British Library

The Random House Group Limited supports The Forest Stewardship Council (FSC), the leading international forest certification organisation. All our titles that are printed on Greenpeace approved FSC certified paper carry the FSC logo. Our paper procurement policy can be found at www.rbooks.co.uk/environment

To buy books by your favourite authors and register for offers visit www.rbooks.co.uk

Photography and design: Vanessa Courtier

Printed and bound in Italy by Graphicom

ISBN 9780091930455

Contents

Recipe notes

Southern-Italian cooking is straightforward and relies heavily on the quality of ingredients. Seasonal and local are second nature to the lucky cooks of the South. To enjoy these dishes at their best build up the flavours with these few guidelines.

• All recipes serve four unless otherwise specified; for example, where a dish may be more likely to be prepared for one person, or where ingredients are a real luxury and so the dish may be prepared as a treat for two.

• All spoon measures are level, unless otherwise specified.

• All vegetables, including garlic and shallots, should be peeled, unless stated otherwise. Garlic is used sparingly in Italian cooking, to give a subtle flavour rather than an overpowering taste. Use seasonal garlic wherever possible.

• Choose fruit and vegetables that are locally grown and harvested in season when you can. I use organic courgettes, carrots, herbs and salads because they have a lower water content than forced varieties, and therefore more flavour. All fresh fruit, salad ingredients and herbs should be washed in cold water before use.

• For best flavour choose cold-pressed extra virgin olive oil for all cooking, except for deep frying where you should use olive oil, sunflower or rapeseed oil.

• All eggs should be large and free range unless stated otherwise.

• Meat and poultry should ideally be free range, ethically reared and locally sourced if possible. Do source fish from a good fishmonger and use it as fresh as possible, preferably within 24 hours of purchase. All fish should be rinsed in cold water and patted dry before use.

• Choose sea salt for seasoning and table salt for boiling pasta or vegetables. I prefer Maldon sea salt. Pepper should always be freshly ground; I use Parameswaran's Special Wynad black pepper.

• Like most southern-Italian cooks, I dry my own supply of '*peperoncini*' (hot red chillies). For the recipes in this book, I suggest you buy whole dried chillies and crush the amount you prefer into your dishes. Use according to your tastes; dishes should have a heat but not be overpoweringly spicy. Mexican or South American chillies have a completely different flavour.

• '*Soffritto*' (an Italian culinary term translated as 'to suffer') refers to the root of many Italian recipes, which is a base of flavour made up of extra virgin olive oil with a combination of some or all of the following: garlic, *peperoncini*, onion, celery, carrot, parsley. Depending on the flavour required the ingredients will be finely chopped, sliced or whole. The simple rule is always they should be slowly cooked in the oil with a gentle heat and never allowed to burn.

• '*Sugo*' is the Italian term for a pasta sauce, often tomato-based.

Open for business

I AM AT MY HAPPIEST when I am cooking for family and friends – a pot of my favourite *sugo* (a tomato sauce for pasta) simmering on the stove, the table set for supper and a bottle of wine open, ready to pour. My kitchen at home is warm and welcoming and my greatest pleasure is preparing food there, the more the better. I have cooked since I was very young – growing up as the third-oldest in an Italian family of eight children I had no option – and I cook from the recipes I have learned from my mother, mother-in-law and my grandmothers.

The dishes I cook follow the traditions, rituals and feasts of the Catholic calendar, and are in turn inextricably linked to the seasons and harvests of the south of Italy and use the natural ingredients it produces. Although strict abstinence such as 'no fish on Friday' has fallen by the wayside, some traditions are so ingrained in my family they may never change. *Baccalà*, salt cod, on Good Friday and roast *abbacchio*, milk-fed lamb, on Easter Day are sacrosanct, as are big family picnics on 15 August, *Ferragosto*, whether it is raining or not. I cook pasta in exactly the same way as when I was young and our favourite dishes have the tastes I remember from my childhood.

At our family shop, Valvona & Crolla, the same seasonality dictates our work. For over four generations we have been supplying goods imported from Italy and sourced from

Scotland from small families who have grown up and developed alongside our company. And to our many customers who have known and loved our shop, it is those very smells of Italian cooking, coffee simmering and ripe cheeses mingling with salty hams and salamis that evoke the feeling of familiarity and trust they associate with Valvona & Crolla.

Things change, of course. Each generation of the family has reacted to circumstances and steered the business through good times and bad, making decisions and taking risks that have taken the company forward and left their mark. The company was started by Alfonso Crolla, my husband's grandfather, an immigrant shepherd from the south of Italy, who in 1934 took a share in a wholesale continental food importer called R. Valvona. Within two years he had moved the business to its present premises, a tall, narrow shop in an unassuming street at the top of Leith Walk in Edinburgh. Not long afterwards Valvona himself opted out of the business. Then, tragically, in 1940, when Italy declared war on Britain, Alfonso and his immigrant compatriots became enemy aliens and he lost his life on the *Arandora Star* as he and countless other Italian immigrants were being transported to Canada.

After the war, Alfonso's sons, Victor and Dominic, took over the running of the business and with their new brother-in-law, Carlo Contini, they built up a thriving trade serving the local Italian community and the returning British soldiers and officers who had experienced the joys of Italy during the war for the first time. The shop became a haven for anyone nostalgic for Italy, or wanting exotic produce and freshly roasted coffee served with a healthy dose of Italian charm.

In the early 1980s when Carlo's son Philip Contini took over the shop, change was afoot in the market. The new, exciting, one-stop supermarkets were starting their journey to food dominance and the survival of small, specialist food shops was under threat. Philip decided to source all our food direct from the producer and, sensing Italy's desire to expand its wine exports beyond domestic shores, moved to supply top-quality Italian wine. Gradually Valvona & Crolla gained a name for sourcing the best of everything it offered its customers. These were exciting times.

When, in 1995, we opened a small Caffè Bar at the back of the shop we were able to share our home cooking with our customers for the first time and prepare for them the recipes that we had learned from our families, handed down through the generations by word of mouth. Our customers loved it!

We still cook fresh food daily in the Caffè Bar, made from the best local and imported ingredients. Today we import fruit and vegetables from Italy, but more and more we find that what we need to have close at hand are the local smallholdings and farms that surround the city of Edinburgh. Fresh meat and fish of excellent quality are abundant in Scotland, and with seasonal produce delivered straight to our door our customers can eat the dishes in the Caffè then buy the fresh ingredients they need to cook them at home.

We have also had the pleasure and privilege of meeting many talented cooks and food writers, wine and cheese producers who have talked about their produce and shared tips and ideas with us, resulting in a whole new collection of recipes which we enjoy both in the Caffè and at home.

There has never been a better time to cook. Fresh local ingredients have never been so widely available; seasonal produce is abundant in farmers' markets and for you, the cook, the producer has never been more accessible. Preparing food from an Italian kitchen can be frugal and healthy or exotic and indulgent – the mood and the choice is yours. All I recommend is that you choose the best ingredients you can find, use fresh, locally grown vegetables and judge using your own palate – taste as you cook. I do hope you enjoy making and sharing these recipes with your own family and friends.

DI SARONNO
AMARETTI
DI SARONNO
PROVVEDITORI
DI SARONNO
SARONNO
DI SARONNO

WINTER

inverno

IT IS WITH great anticipation that my husband Philip and I, with our teenage daughter, board our flight on 1 January, off to join in the continuing New Year celebrations in Rome. Christmas in Italy extends right through to *La Befana* (Epiphany) on 6 January, so when we arrive tired but exhilarated late on New Year's Day, the festivities are still in full swing. How easy to slip into party mode, and where better than Rome? In a lovely old hotel just a stone's throw from the Spanish Steps we unpack our bags. Then, leaving the cares and exhaustion of business behind us, we spill out into the throngs that parade up and down the Via del Corso late into the night.

Rome over New Year is buzzing. Long, narrow streets are decked with sparkling lights and gaudy garlands. Every corner turned reveals more elaborate decorations, more stunning displays. New Year tradition in Rome sees locals opening their windows and throwing out unwanted household articles – old beds, pictures of former lovers, anything. A great commotion ensues; good-natured hilarity pervades the air.

Tiny alleyways strung with garlands of sparkling stars give way to famous piazzas full of jostling and joyous people being entertained by itinerant musicians, mime artists and street theatre. *Strega Nonna*, the grandmother witch who brings gifts to children on the Epiphany, sits menacingly in a sleigh harnessed to moth-eaten, life-sized stuffed reindeer, and cackles to designer-clad children who line up to be terrified and excited in anticipation of gifts and treats.

Piazza Navona is transformed into a fairground, with rides and shows and food stalls piled high with fantastic-looking sweets: *struffoli*, tiny fried dough balls dipped in honey and sprinkled garishly with hundreds and thousands; *torrone*, hard nougat studded with almonds, pistachios and chocolate and piled high like bricks in a builder's yard; glossy slabs of nut brittle; gaudy pink, blue and green candyfloss; Nutella-smeared crêpes; giant toffee apples. Appetising smells fill the air: hot chestnuts roasting over wood-burning braziers and boiling *peri'o'mus*, white wrinkled slabs of tripe, prepared by Neapolitans and eaten in the street with salt and olive oil, just as we would eat fish and chips.

It is as if all of Italy converges on Rome; dialects are heard from all over the land – Sicilian, Neapolitan, Venetian and Florentine. Large family groups, with four and five generations shouting and laughing, are strolling together, eating and singing and celebrating the end of the past year.

And, of course, the Baby Jesus is fêted and celebrated everywhere you turn. Larger than life-sized cribs with a full cast of leading characters are displayed in every available space: churches have cribs inside, outside, on the altar, in the crypt. Halfway up the Spanish Steps a 'little town of Bethlehem' is on view, complete with harassed innkeepers, guilty despots, majestic angels and ox and ass. Windowsills, doorways and shop windows all exhibit something acknowledging the birth of Christ. The most impressive is at 'head office', in Piazza San Pietro, in front of the Vatican, where you'll find the biggest, most magnificent display of all – the crib of cribs.

If we are organised and book ahead, our first meal is enjoyed in Sora Lella, a small family-run *ristorante* on the Isola Tiberina, which is also home to an ancient church, San Bartolomeo, and Rome's main hospital. 'You can't go wrong!' as my father would say. The restaurant is run by two brothers, sons of Elena, the original owner and an exceptional cook who was the youngest sister of a famous Roman film star in the 1950s, the era of *La Dolce Vita*. The taller, thinner brother is the chef-patron, who prepares a traditional Roman menu, typical of our own home cooking: *Gnocchi all'amatriciana, Rigatoni con sugo di coda alla vaccinara, Polpettini alla nonna, Pasta e fagioli*. The second brother acts as maître d' and holds court front of house. Jovial and enthusiastic, he describes each dish with such joy that you can almost taste the flavours as he talks.

Rome has an abundant choice of *trattorie* and restaurants, some wonderful, authentic and full of locals, others tourist traps, expensive and disappointing. They say the best trick in Rome is to follow a priest at lunchtime and you will always eat well. I must admit that we have often put this to the test and have always been lucky. The best *abbacchio* (spring lamb) I have ever eaten has been in an unassuming *trattoria* behind the Vatican, which from noon until well after three is full to bursting with happy, hungry families, almost all of which have one or two priests dining with them. (We once bent this rule and followed two nuns into the basement of a dodgy-looking *trattoria*. Needless to say, it was not a good idea: we had the worst meal of our lives, and so did the poor nuns!)

Beginning our year away from Edinburgh is invigorating and exciting. The combination of familiar tastes and new dishes means we start the year full of ideas and return to work inspired, ready to recreate the joys of Roman eating at home.

Winter minestrone with green vegetables and spelt

minestra di verdure e farro

Farro or spelt is an ancient grain that still crops up at feasts and festivals, most notably 5 December in Monteleone di Spoleto, where they celebrate the feast of San Nicola (Santa Claus) and the parish priest gives *Zuppa di farro* to the poor. High in protein and low in gluten, spelt cooks like good, old-fashioned Scottish barley, and you can easily substitute one for the other.

The richness, flavour and creaminess of the soup can be enhanced by adding a *battuto*, a blend of garlic, dried chilli, parsley and Italian lard, which melts into the soup at the end, helps it thicken and adds a rich, intense flavour. Tuscan *Lardo di Colonnata* is made from the fat under the pig's back and is cured with salt, garlic, peppercorns and spices, slowly air-dried to give a creamy, full-flavoured lard. It is traditionally eaten plain on toasted bruschette, like luxurious bread and butter. If you can't find it, you can use unsmoked pancetta instead. This soup tastes better the next day, so make it in advance if you can.

150 g farro (spelt)
1 large onion
2 sticks celery
1 leek
2 carrots
4 tbsp extra virgin olive oil
1 garlic clove
1 small peperoncino (dried chilli), crushed
large bunch of cavolo nero or curly kale
large bunch of bietola or Swiss chard
1 large potato
2 litres boiling water
sea salt

For the battuto
100 g Lardo di Colonnata
1 garlic clove
1 peperoncino (dried chilli), crushed
bunch of flatleaf parsley, chopped

Cover the farro in plenty of cold water and soak overnight.

Chop all the vegetables into similar-sized cubes. Heat the olive oil in a heavy-based saucepan. Add the garlic and peperoncino and warm through to flavour the oil. Add the onion, celery, leek and carrots and sauté until softened.

Add the greens, potato and the drained farro. Cover with the boiling water, then stir in a teaspoonful of salt. Bring to the boil, then simmer for 30 minutes or so, stirring occasionally as the farro swells and thickens the soup. Add more boiling water if necessary. It is ready when all the vegetables are cooked and the farro is swollen but still has some bite. If possible, set aside for 24 hours at this point as it improves the flavour.

Make the battuto just before serving the soup. Lay the lardo on some greaseproof paper and add the garlic, peperoncino and parsley. Fold the paper over and use a rolling pin to beat everything into a paste.

Reheat the soup and adjust the consistency and seasoning as necessary. Add the battuto and simmer until the lardo has melted and the flavours have combined.

Lentil soup with smoked ham hock

zuppa di lenticchie con prosciutto affumicato

In the food markets of Rome you see piles of pigs' trotters lined up with their toes pointing towards you. They are often blanched, white and anaemic – a bit unappetising. I prefer the smoked ham ends that you see in Scottish butchers' – easily cooked and making a lovely soup and meal in one pot.

1 x 300 g smoked ham hock, soaked in water overnight
250 g Castelluccio or Puy lentils, or 1 x 400 g can brown lentils, drained
4 tbsp extra virgin olive oil, plus extra for drizzling
1 garlic clove, chopped
1 small peperoncino (dried chilli), crushed
1 large Spanish onion, chopped
2 sticks celery, chopped
1 bay leaf
1 sprig rosemary
2 plum tomatoes (from a can)
sea salt and freshly ground black pepper
handful of chopped flatleaf parsley, to finish

Cover the ham hock with cold water and bring to the boil. Simmer for about 1 hour, skimming off any scum that rises to the surface.

Unless the lentils have been hanging around in your cupboard since last year, there is no need to soak them. Just rinse them in a bowl of cold water.

Warm the olive oil in a saucepan. Add the garlic and peperoncino and sauté gently to flavour the oil. Add the onion and celery and cook to soften. Drain the lentils and add to the saucepan along with the herbs. Stir for a few minutes so that they start to absorb some of the flavours.

Add the ham hock and its boiling stock, then stir in the tomatoes. The liquid should be about 5 cm above the lentils, so top up with boiling water if necessary. Simmer on a low heat for about 45 minutes, until the lentils are soft.

Lift the ham hock out of the saucepan and pull the meat from the bone: it should fall off.

Remove the bay leaf and rosemary sprig from the pan. Take about half the lentils and pass them through a mouli or sieve (not a food processor as it makes the soup gluey). Return the puréed lentils and ham to the soup, then warm through.

Check the seasoning and consistency, adding hot stock or water to taste (I like my soup quite thick).

Serve piping hot with a drizzle of extra virgin olive oil, a sprinkling of parsley and plenty of black pepper. Alternatively, if there is a lot of ham, serve it as a main course after the soup with Nonna Caffè's Mashed Potatoes (see page 120).

Chestnuts

Hot-chestnut sellers are a fixture on every street corner in Rome during the winter. The smell is so enticing that we often stop and buy. The best ones come from the older men who stand over their braziers like Michelin chefs, carefully smoothing the shell of each glossy *marron* before scoring it and placing it in just the right spot on the burner to cook it slowly and crack open the shell. Irresistible! Strolling in Rome at night, wrapped up warm against the cold, absorbing the sounds, smells and chaos of New Year and nibbling hot chestnuts. What more could you ask for?

Available from November, chestnuts are classified by size. Choose large, glossy ones as these are most likely to have a single large nut inside rather than two or three smaller ones. Wash them, as they might be grubby, and score with a stubby knife before boiling them for 10 minutes. Roast in a hot oven for another 10 minutes or so, then peel them while still warm so that the inner papery covering comes away easily.

Alternatively, use the excellent French, vacuum-packed, ready-cooked chestnuts that are widely available. For a quick snack, warm them through in a hot oven with a drizzle of olive oil and some salt, then serve them in a paper cone. You can pretend you're in Rome!

Canned cooked chestnuts in water are also very good, while sweetened chestnut purée is excellent for cakes. The cooked chestnuts are sweetened with sugar and pushed through a potato ricer to make a drizzling of chestnut to serve over whipped cream or ice cream.

Cream of chestnut soup with smoked pancetta

zuppa di castagne e pancetta affumicata

This rich festive soup uses smoked pancetta instead of smoked bacon; it has a sweeter, creamier flavour that matches the chestnuts perfectly.

2 tbsp extra virgin olive oil
1 garlic clove
1 small peperoncino (dried chilli)
200 g smoked pancetta, cubed
2 shallots, finely chopped
2 celery sticks, destringed and chopped
400 g vacuum-packed ready-cooked chestnuts
2 potatoes, cubed
1.5 litres boiling water
2 tbsp dry sherry
sea salt and freshly ground black pepper
125 ml double cream (optional)
fresh fennel fronds or flatleaf parsley

Warm the olive oil in a sauté pan and gently cook the garlic and peperoncino for a few minutes to release their flavour. Transfer to a plate.

Add the pancetta to the pan and cook until browned. Set aside 1 tablespoon to finish.

Add the shallots and celery and sauté until soft and translucent.

Add the chestnuts, stirring for a few minutes to coat them in the sautéd vegetables. Transfer a couple to a plate for the finish.

Add the potatoes, boiling water and sherry. Simmer for 20 minutes or so, until the potatoes soften.

Whiz with a hand blender, then pass through a sieve. Return to the pan and bring back to a simmer.

Adjust the consistency with cream or water depending on the thickness required, and season to taste. Serve the soup with a swirl of cream, some of the reserved pancetta and chestnuts, roughly chopped, and a scattering of chopped fennel or parsley.

Millerighe pasta with oxtail sugo

millerighe al sugo di coda alla vaccinara

Philip's big cousin Joe Conetta has taken over the role of *Capo dei Capi* (Boss of Bosses) among the family's third-generation Scottish–Italians. A fiercely competitive businessman, he transformed his father's lucrative fish and chip shops of the 1940s and 1950s into a multimillion-pound restaurant business, Di Maggio's. So successful is he that he retired before he was fifty and lives the life his immigrant forebears only dreamed of. Nevertheless, he is a man with a weakness: his mother, Auntie Phyllis, used to make oxtail sugo every Sunday, but didn't teach her son, Big Cousin Joe, how to cook it. This recipe is a personal gift for the man who has everything!

Oxtail might sound a bit fearsome to cook, but it is simplicity itself. All you need is a good butcher and some time, because it needs a slow, gentle braise. The interesting thing is that while you might expect it to be greasy, chewy or too strongly flavoured, the opposite is true. It is lean, the gelatinous fibres melting down to creaminess, and the meat that falls from the bone is sweet and deliciously flavoured.

Although this recipe makes a large quantity, it freezes perfectly in small batches. If you want to make a smaller amount, just halve the quantities, but it is best cooked in a large batch.

Serves 10

1 oxtail (750 g–1 kg), cut into 5–6 rounds
4 x 425 g cans good Italian tomatoes (Vitale or Cirio)
3–4 tbsp extra virgin olive oil
2 garlic cloves
2 small peperoncini (dried chillies), crushed
2 Spanish onions, finely chopped
2 fresh bay leaves
sea salt and freshly ground black pepper

To serve

80–100 g millerighe or rigatoni (or any chunky ridged pasta) per person
freshly grated Parmigiano Reggiano

Cover the oxtail in cold water and leave for 30 minutes to rinse out any impurities.

Open all the cans of tomatoes and whiz in a liquidiser or with a hand blender.

Heat the oil in a saucepan. Add the garlic and peperoncini and heat through to flavour the oil.

Remove the oxtail from the water and pat dry with kitchen paper. Season well with salt and pepper.

Without overcrowding the saucepan, add a few pieces of oxtail and brown well on each side. Don't let the garlic burn; take it out if it shows signs of doing so. Transfer the oxtail to a warm plate and brown the remaining pieces. Set aside.

Once that is done, add some more olive oil to the pan if there is not enough and cook the onions slowly until they are softened and translucent. That's all the hard work over!

Return the oxtail to the saucepan, add the bay leaves, then pour in the blended tomatoes. Add a good drizzle of olive oil (the oxtail is very lean, so it's needed – Auntie Margaret

would have had about 2 cm of oil on top of the sugo). Add 2 teaspoons of salt, a good grinding of black pepper and stir well.

Place a wooden spoon across the saucepan, balance the lid on it, then simmer slowly, slowly, slowly for 3 hours. The gap around the lid lets some steam escape, but most stays in the pot, allowing the sugo to cook slowly without getting too concentrated.

Once it is cooked, leave the sugo to cool. It is best left for a day to allow the flavours to settle.

When you are ready to eat, reheat the oxtail and sugo until piping hot, about 30 minutes. Check and adjust the seasoning. You can either serve a whole piece of oxtail with the pasta, or take the meat off the bone and return it to the sugo.

Cook the pasta in plenty of salted boiling water until al dente. Drain well and pour into a large warmed serving bowl. Stir in lots of oxtail sugo and serve with plenty of freshly grated Parmigiano Reggiano.

And to drink...

The wine you are most likely to see on our table when I cook this old-fashioned, homely tomato sugo is Montepulciano d'Abruzzo, which comes from the hills south of Rome, where our family originated. The light, fruity wines of this region are plummy and very easy to drink. They suit the pasta perfectly, and as you always have a second portion of *millerighe*, so you can have a second, or third, glass of wine as well. At least, that's what we do!

Tomato and smoked pancetta sugo

sugo all'amatriciana

This sugo is typical of Roman cuisine, seen on nearly every menu in the city, more often than not with *bucattini*, long pasta with a hole down the middle. The recipe comes from the town of Amatrica in L'Aquila, the capital of Abbruzzo, south of Rome. In the hills around Rome there is a strong tradition of producing pecorino (sheep's milk cheese), so use grated pecorino rather than Parmigiano Reggiano, which is cows' milk cheese from the north of Italy. To be fair, grated pecorino is rarely served in Roman restaurants, but do try some – it's exceptional.

The other classic ingredient in this sugo is *guanciale*, cured hog's cheek, which looks like *lardo* with a slash of red flesh through it. This speciality involves rubbing the cheek with salt, black pepper and herbs and slow-curing it for forty days, creating a unique ingredient that melts when warmed, imparting a sweet, evocative flavour, noticeably richer than pancetta. It is unsmoked, so use *pancetta coppata* (rindless unsmoked bacon rolled up with some neck pork) if you can't find *guanciale*.

4–5 tbsp extra virgin olive oil
150 g guanciale or pancetta coppata (see above), thinly sliced
2 small peperoncini (dried chillies), crushed
1 large Spanish onion, finely chopped
2 x 425 g cans good Italian tomatoes (Vitale or Cirio), sieved

To serve
80–100 g buccatini or Home-made Gnocchi (see page 22).

Heat the oil in a heavy-based saucepan. Add the guanciale and allow it to soften rather than brown.

Add the peperoncini and stir to release their heat. Add the onion and cook slowly until it is softened and translucent.

Stir in the sieved tomatoes. Simmer gently, half-covered with a lid, for about 45 minutes. Check the seasoning.

Home-made gnocchi

gnocchi di patate

Packet gnocchi, from brands such as De Cecco, or shop-bought 'fresh' gnocchi are very good kitchen standbys, but if you really want a treat, nothing beats home-made. They are fairly easy to make, and if frozen in layers between sheets of greaseproof paper, can be cooked straight from the freezer and are ready in minutes.

The secret of foolproof gnocchi is to make them often and get a feel for them. You need dry, floury potatoes, such as Desiree, King Edwards or Maris Piper, and a good eye. The weight of plain flour to potato should be about half or less. We use a little self-raising flour as insurance against heavy gnocchi. For the same reason, we add a small egg yolk.

Treat gnocchi like fresh or dried pasta and add salt to the cooking water rather than the dough.

200 g '00' flour, sifted
25 g self-raising flour, sifted
500 g unpeeled floury potatoes
1 small egg yolk

Combine the two flours in a bowl.

Boil the potatoes until easily pierced with a skewer. Drain and set aside to cool a little. As soon as you can hold them, peel off the skin and pass them through a potato ricer or mouli, or mash them well. Don't put them into a blender or food processor as this will make them 'gluey'. Work quickly while they are still warm.

Stir in the egg yolk, then add three-quarters of the flour mix and work lightly into a dough.

Take a small nugget of dough, roll it over the back of a fork, then test it in a small pan of salted boiling water. Gnocchi are cooked when they rise to the surface. If the mixture is too wet, the dough will disintegrate in the water. In this case, simply add some more flour and test the dough again.

Once you are happy with the consistency, work quickly, rolling pieces of the dough into narrow sausage shapes. Cut into pieces 3–4 cm long, then roll each piece over the back of an upturned fork to create slight ridges (these will act to hold the sugo once the gnocchi is cooked).

Lay the gnocchi on a floured sheet of greaseproof paper and use within 4–6 hours. Do not refrigerate. Alternatively, freeze as described on the previous page.

To cook, bring a saucepan of salted water to the boil and slip the gnocchi into it. Once they sink to the bottom, give them a gentle stir and wait until they rise to the top. Cook them for a minute or two, then drain and serve with Tomato and smoked pancetta sugo (see page 21) and plenty of freshly grated Parmigiano Reggiano or Gorgonzola sugo (see page 25).

Or you could try...

Gnocchi verdi: Add a handful of cooked, chopped spinach to the potato mixture. Squeeze all the water out of the spinach, season it well, then cut into shreds large enough to give texture but fine enough to combine well with the dough.

Roasted aubergine gnocchi with butter and sage sauce

gnocchi di melanzane con salsa di salvia e burro

We discovered violet aubergines on our first visit to the Milan markets and now import them from Italy all year round. They are particularly sweet and and juicy, need no soaking or salting before cooking, and roast really well.

These gnocchi cannot be frozen, so they should be cooked the same day you make them. Do not refrigerate as they might go soggy.

2–3 violet aubergines
fresh thyme leaves
extra virgin olive oil
300 g floury potatoes (about 350 g unpeeled weight), such as Desiree, Maris Piper or King Edwards
freshly ground nutmeg
200 g '00' flour, sifted
25 g self-raising flour, sifted
2 tbsp chopped flatleaf parsley
sea salt and freshly ground black pepper

For the sauce
200 g unsalted butter
6–8 fresh sage leaves
freshly grated Parmigiano Reggiano

Pre-heat the oven to 230°C/450°F/Gas mark 8.

Slice the aubergines and cut into cubes. Place in a roasting tray and season with salt and pepper. Sprinkle with the thyme, add a few tablespoons of oil and mix well.

Roast in the oven until softened inside and browned and slightly crispy on the outside. Allow to cool.

Boil the potatoes in unsalted water until easily pierced with a skewer. Drain and set aside to cool.

As soon as you can hold them, peel off the skin and weigh out 300 g. Pass through a potato ricer or mouli, or mash them well. Don't put them into a blender or food processor as this will make them 'gluey'. Work quickly while they are still warm.

Add 150 g of the cooled, cubed aubergine to the potato and mash together. Check the seasoning and add some ground nutmeg to taste.

Again working quickly, add the sifted flours and parsley and mix together lightly to form a dough.

Take a small nugget of dough, roll it over the back of a fork, then test it in a saucepan of boiling salted water. If the mixture is too wet, the dough will disintegrate in the water. In this case, simply add some more flour. If it rises, cook it for 1 or 2 minutes, then taste and adjust the seasoning or texture of the mixture as required.

Once you are happy with the consistency, work quickly, rolling pieces of the dough into narrow sausage shapes. Cut into pieces 3–4 cm long, then roll them over the back of an upturned fork to create slight ridges (these will act to hold the sugo once the gnocchi is cooked). Arrange in a single layer on a sheet of greaseproof paper and leave covered until you want to cook them. Do not refrigerate.

To make the sauce, put the butter and sage in a saucepan, place over a low heat and allow the leaves to release their flavour as the butter melts. Keep warm, but be careful not to burn the butter.

Gently warm the reserved aubergine cubes.

Cook the gnocchi in boiling salted water until they float to the top. Cook for a minute or two, then drain with a slotted spoon as they are delicate.

Pour the butter and sage sugo over the drained gnocchi. Top with the warmed aubergine cubes and serve with plenty of freshly grated Parmigiano Reggiano.

Or you could try...

Butter tomato sugo: Place 2 x 425 g cans sieved or liquidised tomatoes, 250 g unsalted butter, 1 teaspoon sugar and 1 small shallot in a small saucepan. Bring to a gentle boil, then simmer slowly for about 30 minutes, just until the butter splits from the sugo. Discard the shallot, add another knob of butter and season with sea salt. Stir in a good handful of torn basil leaves and serve with the aubergine gnocchi and plenty of freshly grated Parmigiano Reggiano.

Gnocchi with Gorgonzola sauce: Place about 60 g Gorgonzola per person in a small saucepan, add a little cream and warm until combined. Sieve to remove any blue veins, as these can be gritty. Reheat, add some torn basil leaves and pour over the gnocchi. Serve with freshly ground black pepper and plenty of freshly grated Parmigiano Reggiano.

Home-made pasta

pasta all'uovo fatta in casa

When making pasta for a crowd, use one egg per person (three yolks and one whole egg makes pasta for four). I nearly always make the pasta and the sugo the day before so that the worry is taken out of the whole thing.

Home-made egg pasta needs twice as much sugo as dried pasta. We traditionally use meat sugo with it (see page 18 or 21). We prefer our traditional treats to be familiar and nostalgic, like those we remember Nonna cooking for us.

This recipe requires a pasta-cutting machine; we use the Imperia brand. Do read the instructions that accompany your machine and note that it should never be wet or washed – the stainless steel rollers will rust and the machine will be ruined. When I've finished using mine, I wipe it with a dry cloth and use a dry pastry brush to whisk away any flour or dough. I then wrap the whole machine in a clean tea towel, and the attachments, handles and clamp in another. Everything is stored in the original box until the next time.

300 g '00' Italian durum wheat flour
2 large eggs
3 large egg yolks

Place the flour on a clean work surface and make a 'well' in it. Put the eggs and yolks in the middle. Use a fork to whisk the eggs, flicking the flour into them so that it is gradually incorporated. The mixture will naturally become denser and eventually form a ball.

Use your hands to press the dough together, tossing it in any flour that is still not incorporated. Try to let the dough take as much flour as is comfortable to handle; it should be quite stiff, but pliable and not sticky. (This stage can be reached using a food processor with the dough attachment. Add more flour if the dough is sticky.)

Transfer the dough to a clean, floured work surface and begin to knead it with the palm of your hands. Push the dough away from you, constantly folding it over, rotating it 90 degrees, and kneading it again. Keep working until it becomes smooth and elastic, dusting it with a little flour if it's sticky. The more you knead the dough and the more flour you can incorporate, the lighter the pasta will be and the better bite it will have. The dough is ready when you ease it apart and can see a smooth, silky surface with no cracks. Cover it with cling film and leave to rest for 30 minutes.

Divide the dough into 6 pieces. Take one, keeping the others covered with cling film. Attach the pasta machine to a table that is a comfortable height for you to work at. Flatten the dough and pass it through the widest setting of the pasta machine. Fold it equally into three along the narrowest side and pass the folded edge through the rollers again. Continue to roll and fold at the widest setting about 6 times.

At this stage you can start to thin the dough. Reduce the width between the rollers each time so that it becomes thinner and longer. It shouldn't be sticky, but if it is, add a sprinkling of flour. Don't fold the dough any more – just pass it once through each setting.

Take the dough down to the second thinnest setting. When the dough is ready, hang it over a clean stick balanced between two chairs. Repeat until all the dough has been used.

Square ravioli filled with buffalo ricotta and mint

quadretti di ricotta di bufala e menta

I love making fresh ravioli but I seldom have time. I have a sneaky suspicion that your pasta machine, like mine, is tucked away at the back of the cupboard and has been since last year. The trouble is, our hand-made *macheroncini* egg pasta from Campofilone is so good that even my big brother Cesidio – self-appointed judge of all home-made pasta – couldn't tell the difference at Christmas! I used the *chitarra* size, which is cut on a square die and cooks in 2–3 minutes.

The town of Campofilone in Marche, on the Adriatic coast, is now famous worldwide for its beautifully presented pasta. Having said that, if you want to make home-made ravioli or stunning lasagne, you will need to get out that dusty pasta machine and do some hard work. As with gnocchi, you can make these ravioli and freeze them for use at a later date, but they are at their best fresh. Don't be tempted to make ravioli and leave them overnight in the fridge because the moisture from the filling can seep through the pasta dough and ruin all your hard work.

This recipe for giant square ravioli has a filling made from ricotta, mature grated pecorino, coarse black pepper and fresh mint – ideally, Roman mint. Its long narrow leaf has a distinctive flavour, more suitable for savoury cooking than garden mint. In the past I brought plants back from the Rome market, but sadly this is now illegal. Instead, we grow our own from packets obtained from Seeds of Italy, a company that imports all manner of Italian seeds. You can grow them in a window box and add real authenticity to your cooking.

1 quantity Home-made pasta (see page 27)
flour, for dusting
1 egg white, beaten

For the filling
300 g fresh ricotta di bufala or cows' milk ricotta
4 tbsp grated pecorino stagionato
squeeze of lemon juice and grated rind of ½ unwaxed lemon
handful of chopped fresh mint
1 egg yolk
sea salt and freshly ground black pepper

Mix together the filling ingredients and add a generous grinding of black pepper. The pecorino is quite salty, so you might not need to add salt at all.

Divide the pasta dough into 5 pieces and flatten each one with your hand. Using a pasta machine on the second finest setting, roll out the pasta in long strips and lay them on a floured work surface with the long side facing you.

Starting at the left, put a neat tablespoonful of filling about a third of the way up from the bottom of the pasta sheet. Continue placing spoonfuls of the filling along the sheet, spacing them 2 finger-widths apart.

Using a pastry brush, paint some egg white around each mound of filling.

Fold the upper part of the pasta sheet over the filling and use your fingers to seal around each mound, pressing the air out and creating large squares.

Use a ravioli cutter or a knife to cut out each square. The folded edge does not need to be cut.

Cook the ravioli gently in boiling salted water for about 5 minutes, until the filling is cooked through.

Serve with Butter tomato sugo (see page 25).

Or you could try...

Quadretti with butter, lemon and mint sugo: Melt 200 g unsalted Italian butter in a small saucepan. Add the grated rind of 1 lemon, 1 tablespoon lightly toasted and roughly crushed pine nuts, and the torn leaves from a small bunch of fresh mint. Warm through for few minutes to release the flavours. Pour over the quadratti and serve with grated pecorino stagionato.

Quadretti filled with roasted aubergine, ricotta and thyme: Cube 1 large aubergine, place in a roasting tray and sprinkle with extra virgin olive oil, thyme leaves and sea salt. Roast in a hot oven (200ºC/400ºF/Gas mark 6) until it is softened and starting to crisp slightly. Once it has cooled, mix with 200 g ricotta, freshly grated Parmigiano Reggiano and plenty of freshly ground black pepper to taste.

Lobsters

I grew up in Cockenzie and Port Seton, a fortunate pair of fishing villages about 10 miles east of Edinburgh. They had two harbours, two fishing fleets and two Italian fish and chip shops – one belonging to my father, Johnny Di Ciacca, the other to his brother, Alex.

In those days, about forty years ago, the fishing industry was a highly successful one and the fishermen were rich. Our house lay right on the shore, halfway between the two harbours, the Firth of Forth literally at the back wall. On a Tuesday morning we could go down on to the 'rocks' and watch the fleet (twenty-five boats at least) leave the harbour on the tide, going out to sea for three or four days.

At the end of the week the boats would 'come in'. You could hear and smell their approach long before they reached home as the seagulls would be circling madly around them, squawking and screeching as they swooped down into the sea, greedily gulping the fish and guts the fishermen threw overboard as they prepared their catch. There the boats sat, swaying gently in the water, waiting for the tide to fill the harbour and get them home.

In those days the catch was mostly haddock; any odd-looking items, such as monkfish, catfish or squid, were thrown overboard before the boats landed their catch. Lucky seagulls! These days, the locals are cannier, and the market for these exotic items has changed dramatically. The fleet has changed as well; now, thanks to overfishing and quotas, there are barely half a dozen boats in the harbour at Port Seton, and just a couple at Cockenzie. The men now fish daily for prawns and lobsters, catching the precious crustaceans in creels (traditional wicker baskets). The seagulls still do well, but this time swooping over the heads of families wandering around the harbour eating Crolla's fish and chips...

The irony of the Scottish fishing industry has always been that its highly prized harvest has found a better market away from its own shores. The North Sea produces fish of a quality not found anywhere else in the world, yet only now, when it is getting scarce, are the Scots starting to appreciate it.

Langoustines, or prawns as they are called locally, are wonderful. When we were young the fishermen would leave bags of live prawns at the back door of my father's shop, happy to swap them for a jug of ice cream or a fried fish supper when they came out of the pub at closing time. Even better, they would leave a couple of lobsters, blue and angry, claws strapped shut with elastic bands, tails kicking in frustration, the pot awaiting!

Nobody cooks lobsters better than my mother. Born to live the high life, she slightly misjudged the cost of having a big family, so she learned to cook at home all the fantastic things she tasted in fancy restaurants on the few holidays she had abroad. Trouble was, she and Daddy used to go away without us for a 'bit of peace' and that inevitably resulted in another brother or sister. At the final count she had had eight holidays!

Grilled lobster

aragosta alla griglia

If you have small lobsters weighing about 500 g each, try this easy way to prepare them.

40 g unsalted butter
1 garlic clove, finely chopped
2–3 tbsp very finely chopped flatleaf parsley
4 small lobsters (1 per person)

Pre-heat the grill to its highest setting.

Mash together the butter, garlic and parsley.

Wearing an oven glove or holding a thick cloth, grasp a lobster and place it claws-down on a wooden board. With a sharp knife, cut straight into the top of the head between the eyes. The tail will jerk, but the lobster is killed instantly. Using the same knife, cut straight down through the shell, cutting the lobster in half right along its length.

Take off the rubber bands and, using a rolling pin, hit the claws just hard enough to break the shell.

Open out the lobster and rinse in cold water, removing the black vein that runs down its back and any gunge behind the head. Repeat this process with all the lobsters.

Cover each lobster generously with the garlic butter, place in a tray to catch the juices and grill for 10–15 minutes, until the shell turns red and the flesh is cooked.

Serve with a crisp salad and Mayonnaise (see page 73).

Lobster salad

insalata d'aragosta

Choose lobsters weighing about 1–1.5 kg, preferably without the roe attached, and store them in the freezer for half an hour before cooking. The local fishermen boil lobsters the traditional way, by immersing them live in a large pot of boiling, well-salted water and holding the lid down to prevent splashing. If the lobster is well chilled, it is unlikely to react when immersed.

4 lobsters (1 per person)
1 quantity Mayonnaise (see page 73)
squeeze of lemon juice
pinch of cayenne pepper

Prepare a large saucepan of boiling salted water. Immerse 1 lobster at a time, holding the lid down tightly in case the lobster kicks out. A second lobster can be added if it is small, but no more than that. Allow to simmer for 10 minutes per 450 g, plus 5 minutes for each additional 450 g. The shell turns from blue to red during the boiling process. Repeat with the remaining lobsters.

Once cooked, remove the lobsters from the liquid and allow to cool. Don't overcook them, as this makes the delicate tissues tough.

To open the lobster, place it on its back on a chopping board and use a heavy knife to split it lengthways down the middle. Open out the shell and remove the tail flesh. Discard the black intestinal tube that runs down the back. Break off the claws and wrap them in a towel to prevent splashing while you crack them open with a cleaver or rolling pin. The tender meat will slip out easily in one piece. Split the head in half, removing the sack of grit. Keep aside any coral (found in females), the grey, creamy tomalley (liver), and any juices that escape. These can be used to flavour soup or a sauce.

Pile the meat back into the empty shell and place on a plate. Repeat with all the lobsters.

Combine the mayonnaise with a little lemon juice and cayenne pepper and offer alongside the lobsters, which should be served cooled or at room temperature, never straight from the fridge.

Or you could try…

My mother's lobster thermidor: This is based on a simple Béchamel sauce. Melt 50 g unsalted butter in a saucepan and stir in 1 tablespoon plain flour to form a roux. Cook well for a few minutes, stirring to prevent burning. Gradually add equal amounts of milk and the lobster cooking water (about 450 ml in all), a bay leaf, 1 tablespoon flamed brandy and a pinch of paprika. Warm through, stirring constantly and cook it gently to form a thick sauce. Add 4 tablespoons freshly grated Parmigiano Reggiano or good strong Cheddar, such as Montgomery's or Mull. Check the seasoning. Pour the sauce over the prepared lobster meat in the shell, add some more grated cheese and sprinkle with a pinch of cayenne pepper. Place under a pre-heated grill until the sauce is bubbling and browned.

And to drink…

You can't do better than a chilled glass of Bianco di Custoza 'Amedeo', made by Luciano Piona on his estate near the town of Custoza, a few kilometres south east of Lake Garda. The wine is made from Garganega, Fernanda and Trebbiano grapes in the Cavalchina vineyard on the estate. It is an aromatic, richly-textured, nutty wine that will not be overpowered by the richness of the lobster. The name Amedeo comes from Prince Amedeo di Savoia who was wounded in the Cavalchina vineyard in 1866 during the Third War of Italian independence. His wounds were tended there and he continued the battle. There is a plaque at the entrance of the vineyard to commemorate this event. The Amedeo wine has perfect balance and drinkability. The late-harvest Trebbiano grape gives structure, the intensely fruity Garganega grape lends itself to barrel ageing and producing rich texture, while the Fernanda grape gives the wine an aromatic quality.

Chargrilled radicchio di Treviso

radicchio di Treviso alla griglia

A stunningly beautiful vegetable, radicchio di Treviso is one of my winter favourites. This member of the chicory family has garnet-red and white leaves, and their intense bitter flavour creates an intriguing iron aftertaste. The eastern part of Venice specialises in radicchio salads because the vegetable has been cultivated there since ancient times.

I first became addicted in Rome, where, in the early winter months, radicchio di Treviso is often served chargrilled alongside grilled meats, as its bitterness is a perfect accompaniment to the griddled flavours. There are countless varieties of radicchio and chicory grown in Italy, each with different flavours, and all worth trying.

2–3 heads radicchio di Treviso
extra virgin olive oil, for drizzling
sea salt

Pre-heat a ridged griddle pan until very hot.

Remove any damaged outer leaves from the radicchio and rinse the head lightly. Pat dry with kitchen paper.

Cut the radicchio in half lengthways, then cut each half into 4 pieces lengthways. Trim away the white stem at the base.

Flatten each piece of radicchio with the palm of your hand, then place in the hot griddle pan.

After 10 minutes or so the radicchio will start to soften and blacken. Turn it over, sprinkle with some salt and drizzle with a little olive oil. Leave it to sizzle and griddle until it has softened and blackened. Be warned: there is a lot of smoke while this cooks, but it's worth it!

Serve cooled, drizzled with more extra virgin olive oil.

Winter leaf salad

insalata d'inverno

The salad leaves available in winter are robust and bitter, full of vitamins and iron. Make up the salad as you prefer, using all or any combination of the leaves suggested below.

yellow leaves of scarola (frisée)
radicchio di Treviso
Castelfranco lettuce (see page 56)
few wild rocket leaves
fennel, thinly sliced
¼ red onion, very finely sliced and soaked in water to soften the flavour

For the dressing
4–5 tbsp extra virgin olive oil
1–2 tbsp red wine vinegar
sea salt

Place all the leaves plus the fennel and onion in a large bowl.

Mix together all the dressing ingredients, pour over the salad and toss well.

Fennel, radish and Camone tomato salad

insalata di finocchio, ravanello e pomodori di Camone

Sardinian Camone tomatoes are best in winter, when they are slightly green with a crunchy skin. If you can't find them, use Pachino cherry tomatoes, which are also good at this time of year.

1 fennel bulb
1 bunch of radishes
200 g Sardinian Camone tomatoes

For the dressing
4–5 tbsp extra virgin olive oil
squeeze of lemon juice
sprinkling of sea salt

Trim the fennel, setting aside the fronds but discarding the outer tough leaves. Slice the bulb into thin rounds.

Set aside the radish leaves, then slice the radishes into rounds.

Refresh the fennel fronds and radish leaves by soaking them in iced water for 10 minutes. Cut the tomatoes into eighths.

Arrange the fennel, radishes and tomatoes on a platter. Decorate with the fennel fronds and radish leaves. Combine the dressing ingredients and pour over the salad.

Radicchio and robiola salad with walnuts

insalata di radicchio di Treviso

Bitter radicchio is a lovely winter salad leaf and combines beautifully with creamy robiola. This recipe can also be made with scarola (frisée) in the springtime, when the first goats' cheeses, *caprini*, arrive from Italy.

Please note: Walnuts and walnut oil should be kept refrigerated and used within six months of opening. If kept too long, they become rancid and can ruin a dish.

1 head radicchio di Treviso
1 heart of scarola (frisée)
few leaves of fresh coriander, basil, parsley and rocket
1 robiola cheese
seeds from 1 pomegranate
50 g fresh walnuts, lightly crushed

For the dressing
100 ml walnut oil
1 tbsp sherry vinegar
1 tsp sea salt

Place the radicchio and frisée leaves in a bowl with a handful of individual leaves and fronds from the fresh herbs.

Combine the dressing ingredients and mix well. Taste and adjust the seasoning as necessary.

Pour most of the dressing over the leaves and toss well. Divide between 4 plates and crumble some robiola over the top.

Scatter with some pomegranate seeds and crushed walnuts and finish with a drizzle of the remaining dressing.

Or you could try...

Serving the salad warm. Place the radicchio leaves on a hot griddle pan, drizzle with extra virgin olive oil, sprinkle with salt and heat them until they are softened and a little charred. Set aside and keep warm. Place the robiola on the griddle and heat through, charring the surface a little. Divide the charred leaves between 4 plates. Dress the frisée and herbs with most of the dressing, then pile on top of the leaves. Lay the griddled cheese on top and scatter with some pomegranate seeds and walnuts. Finish with a further drizzle of dressing.

Risotto with spicy sausage, fontina and griddled radicchio

risotto con salsicce, fontina e radicchio

In this recipe, fresh Italian pork sausages spiced with chilli, fennel and pepper add flavour to the risotto, which is finished off with stringy, melted fontina cheese from Val d'Aosta and perfectly matched with griddled radicchio.

2 tbsp extra virgin olive oil
large knob unsalted Italian butter
1 Spanish onion, finely chopped
4 spicy fresh Italian pork sausages
300 g Carnaroli risotto rice
1.5 litres hot Chicken Stock (see page 115)
1 head radicchio di Treviso
100 g fontina
grated Parmigiano Reggiano
sea salt and freshly ground black pepper

Warm the oil and butter together in a sauté pan. Add the onion and sauté slowly until soft and transparent.

Skin the sausages and cut them into walnut-sized pieces.

Raise the heat under the sauté pan, add the sausage pieces and sauté until brown.

Add the rice and heat through, stirring to coat it in the oil.

Make sure the chicken stock is well seasoned. Add a ladleful to the pan and stir occasionally as it is absorbed into the rice. Continue adding stock, a ladleful at a time, until all the stock has been used – about 20 minutes.

Meanwhile, griddle the radicchio leaves as described on page 40. This will take about 20 minutes.

Take the risotto off the heat as soon as the rice is al dente. Grate the fontina coarsely and stir it into the risotto.

Chop a quarter of the radicchio and stir it into the risotto.

Serve with freshly grated Parmigiano Reggiano and the remaining griddled radicchio on top.

Flash-cooked slices of beef

tagliata di manzo

At Valvona & Crolla January and February are planning and buying months, with several trips to Italy looking for new products and talking to suppliers. I remember a dismal evening in Milan, wandering the streets with Philip and Francesca, looking for somewhere to eat. Chancing upon a nice place to eat is not easy in a big city. Those places that are bright, steamed up and buzzing are invariably fully booked. The dusty, empty restaurant, with the token customer sitting in the window is a high risk. Dodgiest of all are basement restaurants or those where you have to ring a bell to be let in.

So it was with dismay that, having wandered unsuccessfully for over an hour, we stopped at a small, dull bar, the last open establishment for miles, with a neon sign in the window – *Ristorante sotto*.

Contrary to all our prejudices, down the dingy, narrow staircase we found a warren of bright, jolly rooms full of a buzzing young crowd. The highlight of the evening was the discovery of this recipe, which we now serve in VinCaffè as a signature dish.

400 g Aberdeen Angus fillet
1 garlic clove, finely sliced
1 small piece peperoncino (dried chilli), crushed
3–4 tbsp extra virgin olive oil
sea salt

To serve
handful of caperberries
3–4 tbsp very finely chopped flatleaf parsley
2 lemons, preferably Amalfi, cut into wedges

Put the fillet in the freezer or fridge for 30 minutes to firm up.

Using a very sharp knife, cut the fillet into slices as thin you can manage. Place them between 2 sheets of greaseproof paper and beat with a meat mallet or rolling pin until they have doubled in size.

Pre-heat the oven or grill to its highest setting.

Lay the slices of meat in a single layer on 4 plates. (The meat is cooked on dinner plates and served straight to the table, so use heatproof ones, not your favourite fine china.) Sprinkle with salt, a few slivers of garlic and some peperoncino. Drizzle with oil and leave to marinate for 10 minutes.

Put the plates in the oven or under the grill for 4–5 minutes, or until the plate is piping hot and the meat is heated through while still pink. The meat continues to cook from the heat of the plate, so don't be afraid to leave it rare.

Scatter about 8 caperberries on each plate and sprinkle with the parsley. Serve immediately with wedges of lemon.

Stuffed beef slices in tomato sugo

involtini di manzo con sugo

With this kind of comfort food I serve a plate of greens in the middle of the table and plenty of crusty bread.

2 peperoni rossi (red peppers)
12 thin slices Aberdeen Angus braising steak
1 garlic clove, finely sliced
2 tsp chopped flatleaf parsley
1 tsp thyme leaves
250 g Luganega pork sausage
sea salt and freshly ground black pepper

For the sugo
4–6 tbsp extra virgin olive oil
1 garlic clove, finely chopped
1 small peperoncino (dried chilli), crushed
1 Spanish onion, finely chopped
2 x 425 g cans Italian plum tomatoes, sieved

Prepare the peperoni by searing them over a flame until the skin is blackened and the flesh has softened. Place in a sealed plastic bag for 10 minutes, then peel off the skin. It should come away easily. Slice the flesh into slivers.

Lay the slices of meat on a board. Season well, then scatter with the garlic, parsley and thyme. Add some slivers of peperoni and top each with a sausage. Roll them up and secure with a toothpick or skewer.

To make the sauce, heat the oil in a saucepan. Add the garlic and peperoncino and warm through to release the flavours. Stir in the onion and cook gently until soft and translucent.

Raise the heat under the pan, add the involtini (beef rolls) and sauté until brown.

Add the sieved tomatoes and cook for about 45–60 minutes. Taste and adjust the seasoning as necessary.

Serve the beef with Olive oil potatoes (see page 262) and lots of the tasty sugo poured over it.

The branding of Valvona & Crolla

What I find intriguing about Valvona & Crolla is that it was conceived by two immigrants, Ralph Valvona and Alfonso Crolla, who had arrived in Edinburgh by chance at the turn of the twentieth century from a remote, poverty-stricken farming community high in the mountains of southern Italy. By all accounts they had not been educated, and learnt to read and write only after enlisting in the Italian army during World War I. Yet in 1934 they formed a limited registered company with a brand, a logo and a telegraph address (Chianti 001). Most intriguing is their choice of brand – not a doodle on a napkin or a sketch of their home village, but the image of a *fiasco* – a flask of Chianti – which was in itself by then a universal brand of the most famous export of Italy between the wars.

During World War I all exports from Italy were drastically curtailed, but afterwards, under the regime of Mussolini, exports boomed, not least the wine from Tuscany, the now-famous Chianti.

Which begs the question: how was it that a tiny company in Scotland managed to register as a trademark the Chianti flask that was, and is, the universally recognised image of Italian wine? Was Alfonso Crolla an innocent, seeing something in front of him and choosing it as a symbol of his hopes and aspirations, or was he a genius who realised that the brand had not been registered in the UK and grabbed the chance? Who knows?

I grew up in a house where there was a *fiasco* of Chianti on the table every Sunday, bought, I suspect, by my father from the Valvona & Crolla van that drove around the Italian communities every week. I also know that alongside our rigatoni pasta with Nonna's tomato sugo we were all given a splash of Chianti filled up with Barr's lemonade. Try it, it's delicious and, as I remember, makes you giggle!

VINTAGE 2007
CHIANTI
Established 1934
750 ML
DENOMINAZIONE DI ORIGINE
CONTIENE SOLFITI
IMBOTTIGLIATO DA CANTINE LEONARDO
per DALLE VIGNE

Pan-fried herbed and marinated chicken thighs

pollo in padella

I love Linda Dick...and her chickens. A farmer's wife from the Borders near Peebles, whose son wanted to keep a few chickens, she is now, ten years later, the supplier of the best free-range poultry in Scotland. I kid you not – and I will probably regret telling you this when I call Linda and find she is 'stowed out' with orders and can't drop off the freshly laid duck eggs and wonderful chickens I've grown to rely on.

What makes her chickens such good eating is their pampered lifestyle. Fed on a natural diet, they are straw-bedded and not slaughtered until they are at least 12 weeks old. Consequently, they are big birds – one of them will feed 10 easily – and the carcass makes stock that you can dance on when it is set! As they are dry-plucked and hung for a week before eating, they are wonderfully succulent and tasty – truly as I remember chicken used to taste.

12 chicken thighs, skinned and boned
4 tbsp dry breadcrumbs
lemon wedges, to serve

For the marinade
2 garlic cloves, finely chopped
2 anchovies, finely chopped
2 tbsp grated Parmigiano Reggiano
2 tbsp finely chopped flatleaf parsley
1 tbsp finely chopped mint
grated skin of 1 unwaxed lemon
good squeeze of lemon juice
1 tbsp crushed cumin seeds
4 tbsp breadcrumbs
sea salt
3–4 tbsp extra virgin olive oil, plus extra for drizzling

Mix all the marinade ingredients together in a bowl and rub them into the chicken thighs. Leave to marinate for an hour or so.

When ready to cook, pre-heat a ridged griddle pan until very hot. Pat the marinade into the chicken and roll in the dry breadcrumbs, pressing them onto the thighs to seal them and create a crust.

Add a drizzle of olive oil to the griddle. Place the thighs in it and griddle them on all sides until they form a crust. Add a little more oil if necessary. Serve with wedges of lemon.

Polenta with branzi cheese

polenta la taragna

1.8 litres water
1 tsp sea salt
220 g polenta bramata (coarse-grained)
150 g branzi or fontina cheese, cut into cubes
12 thin slices Lardo di Colonnata (see page 14)

Fill a deep, heavy-based saucepan with the water, add the salt and bring to a rolling boil.

Using a funnel or a sheet of greaseproof paper folded into a cone shape, pour the polenta into the water in a steady stream, stirring with a long wooden spoon in an anti-clockwise direction. As the polenta dissolves and thickens, keep stirring in the same direction to prevent it coagulating or sticking to the bottom of the saucepan. Gradually, like porridge or jam, the polenta will take on a life of its own and bubble and splutter like a volcano. Keep an eye on it; purists would say keep stirring, but hey! The polenta takes about 20 minutes to cook and is ready when it leaves the sides of the saucepan clean.

Reduce the heat and stir in the cheese. When combined, check the seasoning: the cheese is quite salty, so you shouldn't have to add much more salt.

Serve piping hot on a wooden board with the slices of lardo melting on top.

Water, water everywhere

Bergamo Alto is a particularly charming hilltop town northeast of Milan. A cable car carries you up from a sprawling suburb of modern Bergamo and takes you back in time, through thick walls into another, ancient world. Almost completely free of cars, the town is a delight. You can wander aimlessly along the winding cobbled streets flanked by high, secretive walls. (It is in some ways reminiscent of Edinburgh's Old Town, especially when you get off the beaten track and away from the tourist areas.) Bergamo Alto is a town full of priests, nuns and monks; countless church bells toll throughout the day, vying with the echo of the lunch bell that rings out over the valley at noon. What a welcome noise!

The town has an abundant choice of restaurants and *trattorie* for such a small town, offering classic, northern-Italian food and innumerable varieties of polenta, salami, cured meat and rich cheese – not a good place for a vegetarian or anyone watching their weight. This is mountain survival food designed to keep out the cold and store up the fat!

On every menu you will find the town's traditional *polenta taragna*, a steaming hot, sticky polenta, cooked in a copper pan and served on a wooden board with lashings of branzi cheese and, to make matters even worse, thin slices of *lardo* (flavoured lard) melting on top. Even in the middle of winter, restaurant tables spill out into the street, a clever trick to encourage a healthy appetite. Tucking into a huge plate of *polenta taragna* in the cold, while wrapped up well and huddled under outdoor heaters with plenty of Valpolicella Amarone to hand, is an experience I look forward to every year.

If you drive further north, high into the hills of Lombardy, you will see the most glorious alpine terrain, with small dairy farms dotted around. This is cheese country, and the source of some of our most popular soft runny cheeses, such as taleggio, robiola and crescenza. Many are made of milk from just one or two farms – a labour of love in small family dairies that have remained remarkably unchanged over the years.

The other famous export of this region is found almost by accident when driving higher into the mountains. You could be forgiven for not noticing San Pellegrino Terme, which boasts little more than a ski lift, a hotel and a long, low factory, the producer of the most popular sparkling water in the world. Now owned by Nestlé, the factory continues to turn out the familiar bottles, and a lorry departs from it on average every 30 seconds. Bottled water is now frowned upon in some quarters, but health-giving water from the limestone and volcanic rocks of the Bracca ravine was legally registered in 1395 and has been consumed ever since. Even Leonardo da Vinci was a fan. Unlucky for the next town up the hill, which bottles San Bernardino water and is not quite as busy as its clever neighbour!

Pan-roasted quail

quaglie in tegame

If you're feeding big men with big appetites, serve these meaty quail with the rich polenta on page 47 and you'll be friends for life. You will need a wide, shallow pan with a tight-fitting lid.

8 fresh quail (French-farmed birds are best)
butter, for greasing
8 slices Lardo di Colonnata (see page 14) or smoked pancetta
grated rind of 1 lemon
8 fresh sage leaves
2–3 tbsp extra virgin olive oil
200 ml dry white wine
sea salt and freshly ground black pepper

Wash the quail and dry them well with kitchen paper inside and out. Rub them all over with butter and season well.

Stuff each bird with some lardo or pancetta, a few strips of lemon rind and a fresh sage leaf (don't be tempted to use dried sage as it overpowers and is too reminiscent of packet stuffing).

Heat the oil in a wide, shallow pan and brown the quails well on all sides.

Arrange the browned birds in the pan so they are snuggled tightly together. Turn the heat up high and pour the wine over them. Allow to bubble fiercely for a few minutes until the alcohol evaporates. This takes 4–5 minutes, and you can tell by sniffing the vapours: the alcohol will no longer catch the back of your throat. Lower the heat, put the lid on tightly and cook on the hob for about 30–40 minutes.

Serve the quail with Polenta with branzi cheese and Wilted bitter greens (see pages 47 and 145).

Food, flirting and fun

About 30 years ago it became very fashionable to eat wild boar (*cinghiale*). I can't remember where or why it started, but it was long before TV chefs could cause a run on cranberries or EasyJet-set customers wanted to replicate what they'd eaten in foreign parts. I'm talking about the days when any new ingredient caused a great stir and became a major talking point for months.

Wild boar was the 'next big thing', and for a time we sold wild boar anything and everything! Wild boar salami and wild boar sausages hung in abundance above the meat counter. Slabs of wild boar prosciutto gleamed on the counter. Thick glass jars of gnarled, chewy *cinghiale salsiccie* peeping though a creamy blanket of lard were stacked enticingly on the shelves. Pictures of wild boar with menacing tusks appeared on bottles of sugo and even on bottles of wine.

In this frenzy we somehow acquired a wild boar's leg. No one remembers where it came from, or where it went, but this ugly, hairy, spiky limb, with its long, narrow hoof and curled toenails, hung in the rafters of the shop beside the prosciutto and salamis and the giant paella pans and leather wine sacks that had hung there for years. Incongruous and menacing, it looked like some satanic talisman, and although we had offers to buy it, slice it, even exorcise it, no one ever dared go near it.

In those days, before the shop was extended, everybody was squashed up together, on both sides of the counter. Cheeses were weighed on ancient scales and random prices were charged depending on who was serving and how pretty the customer was. Slivers of salami and cheese were handed across to the patient customers while they were talked into buying countless products they had never heard of and didn't want. But they loved it!

right Carlo Contini

Accounts were hurriedly scribbled by hand with a pencil retrieved from the back of an ear. Agitated conversations invariably occurred over the size of a bill, the amount of discount and the quality of the produce. Italian was mixed with dialect, dialect with Morningside accents, Morningside accents with Leith twang. The shop was a mecca for anyone who had a passion for Italy, for cheap drink and for life. And many would say it was also for those with a passion for passion. If any woman came in, beautiful or not, young or old, the men serving behind the counter stopped everything they were doing to give maximum attention to the pretty girl while the long-suffering customers who had queued all morning had to stand patiently by and wait their turn.

And who were the men? Victor Crolla, Philip's uncle, who ran the shop for 40 years after his father, the original Alfonso Crolla, perished during World War II; and Dominic Crolla, Victor's younger brother, a born salesman who could charm anyone in seconds with his kindly smile and generosity. Then there was Wilhelm, the Dutch warehouseman who loaded cases of wines and pallets of pasta from the pavement outside the shop down into the cellar through a hole in the ground. And Carlo, Philip's father, tall, handsome, charming and the most wonderful salesman, who would do anything for his customer, unless it was time for his break or lunch. Then, like clockwork, he would down tools and remove himself from the counter until he was fed and watered and ready to return to work.

Then there were the cousins, Dominic's children, all girls, all beautiful and all single: Bruna and Paola, Marina and Gabby, and the lovely Carla, who vied with Gina Lollobrigida and Sophia Loren in the glamour stakes.

There were also the *tenentes*, the young after-school workers, who, as the foot soldiers of the shop, were employed for a few shillings an hour to run up and down stairs and up and down ladders to get anything that the customers needed. They were trained like army recruits: to 'answer the call', to 'never return empty handed' and to agree with an instruction by shouting out 'Rossini', as if they were calling 'Yes, sir' and saluting to a superior officer. I don't know where 'Rossini' came from, except that Uncle Victor Crolla was obsessed with all things operatic. To this day we use this call, and many new staff just think Rossini is Italian for 'will do'!

Behind the small shop was a narrow staircase that wound down to a basement, and up past a low-ceilinged mezzanine floor packed with spices, herbs and sacks of raw coffee beans all the way up to the flat above the shop. Six-roomed, with high Georgian ceilings, ornate cornices and white marble fireplaces, the flat was the storeroom for thousands of products. To impose order on the chaos, Uncle Victor, an irrepressible eccentric, invented a system to organise the stock. Each room was named after a great composer or author, and each shelf was named after a piece of the great person's work. To Victor it was obvious; to the *tenentes* it was a mystery. Just out of junior school, these poor kids had to learn that when Mr Crolla wanted a case of millerighe pasta they had to go to Shakespeare/Hamlet, or Verdi/Aida. In this organised chaos that was Valvona & Crolla in the 1960s, the shop was real live theatre, and the purchase of, say, some high-roast coffee merely a pleasant sideshow.

With the passing of the older generation and the onset of computers, health and safety and double entry accounting, the ban on smoking, tasting, drinking and everything else pleasurable on earth, things have changed. The wild boar's leg was spirited away one night on the advice of some over-enthusiastic official, who deemed it an 'out-of-date health and safety risk'.

Grilled marinated wild boar loin chops

costate di cinghiale marinate alla griglia

Now that wild boar have been reintroduced to the Highlands, the meat has become readily available. There are some enterprising farmers who produce cuts of *cinghiale*, as well as great-tasting sausages and bacons. To me, wild boar tastes likes excellent pork, full flavoured and sweet. It is especially good when marinated to tenderise it, but free-range pork can be used instead. Serve with *mostarda di frutta*, the delicious Italian candied fruits flavoured with mustard that you see piled high in jars and decorated tins in delicatessens. They are also delicious with cold meats and spicy sausages, and add magic to leftover turkey.

4 wild boar or free-range pork double loin chops
1 garlic clove
2 tbsp fresh rosemary leaves
6 fresh sage leaves
2 unwaxed lemons
3–4 tbsp extra virgin olive oil, plus extra for drizzling
sea salt and freshly ground black pepper

Trim most excess fat from the chops, leaving just a little to help keep them moist while cooking. Lay the chops between 2 sheets of greaseproof paper and beat with a meat mallet or rolling pin to flatten and tenderise them.

Place the garlic, herbs, the juice of 1 lemon and oil in a pestle and mortar or small blender and pound or whiz to a paste. Rub the paste all over the chops, then cover and refrigerate for a few hours or overnight. Remove the chops from the fridge 30 minutes before cooking.

Pre-heat a ridged griddle pan until very hot.

Place the chops on the griddle and cook for about 10 minutes, turning and moving them over the heat so that they slightly char but do not burn.

Drizzle with extra virgin olive oil and a squeeze of the remaining lemon. Serve with Roasted winter vegetables (see page 61) and some mostarda di frutta.

Castelfranco lettuce griddled with taleggio and pancetta

lattuga Castelfranco con taleggio e pancetta

Castelfranco comes high on the list of famous salad leaf producers, vying with Treviso for the crown. Castelfranco lettuce is actually a type of radicchio, but has a more open head than radicchio di Treviso, so is always referred to as 'lettuce'. Its beautiful cream-coloured leaves speckled with red have a slightly bitter taste. As well as being used in salads, it is robust enough to be stuffed and griddled. If you can't find Castelfranco, use a round Dutch radicchio instead.

200 g taleggio cheese, sliced
2 large Comice pears, cored and quartered
1 head Castelfranco lettuce
8 slices unsmoked pancetta
extra virgin olive oil
sea salt and freshly ground black pepper

Heat a griddle until medium hot.

Place a slice of taleggio on a pear quarter and wrap in 2 or 3 leaves of the lettuce. Season with salt and pepper, then wrap in pancetta.

Drizzle the parcels with oil and place on the griddle until the pancetta is cooked, the lettuce is charred and the cheese inside has melted.

Serve with grilled meats – absolutely delicious!

Purple sprouting broccoli

broccoletti

500 g purple sprouting broccoli
4–5 tbsp extra virgin olive oil
1 garlic clove
1 small piece peperoncino (dried chilli), crushed
squeeze of lemon juice

Cook the broccoli in boiling salted water until al dente. Drain and refresh in cold water to maintain its bright green colour.

Heat the oil in a frying pan, add the garlic and chilli and fry briefly to lightly flavour the oil.

Add the broccoli and toss in the oil to warm through. Serve at room temperature, adding a squeeze of lemon juice at the last minute (if added earlier, the broccoli will discolour).

Oven-baked chops

costate al forno

Cooking chops in the oven is easy and failsafe: we prepare lamb, veal, pork or wild boar chops in this way. Don't trim off all the fat – it melts during cooking, preventing the meat from drying out in the oven.

4 wild boar or free-range pork or lamb loin chops
2 eggs
4 tbsp plain flour
2–3 tbsp dried breadcrumbs
extra virgin olive oil, for drizzling
sea salt and freshly ground black pepper

Pre-heat the oven to 180°C/350°F/Gas mark 4.

Prepare the chops as described in the previous recipe, but leave a little more fat on them. Season with salt and pepper.

Beat the eggs and season well.

Put the flour on one plate and the breadcrumbs on another.

Line a large baking dish with foil, leaving enough hanging over the sides to eventually enclose the contents. Drizzle some oil in it.

Dip the chops first in the flour, then in the eggs and finally in the breadcrumbs, pressing them down so that they are well coated.

Lay them in a single layer in the baking dish and drizzle with a little more oil. Enclose them in the foil and bake for 25 minutes.

Open the foil, carefully loosen the chops, then turn them over. Return to the oven and bake with the foil open for another 5 minutes or so to allow the chops to brown and become all crisp.

Serve with Roasted winter vegetables or Wilted bitter greens (see page 61 or 145).

Salt cod with chickpeas and potatoes

baccalà con ceci e patate

Salting is an old method of preserving food, which renders it dry and hard. As a result, it must be soaked in several changes of cold water to make it suitable for cooking. The soaking needs to be started about two days in advance. If you prefer, this recipe can also be made with fresh white fish, such as cod, haddock or gurnard.

500 g salt cod
200 g dried chickpeas or 1 x 425 g can chickpeas, rinsed
1 sprig rosemary
1 sprig thyme
2 garlic cloves
extra virgin olive oil, for drizzling and frying
6 floury potatoes, such as Desiree, Maris Piper or King Edwards
1 small piece peperoncino (dried chilli), crushed
handful of flatleaf parsley, very finely chopped
sea salt and freshly grated black pepper

Soak the cod in cold water for 48 hours, changing the water at least 3 times.

Soak the dried chickpeas in cold water overnight. Drain and rinse well.

If using dried chickpeas, place the soaked chickpeas in a saucepan, cover with cold water and bring to the boil. Skim off any scum that rises to the surface, then add the rosemary and thyme, 1 clove of garlic and a splash of oil. Cover and simmer gently for 40 minutes, then season with salt. Continue simmering for a further 20 minutes, or until cooked. The time depends on how old the chickpeas are. (To be honest, canned chickpeas are almost as good and save a lot of time.) Drain, reserving some of the cooking liquid, and set aside.

Boil the potatoes until just cooked, then cut into large bite-sized pieces.

Rinse the salt cod and flake it into pieces, taking care to remove all the bones.

Heat 4–5 tablespoons of the oil in a wide frying pan. Chop the remaining garlic clove and add to the pan with the peperoncino. Allow them to warm in the oil and infuse it. Add the cod and brown it lightly on both sides.

Stir in the chickpeas (cooked or canned) and potatoes, turning them gently in the oil, then add 2 tablespoons of the chickpea liquid to keep the dish moist. Cook for about 15 minutes, until the cod is cooked and the potatoes and chickpeas are heated through and flavoured.

Serve warm with a final drizzle of olive oil, some freshly grated black pepper and a good sprinkling of the parsley.

Roasted winter vegetables

verdure d'inverno al forno

There is a misconception that in Scotland we have no vegetables in the winter except turnips, cabbage and kale. I am glad to say that, thanks to trail-blazing organic farmers and the recent phenomenon of farmers' markets, we now produce an amazing selection of vegetables and greens. Even better is that we can cook them in far more interesting ways than previously; the old habit of boiling everything to death and serving it with a redeeming blob of margarine is long gone.

So what do we have to choose from? Beetroot, parsnips, carrots, turnips, squash and pumpkin, kale, spinach, red cabbage, black cabbage, leeks, broccoli, purple sprouting broccoli and chard. Our Scottish farmers also grow a vast selection of potatoes, including Charlottes, Edwards, pink fir and old varieties, inspired by growers such as Carroll's Heritage Potatoes, who produce more than seventeen varieties.

To add to the choice, Scotland has woody winter herbs – rosemary, thyme, bay and sage – and boasts the most northerly producer of garlic in the British Isles: the Really Garlicky Company.

6 beetroot
3 parsnips
1 large fennel bulb
1 head radicchio di Treviso
2 red onions
1 head garlic
1 sprig rosemary
1 sprig thyme
extra virgin olive oil
splash of balsamic vinegar
sea salt

Pre-heat the oven to 230°C/450°F/Gas mark 8.

Cut the beetroot and parsnips into walnut-sized chunks. Boil in salted water for about 10 minutes, then drain well. Scatter them over the base of a roasting tray.

Cut the fennel lengthways into quarters. Remove the core and trim the stalk just a little.

Prepare the radicchio in the same way as the fennel. Cut the onions into eighths.

Add the fennel, onion and garlic to the roasting tray and drizzle generously with olive oil. Season well and roast for 20 minutes.

Stir the contents of the tray, add the radicchio and the herbs and stir again. Pour in a generous splash of the vinegar and cook for a further 15 minutes or so, until everything is crispy and caramelised.

Broccoli with spicy sausage

broccoli con salsiccia piccante

I defy any person who doesn't like greens to resist this delicious combination! If you don't want a sausage that's too spicy, try the Luganega, which are generally quite mild.

500 g broccoli, cime di rape (turnip greens) or curly kale
2–3 tbsp extra virgin olive oil
1 garlic clove, finely chopped
1 small piece peperoncino (dried chilli), crushed
300 g spicy Italian sausage, such as our paesano piccante, or Luganega, chopped

Trim the broccoli. (The Italian cooks I work with do this very carefully, taking each floret from the stalk and trimming them all to the same length.) Cut the turnip greens and kale into strips.

Cook in boiling salted water until al dente, then drain and refresh in cold water. Set aside.

Heat the oil a large frying pan. Add the garlic and peperoncino and fry for a minute to release the flavours.

Add the sausage and cook for 10 minutes or so, until heated through. Stir in the broccoli or greens and cook for a further 5 minutes.

Serve with grilled meats, or on bruschette as a snack.

Or you could try...

Turning this recipe into a sugo for use with pasta. Simply add an additional 2–3 tablespoons extra virgin olive oil at the beginning, and cook all the ingredients as described. Cook 300–400 g spaghettini per person until at dente, then toss in the sugo, adding a few tablespoons of the cooking water. Toss everything together for a tasty pasta meal.

Roasted garlic

aglio al forno

Garlic is especially good roasted around chicken or lamb, as it enhances rather than overrides the flavour it accompanies. We roast it whole in the oven and serve it with bruschette.

1 head garlic per person
extra virgin olive oil
griddled bruschette, to serve (see page 173)

Pre-heat the oven to 180°C/350°F/Gas mark 4.

Trim the top from the garlic bulb and rub it with oil. Wrap the bottom half in foil, place in a roasting tray and roast in the oven until soft inside, about 15–20 minutes.

Squeeze the softened garlic out of each clove and spread on the bruschette, or cut the bruschette into 'soldiers' and dip them into the softened garlic cloves.

Mixed greens with garlic

verdure all'aglio

The combination of greens and garlic is very common in southern Italy, particularly on pizza. From summer through to winter it is combined with fresh fennel-flavoured pork sausage to make *pizza con friarille e salsiccie*. However, Italians eat greens with every meal in the winter, just as salad is eaten every day in the summer. They can be boiled in salted water, then served warm dressed with extra virgin olive oil and lemon juice, or sautéd, as described below.

500 g broccoli, spinach, kale or cavolo nero (black cabbage)
2–3 tbsp extra virgin olive oil
1 garlic clove, chopped
1 small piece peperoncino (dried chilli), crushed

Prepare the greens or broccoli as described on page 63. Cook in boiling salted water until al dente, then drain and refresh in cold water.

Heat the oil in a large frying pan. Add the garlic and peperoncino and fry for a minute to release the flavours.

Add the greens and turn in the oil until heated through.

Sea kale with grated pecorino

cavolo marino con pecorino

Sea kale or winter asparagus grows wild on the shingle beaches of northern Europe. It is grown commercially by Sandy Patullo (see page 116) in Aberdeenshire, the shoots blanched white to keep them tender and delicate. The perfect accompaniment is pecorino romano cheese. Aged for 5–8 months, it is slightly salty and gives the delicate sea kale a rich, creamy flavour.

200 g sea kale
20 g unsalted Italian butter
pecorino romano
freshly ground black pepper

Cook the sea kale in boiling salted water until al dente. Meanwhile, melt the butter and keep warm.

Drain the kale and toss it in the melted butter. Shave pecorino romano over it and season with black pepper. Eat at room temperature.

Neapolitan-style frisée

scarola alla napoletana

Scarola (frisée) is a favourite in Italian households. I use the yellow inner leaves for salads or in soups. The green outer leaves, which have a distinctive bitter flavour, are best boiled and then sautéd in olive oil, garlic and peperoncino (as in the Mixed greens with garlic recipe, page 64), or given a Neapolitan twist, as here.

I use Taggiasche olives in this recipe as I like their flavour but you can use the type you prefer.

1 large head scarola (frisée)
6–7 tbsp extra virgin olive oil
2 garlic cloves, each cut into 3 pieces
1 small piece peperoncino (dried chilli), crushed
3 anchovies in olive oil
2 tbsp roasted pine nuts
8–10 pitted black olives

Detach the green outer leaves from the scarola and weigh out about 750 g. Boil them in salted water for about 10 minutes, then drain.

Heat the oil in a wide frying pan. Add the garlic and peperoncino and fry for a minute to release the flavours. Stir in the anchovies until they have melted into the oil.

Add the drained greens, stirring well to coat them in the oil. Mix in the pine nuts and olives, just enough to add texture, and serve warm.

Pizza stuffed with frisée, anchovies, olives and pine nuts

pizza farcita di scarola, acciughe, olive e pinoli

We first met Antonio Carluccio when he was filming our family for the BBC *Good Food* show. It was 1993 and the fortieth wedding anniversary of my in-laws, Carlo and Olive. Antonio, together with his wife Priscilla and about ten BBC crew members, descended on us and we had a wonderful time cooking, eating, drinking and arguing about food for three days. He loved our cooking and we loved his!

We were filming at the front counter, talking about cheese, when our cook, Pina Trano, innocently stretched over to put a plate of *scarola*-stuffed pizza out for sale. In the middle of filming, and feeling completely at home, Antonio stretched out and took a slice of the oily, steaming hot pizza. He was in heaven. '*Magnifico*!' he declared. He very kindly still mentions it to this day whenever we meet him. So, Antonio, for you, here is Pina's recipe!

700 g '00' flour, plus extra for rolling out
2 sachets instant yeast
420 ml hand-hot water

For the stuffing
1 head scarola (frisée)
4–5 anchovies in oil
handful of pitted black olives, preferably Taggiasche
handful of lightly toasted pine nuts
3–4 tbsp extra virgin olive oil

First make the pizza dough. Place the dry ingredients in a bowl, make a well in the centre and gradually add the water, mixing by hand until a dough forms. Knead for 20 minutes or so then cover and leave in a warm place until it has doubled in volume.

While the dough is proving, prepare the scarola as described on page 63.

Pre-heat the oven to 230°C/450°F/Gas mark 8.

Divide the dough in two, place one piece on a floured work surface and roll into a rectangle as thin as you can manage.

Lightly oil a baking sheet. Place the rolled dough on it, pulling it with your fingers to stretch it out.

Place the cooked scarola on top, spreading it out evenly. Roll out the second piece of dough on a floured work surface and use to cover the greens. Press around the edges with your fingers to seal the scarola inside. (This is pizza rustica, so don't worry about it looking too tidy.)

Drizzle a little oil over the 'parcel' and bake in the top of the oven for about 10 minutes, until the surface is crisp and brown. Turn it over and bake until the other side has browned too.

Slice and serve warm, or wrap up and serve as part of a winter picnic.

Gratin of fennel with Parmigiano Reggiano

finocchio gratinato al Parmigiano Reggiano

This recipe needs top-quality stock, so don't be tempted to use a stock cube. If you don't have good stock to hand, use plain water instead.

4 large fennel bulbs
400 ml Chicken stock (see page 115)
150 ml double cream
Parmigiano Reggiano
2 tbsp fresh breadcrumbs
sea salt and freshly ground black pepper

Pre-heat the oven 200°C/400°F/Gas mark 6.

Trim the fennel, discarding the fibrous outer leaves, and cut into quarters. Remove the tough core at the bottom.

Heat the stock, add the fennel and simmer until almost cooked. It should absorb all the stock: a little water can be added if necessary.

Grease an ovenproof dish large enough to hold the fennel in a single layer. Place the fennel in it, then add the cream and a generous grating of Parmigiano Reggiano. Toss well and check the seasoning.

Sprinkle the breadcrumbs and some more grated Parmigiano Reggiano on top and bake for 20–25 minutes, until sizzling hot and browned.

Carciofi

The first artichokes (*carciofi*) usually arrive in January; anything imported before then is too expensive. Funnily enough, raw artichokes don't sell very well; they are still treated with suspicion by most people. Of course, they are a lot of work to prepare, but if you get used to it, they are worth the effort.

In Rome, though, people don't have to prepare them at home. In all the markets old *nonnas* sit and prepare artichokes, tossing them into buckets and basins of water acidulated with lemons so that lucky housewives can buy them ready to use. I use the word 'housewives' with reservation. In Italy, like many other countries, there are fewer women than previously who spend their time at home doing domestic chores. In the markets it is mostly older people, sometimes grandparents with grandchildren, who are buying, seldom stay-at-home mothers with young children.

ORTOSA
CARCIOFI
SARDEGNA
€ 1,95
CADAUNO

Stuffed artichokes

carciofi farciti

1 unwaxed lemon, cut in half
6 large artichokes
8 tbsp water
8 tbsp extra virgin olive oil

For the stuffing
8 tbsp fresh breadcrumbs
2–3 tbsp grated pecorino romano
2 tbsp roasted pine nuts
1 tbsp raisins
2 anchovies, finely chopped
1 garlic clove, finely chopped
2 tbsp chopped flatleaf parsley
sea salt and freshly ground black pepper

Fill a bowl with cold water and add the juice of half the lemon. Also add the squeezed lemon half to the bowl.

Holding an artichoke under running water, work your way around its base, breaking off the outer leaves to reveal the pale, edible core. Trim off the stalk. After trimming the stalk you can peel a few centimetres of it as this is still good to eat. Rub the cut surfaces with the remaining half of lemon to stop the artichoke discolouring then place in the bowl of acidulated water until ready to cook.

Cut off the spiky top of the artichoke, then bang that end of it on a work surface. Open out the heart and use a sharp knife or the handle of a spoon to scrape out the tough, inedible choke. (Don't be afraid to trim the artichokes well. There is no joy in eating them if you keep having to spit out inedible bits.)

Place all the stuffing ingredients in a bowl and mix them together. Taste and adjust the seasoning.

Fill each artichoke with stuffing, then place in a saucepan that allows them to sit upright nestled together.

Add the water and oil to the saucepan, then bring to the boil. Cover tightly and simmer for about 30 minutes, until the artichokes are tender when pierced with a skewer.

Serve warm, pouring some of the cooking liquid over them.

Fried artichokes and green sauce with walnuts

carciofi fritti con salsa verde ai noci

Here is an easy way to enjoy artichokes: just dip them in flour and pan-fry. In some restaurants in Italy fried artichokes are often served in heated linen serviettes to keep them hot and crispy. Alternatively, you can simply eat them quickly! Batons of zucchini or aubergines can be used instead of artichokes, but sometimes I make a mixture of all three.

1 unwaxed lemon, cut in half
8–10 young artichokes
extra virgin olive oil, for frying
seasoned flour
sea salt and freshly ground black pepper

For the sauce
4 tbsp flatleaf parsley
handful of fresh basil
handful of fresh mint
2 garlic cloves
3 tbsp chopped walnuts
2 anchovies in olive oil
2 tbsp salted capers, soaked for 30 minutes before use
extra virgin olive oil
1 unwaxed lemon

Prepare the artichokes in acidulated water, as described on page 70.

Cut the artichokes lengthwise into eighths and trim away any coarse spike at the core. Set aside in the acidulated water.

Roughly blend all but the last two sauce ingredients in a food processor. Add enough olive oil to make a loose paste. Season and adjust the acidity with freshly squeezed lemon juice. Sprinkle with the rind of half a lemon to add some zing. Set aside until needed.

Pour olive oil into a shallow frying pan to a depth of 3–4 cm and place over the heat.

Dry the artichoke pieces well and dip in the seasoned flour, shaking them in a colander to get rid of any excess.

Fry in a single layer in the hot oil, turning from time to time to prevent them burning. Drain on kitchen paper and season with salt. Serve piping hot with the green sauce.

Or you could try...

Jerusalem artichokes in place of globe artichokes. Peel and par-cook in boiling salted water, just to soften a little. Dry well and dust in seasoned flour. Fry in hot oil, as described above, but increase the heat towards the end so that they become nice and crisp.

Frittata with grated courgettes, mozzarella and basil

frittata con zucchini, mozzarella e basilico

2 tbsp extra virgin olive oil
knob of unsalted butter
2 shallots, finely chopped
2 zucchini (courgettes), coarsely grated
1 mozzarella di bufala
6 eggs, beaten
handful of flatleaf parsley, chopped
handful of basil leaves, torn
sea salt and freshly ground black pepper

Heat the oil and butter in a 15-cm frying pan and cook the shallots until softened. Add the zucchini and cook until crispy.

Meanwhile, drain the mozzarella and tear it into small pieces. Add to the eggs together with the parsley and basil.

Season the zucchini with salt and pepper. Pour the egg mixture over the zucchini and raise the heat a little. Cover the pan and cook for about 5 minutes, or until the eggs are nearly set. Place a large plate over the frittata and flip it over. Cook for another 5 minutes. Serve warm.

Frittata with pecorino

frittata al pecorino

Every morning when our kitchens open our cooks make a 24-egg frittata. We then put slices of it into fresh *pistolles*, soft white rolls. Served warm, these are the perfect way to start the day.

6 eggs
4 tbsp freshly grated pecorino romano
4 tbsp chopped flatleaf parsley
2 tbsp extra virgin olive oil
sea salt and freshly ground black pepper

Beat the eggs. Add the remaining ingredients and season well.

Heat the oil in a 15-cm frying pan. When hot, add the egg mixture, cover with a lid and cook for about 15 minutes.

Place a large plate over the frittata and flip it over. Cook the other side until it is brown and all the egg has solidified. Serve warm and do not refrigerate.

Sauté potatoes and Jerusalem artichokes

sauté di patate e topinambur

5 floury potatoes, such as Desiree, Maris Piper or King Edwards
10 Jerusalem artichokes
2–3 tbsp extra virgin olive oil or a mild oil, such as rapeseed or groundnut
sea salt and freshly ground black pepper

Cut the potatoes in half and peel the artichokes. Cook them together in boiling salted water until just easily pierced with a skewer. Allow to cool, then slice into 2-cm rounds. Season well with salt and pepper.

Heat the oil in a shallow frying pan. Gently fry the potatoes and artichokes in a single layer until they are browned on both sides. Drain on kitchen paper and keep warm while you cook the rest.

Mayonnaise

maionese

It is easier to make mayonnaise if the ingredients are at room temperature and the bowl is warm.

2 egg yolks
1 tsp French/Dijon mustard
300 ml extra virgin olive oil
1 tsp lemon juice
1 tbsp white wine vinegar
sea salt and freshly ground black pepper

Whisk the egg yolks, mustard and a pinch of salt in a bowl, then add half? the oil, drop by drop, whisking constantly.

Add the lemon juice and keep whisking to make an emulsion. As the mixture starts to thicken, add steady drizzles of the remaining oil, whisking all the time, and alternating them with teaspoons of the vinegar.

Season to taste.

Or you could try…

Green mayonnaise, which goes very well with fried vegetables as it has been pepped up with pungent flavours. Using a pestle and mortar, pound 2 anchovies, in oil, together with 1 teaspoon lemon juice. Drain and chop 2 teaspoons salted capers (soak them for 30 minutes before use). Stir into the anchovy paste, then fold into 1 quantity of the mayonnaise, along with 1 tablespoon very finely chopped parsley.

Blood orange salad

insalata di aranci di Tarocco

The arrival of Tarocco oranges from Sicily towards the end of January is always welcome. Grown on the slopes of Mount Etna, these intensely sweet 'blood' oranges are full of vitamin C, containing more than any other variety. Given the lack of sunshine in Britain, it's easy to understand why we love them so much. We serve them juiced in the morning for breakfast, and also in cakes and salads. Another variety of blood orange, grown in the same region, is the Moro. It is so 'bloody' that it is almost black inside. Its flavour is more unusual, tasting almost of raspberries.

6 blood oranges
3–4 tbsp extra virgin olive oil, preferably Sicilian
1 tsp balsamic vinegar
sea salt
1 head Castelfranco or cos lettuce
18 pitted black olives

Peel and slice the oranges, removing all the pith and seeds.

Mix the oil, vinegar and a sprinkling of salt in a large bowl. Add the lettuce leaves, olives and orange slices, toss well and serve.

Oranges and lemons

arance e limoni

This is a typical Sicilian combination using winter fruits.

6–8 blood oranges
1 Amalfi lemon
1 pomegranate
1 tbsp pistachio nuts, crushed
caster sugar
few fresh mint leaves

Peel and slice all but one of the oranges, removing all the pith and seeds.

Wash the lemon and slice it very finely.

Remove the seeds from the pomegranate, collecting any juices.

Lay the oranges on 4 plates with a few slices of lemon interspersed. Scatter the pomegranate seeds and pistachio nuts over them. Sprinkle with a little sugar, the pomegranate juice and the juice of the remaining orange. Serve chilled, scattered with torn mint leaves.

Like port, sherry and Madeira, Marsala is a fortified wine, and to a large degree owes its popularity to the English. In the 1770s a sherry and Madeira trader, John Woodhouse, landed in Sicily and quickly realised that the local wine from the town of Marsala was similar to the fortified wines he was already trading. As his current stocks were always in demand by the navy (to encourage sailors at war), he decided to increase productivity and set up an export business.

Marsala ranges from bone dry to intensely sweet, and is used in desserts such as Zabaglione, in savoury cooking, in dishes such as Chicken liver pâté (see page 102) and as an aperitif. Our favourite is '*Terre Arse*' (translated as 'stony ground'), a matured, fruity but dry, and intensely concentrated drink, delicious served at both room temperature or chilled.

Orange cake with Marsala mascarpone

torta di arancia con mascarpone al marsala

At Valvona & Crolla we are always asked for cakes that are gluten-free or dairy-free. This recipe, adapted from Claudia Roden and Nigella Lawson, is perfect. We make it with Tarocco oranges and serve it with Marsala-flavoured mascarpone to intensify the Sicilian sensation.

oil, for greasing
6 Tarocco (blood) oranges or Seville oranges
6 large eggs
250 g caster sugar
150 g ground almonds
100 g polenta
1 heaped tsp baking powder

For the mascarpone cream
200 g mascarpone
100 g double cream
1 tbsp caster sugar
2 tbsp Marsala
grated rind of 1 orange

Pre-heat the oven to 190°C/375°F/Gas mark 5. Oil a 21-cm spring-form cake tin and line it with baking parchment or greaseproof paper.

Place 4 of the oranges (about 400 g) in a large saucepan, cover with cold water and bring to the boil. Simmer for 1 hour or so, until they are softened. Drain and set aside to cool.

Cut the cooled oranges in half horizontally and discard the pips. Place the fruit in a food processor and whiz to a pulp.

Beat the eggs and sugar until light and fluffy. Fold in the almonds, polenta and baking powder. Gently mix in the orange pulp.

Cut the uncooked oranges into very thin slices. Use to line the bottom of the prepared tin.

Pour in the egg mixture and bake for about 1 hour. Cover with greaseproof paper if it browns before it is cooked through.

Remove from the oven and allow to cool in the tin before turning it out.

Gently whisk the mascarpone and cream together. Add the sugar, Marsala and orange rind and whisk again. Serve with the cooled cake.

Burnt orange brûlée

crème brûlée all'arancia

There is something both enticing and evocative about the smell of slightly burnt orange toffee, perhaps a memory of January kitchens with marmalade on the go and outside fairs selling toffee apples. Whatever the reason, it is comforting and encouraging in the depressing days of February – maybe the only month of the year when we all deserve to eat anything we fancy as our spirits yearn for light, sunshine and warmth.

300 ml double cream
200 ml full-fat milk
100 ml orange juice
2 tsp orange flower water
¼ tsp pure vanilla extract
5 egg yolks
75 g caster sugar

For the brûlée
6 heaped tsp demerara sugar
finely grated zest of 1 orange

For the decoration
1 orange, finely sliced
demerara sugar, to sprinkle
icing sugar, to dust

Pre-heat the oven to 150°C/300°F/Gas mark 2. Place 6 x 10-cm ramekins (or 7 x 8-cm ones) in a roasting tin.

Put the cream, milk, orange juice, orange flower water and vanilla extract in a saucepan and gently bring almost to the boil. (I can smell the vanilla!)

In a heatproof bowl, beat the egg yolks and sugar together until light and fluffy. Gently pour in the hot cream mixture, stirring all the time. (It must not be boiling or it will scramble the eggs.)

Pour the mixture into the ramekins. Place the tray on the middle shelf of the oven and fill it halfway up the dishes with boiling water. Bake for about 40 minutes, until the mixture is set but wobbles slightly. Set aside to cool.

Pre-heat the grill until it is very hot. Sprinkle the top of each ramekin with the demerara sugar and orange zest, spreading it evenly. Place under the grill until the sugar is bubbling, and remove just as it starts to smell burnt, no later.

Place the orange slices on a baking sheet with a sprinkling of demerara sugar and brûlée them under the grill. Remove as soon as they start to smell burnt. Allow to cool.

Decorate each crème brûlée with a slice of burnt orange and a dusting of icing sugar.

Ricotta

Sometimes we get deliveries of fresh buffalo milk ricotta. It is really a special treat, arriving on our refrigerated lorry from Italy, beautifully packaged in small parcels of white wet paper, soft and creamy inside. It is very rich in flavour and lightly textured – at its best the day it arrives, which is three days after it was made. Ideally, it should be eaten fresh with pears or just on crusty sourdough bread.

About twenty-five years ago, when Uncle Victor Crolla was about seventy years old and preparing himself for retirement after a lifetime of working behind the counter, he decided that we should make our own ricotta. This was in the days when the shop was only a quarter of its present size, and we had no kitchen or back shop. This didn't deter Uncle Victor.

Every morning the pot of milk went on to the gas, and once it came to the boil, the rennet was added and everyone's breath was held until the milk curdled and the curds floated to the top. Uncle Victor was in his element, running up and down the shop with straw baskets dripping grey, sticky whey on the ground as he searched for a place where the ricotta could be left to set. Today, as you can imagine, Mr McCall, our Health and Safety Officer, would throw a fit at such goings-on! In those days life was much better fun.

These days we get wonderful home-made ricotta from a special farm set in the hills of Dumfries. The Loch Arthur Creamery is a working community, part of the Camphill Village Trust, providing community and work for adults with learning disabilities. Barry Graham and his family provide wonderful support for the community, as well as running the farm, a creamery and a shop. They make Loch Arthur Cheddar and Criffel (unpasteurised cows' milk cheese), as well as exquisite light ricotta that is better even than Uncle Victor's.

Lemon ricotta cake

torta di ricotta al limone

125 g melted butter
10 digestive biscuits, crushed
55 g ground hazelnuts

For the filling
675 g ricotta
225 ml mascarpone
200 g caster sugar
5 eggs, separated
55 g candied peel
2–3 drops pure vanilla extract
juice and finely grated rind of 1 unwaxed lemon

For the topping
4 tbsp lemon curd
4 tbsp mascarpone
caster sugar, to taste

Grease a 30-cm spring-form cake tin.

Mix the butter, biscuits and hazelnuts together, then press this mixture into the base of the prepared tin. Line with a piece of cling film, place a plate on top and weigh it down with a can of beans. Transfer to the fridge to solidify, preferably overnight.

Pre-heat the oven to 180°C/350°F/Gas mark 4.

Place the ricotta, mascarpone, sugar and egg yolks in a large bowl. Beat them together using an electric mixer or a balloon whisk.

Whisk the egg whites in a separate bowl and fold them into the mixture. Fold in the candied peel and lemon zest, then add the vanilla extract to taste.

Spoon the mixture into the biscuit base and bake for 40–50 minutes. Remove from the oven and allow to cool.

Meanwhile, whisk together the topping ingredients and chill until needed.

Serve the cheesecake with the lemon curd topping either spread on top or handed around separately.

LA COSTIERA
LA COSTIERA

Chestnut semifreddo with burnt orange syrup

semifreddo di castagne con sciroppo di arancia

Meaning 'half-frozen', *semifreddo* is like a frozen mousse. It's also miraculously easy, as you can make it at home without any faffing about with an ice-cream maker. Having been raised above an ice-cream factory, I am fussy about my ices, but this one is a cracker!

3 large eggs, separated
85 g caster sugar
225 g mascarpone
225 ml double cream, lightly whipped
225 g chestnut purée, from a vacuum pack
3 or 4 marrons glacés, roughly chopped
2 tbsp lemon juice
2 tbsp Marsala

For the syrup
115 g caster sugar
270 ml orange juice
130 ml lemon juice

Line a 1-kg loaf tin or 1-litre pudding bowl with 2 layers of cling film, leaving a few centimetres hanging over the sides.

Whisk the egg yolks with the caster sugar until light and fluffy. Whisk the mascarpone with the cream, then add the egg yolk mixture. Mix in the chestnut purée, marrons glacés, lemon juice and Marsala.

In a separate bowl, whisk the egg whites, then fold them into the chestnut mixture. Pour into the prepared loaf tin or pudding bowl and freeze for 6–8 hours.

Meanwhile, make the syrup. Place the caster sugar in a saucepan and heat until it starts to turn dark brown and smell slightly burnt.

Carefully add the orange juice and lemon juice: the mixture will spit, so don't get burnt. Simmer slowly until the sugar has dissolved. Set aside to cool.

Tip the semifreddo out of the dish and use a knife dipped in boiling water to cut it into slices. Serve with the syrup poured over.

Persimmon sorbet

sorbetto di cachi

The persimmons that arrive in January are, at their best, gorgeous baubles of orange deliciousness. They grow in hilly areas all over Italy, and the winter sunlight makes them look like gaudy Christmas decorations. For a stunning-looking dessert, persimmons can be opened out like water-lilies and filled with sorbet. In this case the flesh should be loosened first.

450 g pulp from about 600 g ripe persimmons
100 g sugar
8 tbsp orange juice

Open the persimmons and scoop out the pulp, collecting all the juices. Weigh to make up to 450 g. Place in a blender with the sugar and orange juice and whiz to make a smooth paste.

Pour the mixture in an ice-cream maker and follow the manufacturer's instructions. Alternatively, place in the freezer and whisk a few times at half-hourly intervals to break up the ice crystals. Return to the freezer until firm. Before serving, allow the sorbet to sit at room temperature for 15 minutes. Eat within a week or so to enjoy the fresh flavour.

Pomegranate sorbet

sorbetto di melagrana

You can buy really good-quality pomegranate juice to use in this sorbet. Or, if you have a juicer, you can squeeze the juice from the seeds of 5–6 pomegranates. The sorbet tastes delicious inside an opened-out persimmon, but the flesh must be loosened first for ease of eating.

1.5 litres pomegranate juice
3 tbsp granulated sugar
1 tbsp lemon juice

Mix all the ingredients until the sugar has dissolved.

Pour the mixture into an ice-cream maker and follow the manufacturer's instructions. Alternatively, place in the freezer and whisk a few times at half-hourly intervals to break up the ice crystals. Return to the freezer until firm. Before serving, allow the sorbet to sit at room temperature for 15 minutes. Eat within a week or so to enjoy the fresh flavour.

SPRING

primavera

SPRING IN ITALY is a joy! Not so much 'green shoots', more an explosion of gorgeousness, with invigorating light, abundant bursting of buds and heavenly scented flowers creating a general spilling out into nature. Coats are discarded, shirts are unbuttoned and skirts are shortened. Life is exciting!

It is not as overtly sexy in Edinburgh: we don't realise how short the days have been or how little light we have enjoyed until the clocks change. However, a palpable lifting of spirits and energy levels is still felt as the glorious days of spring arrive. At last we wake after the dawn instead of before it, and get home from work with time to go out for a walk rather than huddle indoors against the dark outside.

The customers are happier too. Worries and niggles give way to frivolity and flirting again. The need for comfort food and sugar begins to subside, replaced by an appetite for fresh and less calorific dishes. The lighter days and milder weather produce the first crops of spring salads and vegetables, and the local suppliers and growers seem to come out of hibernation as they make their first deliveries.

Even the animals get frisky. We look forward to fresh cheeses made from goat and sheep milk, first from Italy and then, about 4–6 weeks later, from our Scottish farms. Then comes the first spring lamb and the first wild salmon.

Young salads are full of vitamins, serotonin and health-giving properties. As spring approaches, it's a good idea to start your meal with a light salad dressed in extra virgin olive oil and lemon juice. The effect is to calm the appetite and adjust the palate to eating less. Choose from fresh and wild young salad leaves, organic if possible.

I keep several salad heads in the bottom drawer of the fridge and mix and match as I see fit. Little Gem, romaine, cos and frisée are all lovely and will last at least a week in the fridge. Watercress, land cress and pea shoots are all widely available.

Herbs, such as chives, mint, coriander, chervil, tarragon and parsley, can be added to salads for bite and interest, but use sparingly as the flavours can be strong. This also applies to the spiky, narrow-leaved wild rocket, which is particularly spicy and peppery. Use it as a herb rather than a salad leaf so that it doesn't overpower the delicate flavours of other leaves.

It's become rather fashionable to pick your own wild herbs, but if you do so, pick only small leaves from plants that have not yet flowered. (Viviene Weise's little paperback called *Cooking with Weeds*, published by Prospect Books, 2007, is a perfect pocket companion on a country walk.) Young nettle leaves, sorrel and tips of dandelion leaves are all delicious. Wild garlic, which is prolific near Scottish riverbanks, is another good pick: the leaves are good in soups or with roasted fish.

Add volume and texture to salads with fresh peas, pea pods, asparagus tips and young broad beans. White-tipped radishes are beautifully peppery and crunchy, and when sliced into a salad add colour and bite. Use the leaves as well – they taste similar to rocket.

If at all possible, choose organic produce, but be aware that naturally grown and unsprayed salads may contain 'wildlife'. I wash leaves in a clean sink of salted water, allowing any unwanted species to float to the top where they can be easily removed. Excess water can be removed in a salad spinner, or by dabbing the leaves with a clean tea towel or kitchen paper.

Spring vegetables with bagna cauda

verdure miste con bagna cauda

Nothing is more appealing than a pile of young spring vegetables. Farmers' markets and allotments are the best picking grounds. Here they are served with *bagna cauda*, literally 'hot bath', but in this case a warm garlic and anchovy dressing, which is typical of Piemonte in the northeastern corner of Italy. Also typical is that it contains butter and is offered in a small terracotta pot heated by a candle underneath. (You can find something similar in camping shops.) The sauce simmers gently, filling the air with the enticing aroma of garlic. However, it's not for the faint-hearted. You might want to offer some parsley alongside it to temper the after-effects.

Various spring vegetables, cut into finger-sized pieces:
small carrots, tops still attached
central celery sticks, pale leaves still attached
narrow sprue asparagus fronds
inner leaves of Belgian endive
ruby red radishes, stalks still attached
fennel heart, fronds still attached
red radicchio fronds
handful of young pea pods

For the bagna cauda
200 g unsalted Italian butter
200 ml extra virgin olive oil, preferably Ligurian
3–4 new-season garlic cloves, crushed
4 salted anchovies, rinsed, boned and chopped

Arrange the vegetables on a serving platter.

Heat the butter and oil in a frying pan. Add the garlic and anchovies and simmer together, stirring with a wooden spoon to melt them into the oil.

Transfer the sauce to a dish that can be placed over a flame or on a warming plate – it must be kept warm.

Dip the vegetables into the sauce and eat with plenty of crusty bread.

Spring leaf salad

insalata di primavera

large handfuls of salad leaves, such as Little Gem and young cos
handful of fresh pea shoots
small handful of wild rocket
20 leaves of flatleaf parsley
20 leaves of coriander
small handful of asparagus tips
small handful of fresh peas

For the dressing
sea salt
6–8 tbsp extra virgin olive oil
2 tsp freshly squeezed lemon juice

Place all the salad ingredients in a large salad bowl.

Whisk together the dressing ingredients, pour over the salad and toss well.

Bitter salad

insalata amara

Using bitter leaves gives a more robust salad, so it needs a robust dressing to go with it, like the one given below, which includes garlic and anchovies. I like to use wild garlic cloves, which resemble tiny pearls encased in gauze – a fiddle to prepare, but worth the effort. The dressing is also wonderful on *puntarelle*, the bitter, crunchy chicory from Rome, and drizzled on grilled peperoni rossi (red peppers) topped with some capers, pitted black olives and chopped flatleaf parsley.

large handfuls of Belgian endive, chicory, young rainbow chard, young spinach leaves and radicchio
handful of fresh watercress
small handful of tips of young dandelion leaves
6 wild garlic fronds, shredded
handful of flatleaf parsley leaves

For the dressing
4 salted anchovies
8 wild garlic cloves or 1 ordinary garlic clove
sea salt
6 tbsp extra virgin olive oil
2 tbsp red wine vinegar
1 tbsp finely chopped flatleaf parsley

Place all the salad ingredients in a large bowl.

Rinse the anchovies and remove the bones. Place the fish in a pestle, add the garlic and a sprinkling of salt, and use the mortar to pound to a paste.

Mix in the olive oil, vinegar and parsley. Taste and adjust the seasoning.

Pour the dressing over the salad leaves and toss well. Serve with plenty of crusty bread.

Warm French bean salad

insalata di fagioli verdi

400 g French beans
3–4 tbsp extra virgin olive oil
2 tsp balsamic condimento (see page 275), or 1 tsp red wine vinegar
2 garlic cloves, chopped
3 tbsp flatleaf parsley

Top and tail the beans and cook in boiling salted water until tender but still crisp. Refresh in cold water.

Heat the oil in a saucepan and toss the beans in it, warming them through. Transfer to a serving plate. Drizzle with the balsamico condimento or red wine vinegar and sprinkle with the garlic and parsley.

And to drink...

Our favourite drink in the spring is Pinot Grigio Specogna, which goes beautifully with all the light seasonal dishes. Its pink colour is reminiscent of an East Lothian sunset.

Specogna is the family name of a wine estate in Friuli, northeast Italy. On the E55 motorway from Venice to Vienna, bear right at Udine, head for Rocca Bernarda and you have arrived. Our first introduction to the wine of this estate was at VinItaly four years ago. Specogna had a stand at the fair and we tasted this Pinot Grigio for the first time. It was pink! Not bright pink but a gentle, almost faded rose pink. The nose was stunning – it flew out of the glass, not unlike a Sauvignon – all grassy and gooseberry. The flavour was deep and intense, quite unlike any Pinot Grigio we had tasted before.

This is not a modern concoction but a wine-making tradition that reflects the true quality of the Pinot Grigio grape. If you think about it, if Pinot Noir is black and Pinot Bianco is white, Pinot Gris must be somewhere in between. The Specogna estate, following tradition, produces a *ramato* (copper) Pinot Grigio from grapes that are allowed to stay on the vine long enough to change from green to a pretty shade of coppery pink. Giving the wine a bit of skin contact during fermentation means that it takes on that pinkness, and also acquires a distinctive, elegant and full-bodied flavour.

We shipped some of this wine to Valvona & Crolla via our friend David Gleave, its UK agent. It was an immediate hit – and still is. We simply cannot get enough of this wine. Signor Specogna has customers all over the world and every merchant gets a share. Our allocation arrives in June and we sell out by January, longing for June to come again. The rule is that when you see it on the shelf, buy it!

O IL FORN
LI FRANCA
SPECIALITÀ GRISS
TIRATI A MANC
MONC
60448
Break
PIZZA AL TAGLIO

The art of living

Italians love life. And to live well, you need to eat well. '*Cosa ai mangiato*?' ('What have you eaten?') is the most common discussion. Sounds like a good philosophy!

Breakfast is no-nonsense – an espresso or cappuccino and brioche, usually eaten quickly, standing at the local bar on the way to work or school. Lunch is sacrosanct – an hour, maybe two, eaten at a table, not at a desk. Dinner is late, often after nine, either simply cooked at home or enjoyed in a local caffé or restaurant, hardly ever eaten alone. Italians love to eat in groups; the later in the week, the bigger the groups, the more they enjoy eating!

A regular part of this busy culinary day is time for an after-work aperitif, to relax and wind down. With that, perhaps, will be a light snack before dinner. *Cichetti*, anything you can eat with your fingers, or *stuzzichini*, items you can spear with *stuzzicadenti* (toothpicks) are the usual choice. These include mixed olives, sun-dried tomatoes stuffed with mozzarella, tiny hot peppers filled with tuna paste, cubes of grilled polenta spread with Gorgonzola, and thin slices of bread, *sfilatini*, topped with smooth liver pâté. All cheap and tasty, these are shared with friends in the local *enoteca* (wine bar). This is the highlight of the day, with much kissing and hugging and bonhomie.

In fact, life in Italy has always been like this. In the ancient ruins at Ostia Antica, just outside Rome, are the remains of a 2000-year-old *enoteca*. The main bar fronted directly on to the street so that passers-by could easily stop for a drink and encourage others to join them. Just like my *nonna* used to say, 'A queue makes a queue. Keep your shop front narrow and make them spill out into the street.' The 'them' were her customers!

The Hosteria della Chiucchiolino, founded in Ferrara in 1453, is recorded as the oldest trading *enoteca*. The fact that its name translates as 'The Drunkard' is a joke rather than a slur on the locals. Although Italians drink alcohol regularly from an early age, there is no culture of drunkenness or binge drinking.

When in Florence, you might stumble across the smallest *enoteca* in Italy, which is literally a hole in the wall. The small counter has to be cleared and lifted to allow the single member of staff to squeeze in and serve. The 'kitchen' is just a slicing machine and a sink, and the choice of alcohol is a local red or white wine, or a few aperitifs. What more does the passing customer need?

In Venice it is just the same, except perhaps they don't wait until evening to enjoy socialising. Groups of stylishly dressed workers spill out of various bars along the canals, enjoying the current fashion for *una coppa di Prosecco e cichetti* (a glass of bubbly and some nibbles). Prosecco, everyday sparkling wine from northeastern Italy, is only 10 per cent proof, so is light, easy drinking. It ranges from almost dry to relatively sweet, from slightly fizzy to fully sparkling. The best comes from around the town of Conegliano, north of Verona. Many people in the UK have adopted it as their fizz of choice because it is lighter in price and in alcohol than champagne. Nigella Lawson calls it 'Prozaco', and I get her meaning. It is a natural pick-me-up, better than countless cups of coffee.

Potato croquettes

crocchette di patate

Italians are very fond of these croquettes. You can make them with leftover mashed potatoes, but I never seem to have any, so I always make them specially.

4–5 medium-sized floury potatoes, such as Maris Piper or Kerr Pink
knob of unsalted butter
2 tbsp freshly grated Parmigiano Reggiano
1 egg, beaten
freshly ground nutmeg
plain flour, for dusting
sunflower oil or extra virgin olive oil, for frying
sea salt and freshly grated black pepper

For the coating
4–5 tbsp seasoned plain flour
2 eggs, seasoned and beaten
4–5 tbsp fresh breadcrumbs

Boil the potatoes in salted water. Drain well and mash with the butter. Stir in the Parmigiano Reggiano and the beaten egg. Season well with salt and pepper and a good grating of nutmeg. Cool in the fridge.

Dust your hands in flour, then pick up a tablespoonful of potato and roll into a small sausage shape. Repeat with the remaining potato.

Place the coating ingredients on 3 separate plates. Roll the potato sausages first in the flour, then in the egg and finally in the breadcrumbs. Chill in the fridge for 30 minutes to set the coating.

Heat some oil in a shallow frying pan, enough to fill it about a quarter full. When hot, gently fry the croquettes until browned and cooked through.

Or you could try...

Varying the flavour of these croquettes, as with the arancini on page 97. Just stir the chopped flavourings into the potato after you have mashed it. Always check the seasoning of the mixture before you roll and fry the croquettes.

Deep-fried courgette chips

zucchini fritti

Managing the temperature of the oil is the key to achieving a crisp result with these delicious chips, but they must also be eaten quickly because they lose their crunch as they cool. Organic zucchini are best for this recipe because they have not been pumped full of water in order to make them grow quickly. The drier flesh cooks more crisply, which is just what you want. Some Venetian restaurants serve them beautifully wrapped in a warm, white linen serviette to keep them hot. Classy or what!

3–4 large organic zucchini
seasoned plain flour
sunflower oil or extra virgin olive oil, for frying
sea salt and freshly ground black pepper

Cut the zucchini into long strips 2–3 mm thick. Lay them on kitchen paper for a few minutes to get rid of any excess water, then cut into sticks or chips of whatever size you want.

Put the seasoned flour into a plastic bag. Add a small batch of zucchini chips and shake to coat. Empty the bag into a colander placed over a tray and shake to get rid of the excess flour. Repeat with the remaining zucchini just before you want to fry them.

Heat some oil in a frying pan, enough to fill it about a quarter full. When hot, test the temperature with a little piece of zucchini: it should sizzle straight away.

Fry the zucchini in handful-sized batches until nice and crisp. Drain on kitchen paper, season with salt and serve immediately.

Deep-fried rice balls

arancini di riso

These little balls of rice stuffed with mozzarella are often made with leftover risotto. We serve large ones as a starter with salad, and make walnut-sized ones to serve as *cichetti*.

250 g Arborio rice
2 tbsp extra virgin olive oil
knob of butter
300 ml hot Chicken stock or Fresh vegetable stock (see page 115 or 109)
100 g Parmigiano Reggiano, grated
1 tbsp finely chopped flatleaf parsley
2 eggs, beaten
sunflower oil or extra virgin olive oil, for frying
sea salt and freshly ground black pepper

For the stuffing
125 g mozzarella di bufala, cut into 2–3 cm cubes
4–5 tbsp seasoned plain flour
2 eggs, seasoned and beaten
4–5 tbsp breadcrumbs

Cook the rice simply in salted water.

Heat the oil and butter in a saucepan, add the rice and turn it in the oil to coat it.

Add the hot stock 100 ml at a time and stir occasionally as the rice absorbs it and plumps up. While it is still al dente, remove it from the heat and stir in the Parmigiano Reggiano, parsley and beaten eggs. Check the seasoning.

Spread the rice on to a baking sheet and allow to cool. (Remember, rice must be cooled quickly and then refrigerated as soon as possible because it can harbour bacteria.) When the rice is cold, put the stuffing ingredients on to 4 separate plates.

Dust your hands with flour and pick up a walnut-sized portion of cold rice. Make an indentation with your thumb and push in a cube of mozzarella. Roll it into a small ball, and dip it first into the flour, then into the egg and finally into the breadcrumbs. Repeat with the remaining rice, placing the finished balls on a tray.

Place in the fridge to firm up for at least 30 minutes, or up to 24 hours.

Heat some oil in a shallow frying pan, enough to fill it about a quarter full. When hot, fry the rice balls in batches, keeping a lively heat so that they brown nicely and are cooked right through. Drain on kitchen paper and sprinkle with salt.

The rice balls are best served warm, while the mozzarella is still hot and gooey – delicious!

CREMONA
(ITALY)

Baked stuffed mussels

cozze gratinate

Do you remember when Shirley Conran proclaimed, 'Life's too short to stuff a mushroom'? It was 1975, the year *Superwoman* was published – a rallying cry to all women to free themselves from the kitchen sink and get out to work. What a daft idea! Now we work all day so we can pay other people to raise our children. We buy frozen meals and drive half an hour to buy ready-made mashed potatoes from out-of-town supermarkets. Life's certainly too short to live like that! If you're going to stuff anything, try these mussels.

2 kg (approx. 30) large mussels
extra virgin olive oil, for drizzling

For the stuffing
2 tbsp fresh breadcrumbs
2 garlic cloves, finely chopped
2 tbsp flatleaf parsley
grated zest of 1 unwaxed lemon
sea salt and freshly ground black pepper

Pre-heat the oven 180°C/350°F/Gas mark 4.

Clean and de-beard the mussels, discarding any that are broken or stay open when tapped. Place in a heavy saucepan with a tight-fitting lid and heat for 3–4 minutes, until they are just open. Discard any that remain closed.

Mix the stuffing ingredients together and check the seasoning, remembering that mussels are naturally salty.

Remove the mussels from their shells. Break the shells in half and fill the biggest of them with two or three mussels. Cover with a teaspoon or so of stuffing.

Place the stuffed mussels on a baking sheet and drizzle each one with some extra virgin olive oil. Bake for 10 minutes until piping hot and crispy on top.

Or you could try...

Cape sante gratinate (Grilled scallops): The stuffing used above with the mussels can also be used with scallops. We use hand-dived Queenie scallops from the west coast of Scotland. They are about 7 cm wide and the flesh is sweet and tender to eat. Rinse the scallops and prise open the shell. Take off the top half and loosen the scallop. Cover with the stuffing mixture, drizzle with extra virgin olive oil and bake or grill for 10 minutes.

LVONA & CROLLA

In the Caffè Bar we sometimes serve bite-sized morsels of main dishes and starters as *cichetti* (appetisers) or *assaggini* (tastes). A similar idea to Spanish tapas, they are served on skewers, with a toothpick, or in a small terracotta dish so that they can be shared and eaten with ease, and lots of flavours can be tasted.

This idea can be tried at home. Buy a selection of *salumi* (cured meats and salami) and ask for them to be cut by hand into thick chunks rather than the usual thin slices. Push them onto skewers or toothpicks in various combinations and allow people to help themselves. The knuckle end of prosciutto is particularly tasty when thickly cut and served with plenty of black pepper. Alternatively, cut triangles of mortadella about 5 cm thick and combine with a long, green pickle (*cetrioli*) or gherkin. For a larger appetiser, you could also push four or five thick slices of spicy sausage interspersed with olives onto a skewer.

Other good recipes to serve as tasters include Saltimbocca, Pizza Farcita, Calamari Grigliati and Spiedini di Gamberoni (see pages 270, 66, 178 and 213). You simply choose what you fancy to go with a chilled glass of Prosecco and relax away the day's cares and woes.

Here's a simple but delicious idea: bite-sized pieces of sourdough bread are toasted, drizzled with a little extra virgin olive oil and topped with anything appetising. Try the ideas below, or any of the pâtés that follow.

Creamy Gorgonzola and crushed walnuts
Smoked salmon, ricotta and caperberries
Artichokes preserved in oil with a slice of smoked pancetta
Mozzarella and sun-dried tomato with a basil leaf
Anchovy and a slice of spicy sausage, such as Fonteluna
Rolled slice of Coppa di Parma with sautéd fennel

Baked polenta and cheese toast

polenta e formaggio al forno

Cold polenta is often used as a crostini, either toasted in cubes or warmed on a griddle pan in wedges, and topped with something tasty – chunks of salami, thick slices of prosciutto, cubes of cheese, or just a sun-dried tomato perched on a basil leaf.

cold polenta
Gorgonzola or Fontina cheese
extra virgin olive oil

Pre-heat the oven to 180°C/350°F/Gas mark 4.

Cut fingers or triangles of cold polenta and sandwich them together with a slice of cheese. Drizzle with olive oil, place on a baking sheet and bake in the oven for 10–15 minutes, until crisp on the outside and the cheese is melting in the middle.

Alternatively, fry the sandwiches in hot olive oil until crispy on both sides.

Mushroom pâté

pâté di funghi

2–3 tbsp extra virgin olive oil
2 garlic cloves, finely chopped
1 small piece peperoncino (dried chilli), crushed
500 g Cremini, chestnut or Paris brown mushrooms
leaves from 2–3 sprigs thyme
2 tbsp finely chopped flatleaf parsley
salt and freshly ground black pepper

Heat the oil and sauté the garlic and peperoncino for a minute or so to release the flavours.

Brush, trim and slice the mushrooms. Add to the frying pan with the thyme leaves and sauté until the juices released from the mushrooms have been concentrated. Season with salt and pepper, then set aside to cool.

Transfer the mushroom mixture to a blender or food processor and whiz to make a coarse paste. Add the parsley and serve.

Chickpea pâté

pâté di ceci

This is quick and easy to make if you use canned chickpeas. Or you could try using cannellini beans, flavouring them with crushed coriander seeds and chopped coriander instead of parsley.

3–4 tbsp extra virgin olive oil
1 garlic clove
1 small piece peperoncino (dried chilli), crushed
1 tsp crushed cumin seeds
squeeze of lemon juice
1 x 450 g can chickpeas, drained and rinsed
finely chopped flatleaf parsley
salt and freshly ground black pepper

Heat the oil in a frying pan and sauté the garlic, peperoncino and cumin seeds for a minute or so to release their flavours.

Add a squeeze of lemon juice, then stir in the chickpeas and cook until hot. Check the seasoning.

Put half the mixture into a blender or food processor and whiz to a paste. Return to the pan and mix with the whole chickpeas, adding more oil if it looks too dry. Stir in the parsley and serve with Crostini (see page 102).

Cream of salt cod

baccalà mantecato

I don't like the flavour of salt cod, but I love this! It is irresistibly moreish – perfect with a glass of Prosecco. Like all salt cod recipes, this one must be started two days in advance as the fish must be soaked before cooking.

250 g salt cod
1 garlic clove, chopped
2 anchovy fillets
freshly ground black pepper
5 tbsp extra virgin olive oil
2–3 tbsp warm milk
2–3 tbsp finely chopped flatleaf parsley, to finish
lemon wedges, to serve

Soak the cod in cold water for 48 hours, changing the water 2 or 3 times.

When ready to cook, rinse the cod again, then place in a saucepan, cover with fresh water and bring to a slow simmer. Cook for about 15 minutes, then allow to cool.

When the fish is cold, remove the skin and bones, pressing it all over to catch any hidden bones.

Put the cod, garlic and anchovies into a bowl, add a generous grinding of black pepper and start to mix with a hand-held blender. (Don't use a food processor as it will make the mixture gluey.) Gradually add the oil, blending constantly. Add the milk and blend again. The mixture should take on a creamy, fluffy consistency.

Check the seasoning and serve on warm Crostini (see page 102) sprinkled with chopped parsley. Offer wedges of lemon for squeezing over.

Chicken liver pâté

pâté di fegato

Order the chicken livers from your butcher, asking him for livers from corn-fed or organic chickens. To make a smaller quantity of pâté, simply halve the quantities below.

500 g chicken livers
100 g fresh pork back fat
100 g unsalted butter, plus extra for greasing
100 g shallots, finely chopped
1 garlic clove
2 sprigs fresh thyme, leaves only
2 tsp mustard
freshly ground nutmeg
splash of Marsala or cognac
2–3 tbsp water
1 tbsp finely chopped flatleaf parsley
8 slices smoked pancetta
sea salt and freshly ground black pepper

Pick over the livers, removing any debris. Chop the pork back fat into small cubes.

Melt the butter in a frying pan and sauté the shallots and garlic until softened. Add the chicken livers and cook for 5–10 minutes; they should still be pink in the middle.

Add the thyme and mustard, a grating of nutmeg and the seasoning. Stir in the Marsala. Allow to cool, then transfer to a blender or food processor and whiz to a paste, adding some cold water as necessary. The pâté should be smooth with the consistency of thick double cream. Add the parsley and adjust the seasoning.

Pre-heat the oven to 150°C/300°F/Gas mark 2.

Lightly butter an 800-ml terrine and line it with the slices of pancetta.

Pour the liver mixture into the terrine and cover with foil. Place in a deep roasting dish, then put in the oven and carefully pour in boiling water to come two-thirds of the way up the sides of the terrine. Cook for about 1 hour.

Allow to cool, then place a plate and a weight on top of the pâté and refrigerate until set. It will keep for 5 days.

Wine, women and Scotland

Uncle Victor Crolla spent his whole life in the shop. He worked 14 hours a day, seven days a week in Valvona & Crolla, a bachelor married to his trade. Eccentric in working life, he was also eccentric in retirement. On the last day of 1985 he called his nephew Philip, an eager 32-year-old, into his office and gave him the keys of the shop. 'It's your job now, Pippy. I'm out. You'll work hard, live a good life, but I warn you, you'll never be rich!' Uncle Victor came back only once, when we extended the back shop to open the wine department.

Maybe he'd sensed the change in the market and instinctively decided it was time to get out. The supermarkets were just starting to open and Uncle Victor's philosophy of pile it high and sell it cheap started to be challenged. No longer could we expect to be the only people in Edinburgh selling exotic produce, such as Parmigiano Reggiano and salami, and the cheapest Scotch whisky. He didn't know it but at the same time two revolutions were occurring in the food world, both of which would have a profound influence on our working life.

The first was the fundamental change afoot in Italy led by wine-makers such as Gaja and Antinori. They realised that the image of Italian wine abroad, especially in Britain, was pretty poor: people thought of it as 'good cheap plonk'. In fact, Italy had a wine-making tradition as old as that in France, and produced wines that could challenge any from the great French chateaux. The trouble was marketing. No one either inside or outside Italy knew or understood the Italian heritage of wines other than in the regions in which they were produced.

This is particularly odd, given that every April since 1967 Verona has hosted VinItaly, the world's largest wine fair. The sheer size and scale of it is breathtaking – think of a dozen giant aircraft hangars housing 4000 exhibitor stands and over 180,000 different wines. The programme resembles a telephone directory.

right Victor Crolla

FRIULI VENEZIA GIULIA
HALF BOTTLES

Philip became a regular visitor to the fair, but it was not until he took over Valvona & Crolla that we started to be associated with the best of Italian wines. This resulted in his winning *Wine Magazine*'s wine merchant of the year award in 1990.

Meanwhile, a handful of restaurants came to prominence across Scotland, each of them created by chefs who had travelled widely in France and Italy and recognised the poor image of Scottish produce at home and abroad. Their quiet food revolution would irreversibly change the perception of Scotland's Larder.

Independent of each other, and all in remote locations away from the cities, these restaurants broke new ground. Each was run by a couple and, in another change to the norm, they all had women chefs. Uniquely, they offered a strictly seasonal menu based on local produce.

The new restaurateurs shocked the complacent trade. Here were chefs preparing fresh seasonal food, using Scottish ingredients, and even having the audacity to offer set menus!

The women chefs who changed the face of Scottish cuisine were Gunn Erikson at Altnaharrie Inn in Ullapool, Hilary Brown at La Potinière in Gullane, Betty Allen at Aird's Hotel in Port Appin, and Shirley Spear at the Three Chimneys on the isle of Skye. The cook and food writer Claire Macdonald, owner of Kinloch Lodge on Skye, was also a huge influence and inspiration.

As Philip was inspired by the wine makers in Italy, I was inspired by these great cooks and in many ways their quiet example led us to search out the small Scottish and European suppliers and source our produce direct from producers all over the country. It can be said that by creating a market they helped save the country's farming and fishing industries.

Parsley and poached egg soup

zuppa di prezzemolo e uovo

Musselburgh, six miles east of Edinburgh, has long been famous for its mussels and leeks, but production all but disappeared in recent years. Now a resurgence of interest in local produce has seen a proliferation of working farms and the famous Musselburgh leeks are once more available, and used in this recipe. Let's hope that sooner rather than later the mussel beds are rescued as well.

In the spring we get pullets' eggs, from 'teenage' hens, less than a year old! They are perfect for this soup.

30 g unsalted butter
1 onion, finely chopped
white parts of 2 large leeks, finely sliced
large bunch of flatleaf parsley
2 large potatoes, grated
sea salt
½ lemon
1 small carton single cream
4 pullets' eggs or other small eggs
freshly ground nutmeg

For the vegetable stock
1 shallot, quartered
1 leek, white parts only
3 sticks celery
2 carrots
large bunch of parsley

First make the vegetable stock. Put all the ingredients in a saucepan and cover with 1 litre of water. Simmer gently for about 30 minutes, then set aside to cool then strain.

Heat the butter gently and add the onion and leeks. Sauté gently, making sure the onion doesn't burn.

Add the parsley stalks and half the leaves, the grated potato and the boiling stock. Simmer for 20 minutes until the potato has cooked. Blend the soup until smooth. Return to the saucepan and reheat. Season with salt, then add a squeeze of lemon juice and enough single cream to maintain the light broth.

Boil some water in a shallow saucepan and lightly poach the eggs – about 2–3 minutes.

Pour the hot soup into 4 individual bowls and add a poached egg to each one.

Finely chop the remaining parsley leaves and sprinkle over the soup, together with a grating of nutmeg and swirl of cream.

Fennel, rice and wild garlic soup

zuppa di finocchio, riso e aglio selvatico

I love fresh fennel, with its crisp white bulb and feathery fronds, and use it a lot, often roasted or in salads. In this soup we use it in a light, fresh way – ideal for spring.

Wild garlic (*Allium ursinum*) grows abundantly from March to May, often near river walks and marshes, where its pungent, lingering aroma alerts you to its presence. The broad, ribbed leaves have pretty white starlet flowerheads, which have the most flavour. The tiny, pearl-like bulbs can be used to impart a lively garlic taste. Use fresh, new-season garlic if you can't find wild. Old garlic will overpower.

2–3 fennel bulbs (about 350 g)
4–6 bulbs, leaves and flowers of wild garlic or 2 bulbs new-season garlic
knob of unsalted butter
2 tbsp extra virgin olive oil
2 handfuls of Arborio rice
500 ml hot Chicken stock (see page 115)
sea salt
1 tbsp very finely chopped flatleaf parsley

Trim the fennel, removing any coarse outer leaves, the base and the solid core. Reserve the fronds. Slice the bulbs lengthways.

Trim the wild garlic, separating the bulbs, leaves and flowers.

Heat the butter and oil in a saucepan. Add the garlic bulbs and sauté for a minute or two. Add the fennel and sauté gently until it softens: do not allow it to burn.

Add the rice, chicken stock and wild garlic leaves and simmer for 15 minutes. Check the seasoning and add more water if necessary. The soup should be a light broth.

Serve sprinkled with the chopped fennel fronds and parsley, and place a wild garlic flower on top.

Broad bean and pancetta broth

brodo di fave e pancetta

When broad beans are very young, nestling tiny and luminescent inside their duvet-lined pods, they can simply be enjoyed raw. In Italy they are often served as an appetiser with pecorino cheese, podded and nibbled at the table. As the beans get older, they develop a tough outer coating that needs to be eased off with a paring knife. Alternatively, blanch them in boiling water, refresh in iced water and the beans will slip easily from their outer skin.

Our first beans arrive from Puglia in early March. Six weeks later they are harvested in East Lothian from seeds planted for us by Patricia at Phantassie Farm, so we get the luxury of an extended supply.

3 tbsp extra virgin olive oil
1 garlic clove
1 onion, finely chopped
100 g smoked pancetta, cubed
4 sticks celery, destringed and chopped
750 g broad beans, about 400 g podded weight
1.5 litres hot Chicken stock (see page 115)
sea salt
fresh basil leaves, to finish
100 g fresh pecorino, skinned and cut into small cubes, to serve

For the croûtons
2–3 tbsp extra virgin olive oil
2–3 slices stale crusty bread, cubed
1 tbsp finely chopped parsley

Heat the olive oil in a saucepan and sauté the garlic for a few minutes to release its flavour. Remove it from the saucepan and add the onion. Sauté until soft, then raise the heat and add the pancetta. Cook until browned, taking care not to burn the onion.

Add the celery and broad beans to the saucepan. Pour in enough hot stock to cover them by about 10 cm and season with sea salt. Simmer for about 20 minutes.

Meanwhile, make the croûtons. Heat the oil in a frying pan and fry the bread cubes in it until crisp all over. Remove from the heat, season with salt and toss in the parsley.

When the soup is cooked it should have the consistency of a broth. Season to taste.

Serve hot with some torn basil leaves, warm croûtons and small cubes of fresh pecorino.

Pea soup with ricotta and cucumber

zuppa di piselli con ricotta e cetrioli

This recipe is inspired by Hilary Brown. She believed that a fresh soup did not need stock, as the flavour of the ingredients themselves should be good enough. She advised not to overcook vegetable soups as they lose their brightness of flavour, and always to add boiling water to stop the vegetables sweating. In addition, she never used black pepper in delicate dishes as she said the flavour of the pepper spoilt the result instead of enhancing it.

Fresh peas are used below, but even frozen ones give a good result.

30 g unsalted butter
2 shallots, finely chopped
2 sticks celery, destringed and finely chopped
approx. 1 kg fresh peas, shelled weight
½ litre boiling water
2 tbsp single cream
sea salt

To finish
1 small piece cucumber, peeled and sliced
200 g fresh ricotta
extra virgin olive oil
1 tbsp very finely chopped parsley

Melt the butter in a saucepan, add the shallots and celery and sauté until soft. Add the peas, turn in the butter, then pour in the boiling water. Simmer for 15 minutes, then set aside to cool.

When the soup is cold, whiz in a blender or food processor, then pass through a sieve to make it smooth.

Reheat the soup, stir in the cream and season with salt. Serve hot with a few slices of cucumber on top and a teaspoon of fresh ricotta mixed with a little extra virgin olive oil and finely chopped parsley.

Chicken broth with little meatballs and greens

brodo di pollo con polpettine e scarola

We boil chickens every day in the kitchens to make stock and get chicken for our sandwiches. The stock is used for risotto or soups, this recipe being a favourite.

At home I serve the boiled chicken with creamy mashed potatoes, the sweet boiled celery and some Salsa verde (see page 263). You can also spoon a little broth over the chicken to moisten it. I'm lucky: to me the tastiest bits are the legs and wings, but everyone else likes the breast. At New Year we are more likely to eat the chicken with *cotechino* (pork sausage) and spiced lentils plus some *mostarda di frutta* (see page 56).

Note: You can also use the broth below as chicken stock in any recipe that requires it. I store small amounts in the freezer for easy use.

1 boiling fowl or chicken, or 500 g chicken pieces
1 red onion
1 carrot
4–5 stalks celery, plus the leaves
large bunch of flatleaf parsley
sea salt
plain flour, for dusting
2 handfuls of yellow scarola (frisée) leaves, roughly chopped
Parmigiano Reggiano, to serve

For the polpettine
80 g minced beef
80 g minced pork
2 tbsp dried breadcrumbs
2 tbsp grated Parmigiano Reggiano
small handful of pine nuts
2 tbsp finely chopped flatleaf parsley
1 small egg, beaten
sea salt and freshly ground black pepper

Wash the chicken inside and out, then place in a saucepan in which it fits snugly. Cover with cold water and bring to a simmer. Use a tea strainer to remove any scum that rises to the surface, and wipe around the sides of the saucepan with kitchen paper.

Cut the onion, carrot and celery into quarters. Add to the soup along with the parsley stalks. Simmer gently for 2 hours with the lid ajar to allow some evaporation.

Season the stock with just a little salt after it is cooked; you will be surprised how little you need to add. Allow to cool, then strain.

Mix all the polpettini ingredients in a bowl and season well.

Dust your hands with a little flour and roll the mixture into small balls about the size of a hazelnut. Set aside.

Heat about 1 litre of the strained broth to a simmer. Add the polpettini and the scarola and simmer gently for about 20 minutes. Check the seasoning and serve piping hot with freshly grated Parmigiano Reggiano.

Best Scottish asparagus

It's 20 years since a tall, healthy-looking farmer walked into the shop one spring morning with his arms full of bunches of thick, dark green asparagus. It had been picked from his farm in Perthshire barely three hours before. Traditionally a potato and cereal farmer, he had seen how well asparagus grew in his kitchen garden, so he decided to specialise and grow asparagus commercially.

He's a canny man, Sandy Patullo. He not only realised that asparagus grew well in the sandy soil and mild climate of the east coast, but that the season is ahead of the English one. He now boasts the most northern asparagus farm in the UK, and gets his crop to the market ahead of the Sassenachs! (He also grows sea kale, a blanched type of mild celery that is harvested in March.)

The first Italian asparagus arrives from Venice at the end of March. It takes three days rather than three hours to reach us, but its sweetness and intensity of flavour compensates for the delay. The older the asparagus, the higher the natural break of the stem when you snap it, indicating that more of the sugars have converted to carbohydrate, a process that turns soft eating into stringy chewing!

We also get deliveries of the thick, creamy white asparagus favoured by the French and Germans, which is grown in northern Italy. It's very good, but very expensive. We try to please all our customers.

Best, though, is Patullo's Scottish asparagus, arriving as the weather warms towards the last week in April, dropped off by Sandy barely hours after harvest. We get regular deliveries until mid June, when the supply stops abruptly and the season is over...until the next year.

Roasted asparagus with ricotta, anchovy and lemon

asparagi arrosto con ricotta, acciughe e limone

Since we have asparagus for such a short time, we indulge ourselves by eating it often and in all sorts of ways. Asparagus roasted in a hot oven with extra virgin olive oil and abundant shavings of Parmigiano Reggiano is ridiculously easy and fabulous. I also love it steamed and served with a thick blob of creamy hollandaise sauce. No less wonderful are the thinnest shoots of sprue asparagus, tossed in salad or cooked on a pizza with smoked pancetta and creamy mozzarella.

450 g thick asparagus
4–5 tbsp extra virgin olive oil
1 new-season garlic clove
3–4 anchovy fillets, chopped
juice of ½ lemon
2–3 tbsp chopped flatleaf parsley
400 g Loch Arthur or other fresh ricotta (see page 79)
freshly ground black pepper

Trim the asparagus by breaking off the base of the stem where it snaps naturally and using a potato peeler to shave down the remainder of the stem to remove any spikes.

Stand the asparagus in a deep saucepan of boiling salted water so that the delicate spears steam rather than boil. (You can tie them together to keep them upright.) Cook for 5–6 minutes, until just al dente. Drain and set aside.

Heat the oil in a frying pan. Add the garlic clove and fry for a minute or so to give a hint of flavour. Remove the garlic and add the anchovies, stirring to melt them into the oil.

Add the drained asparagus and sauté gently, just long enough to warm them through. Stir in a squeeze of lemon juice and the parsley.

Serve the asparagus with some fresh ricotta crumbled on top and a grating of freshly ground black pepper.

Pancakes stuffed with roasted asparagus and fontina

crespelle con asparagi e fontina

Crespelle are thin savoury pancakes that can be filled and baked. The filling used here is roasted asparagus coated with creamy Béchamel sauce and sprinkled with fontina cheese, a delicious combination that melts and bubbles, creating an appetising aroma. Prepare them ahead of time for a stunning but easy supper.

Makes 4 medium-sized pancakes

2 large eggs
250 ml milk
90 g plain flour, sifted
unsalted butter
sea salt and freshly ground black pepper

For the filling
500 g asparagus
extra virgin olive oil
sea salt
250 ml full-cream milk
1 shallot
1 fresh bay leaf
50 g unsalted butter, plus extra for greasing
2 tbsp plain flour, sifted
freshly grated nutmeg
6–8 tbsp grated fontina cheese
freshly grated Parmigiano Reggiano

To make the pancakes, beat the eggs in a bowl and mix in the milk. Season well, then whisk in the flour.

Melt a knob of butter in a frying pan. Add 2 tablespoons of the batter, tilting the pan to make the pancake as thin as possible. Cook until the underside is brown, then flip over to cook the other side. Transfer to a plate and repeat the process with the remaining butter and batter. The pancakes can be made in advance and stacked on a plate, separated by leaves of greaseproof paper.

Heat a griddle pan until very hot, or pre-heat the oven to 230ºC/450ºF/Gas mark 8.

Meanwhile, break the asparagus stems where they snap naturally and discard the woody part. Rub with oil and season with salt. Griddle until tender, turning as necessary, or roast in the oven for 15–20 minutes, until slightly charred at the edges. Lower the oven temperature to 190ºC/375ºF/Gas mark 5, or pre-heat it now if you used a griddle pan earlier.

Place the milk, shallot and bay leaf in a small saucepan, bring to a simmer and heat gently for 5 minutes or so to infuse the flavours. Strain, then set aside to cool.

Melt the butter in another small saucepan, add the flour and stir to make a 'roux'. Add a quarter of the infused milk, stirring well with a wooden spoon until the lumps disappear. Gradually add the remaining milk until you have a thick sauce. Bring to a simmer to cook out any floury taste. Season well with salt, pepper and a grating of nutmeg.

Butter a large ovenproof dish.

Place a pancake on a work surface and coat with Béchamel sauce. Add some roasted asparagus and grated fontina cheese, then roll up and place in the prepared dish. Repeat with the remaining pancakes.

Once all the pancakes are in the dish, drizzle the remaining Béchamel over them, sprinkle
with more fontina and grate some Parmigiano Reggiano over the surface. Bake in the oven for 20–25 minutes, or until bubbling hot and the cheese has started to go brown and crispy on top.

Or you could try...

Adding some sautéd pancetta to the basic filling. Crespelle can also be served with Butter tomato sugo (see page 25).

Nonna Caffè's mashed potatoes

patate alla nonna

My Nonna Marietta made the best mashed potatoes. Although she worked in her ice-cream shop all her adult life, her morning was always spent cooking lunch. During my childhood all the women in my life lived like this. These working mothers were fortunate enough to 'live above the shop' and could prepare food for their families while being at work. They became expert natural cooks, never reading a recipe book, but cooking by instinct. Time was not a luxury as it is today, and they took great care and many hours to produce everything to perfection. As children, we called Marietta 'Nonna Caffè', because that is where we could always find her.

Nonna Caffè cooked in an old coal-fired Aga. Her kitchen was always warm and snug, and delicious things were always being miraculously produced from the cream-coloured oven doors.

You need good fluffy potatoes for this mash – Maris Piper or King Edward. I buy my potatoes at my local greengrocer's as they offer seasonal, freshly harvested potatoes from around East Lothian. I find supermarket potatoes have often been stored badly and either fall away or cook unevenly.

100 g unsalted butter, plus extra for greasing and topping
750 g Maris Piper or King Edward potatoes
sea salt
125 ml full-fat milk (more if the potatoes are dry)
150 g freshly grated Parmigiano Reggiano
freshly ground black pepper
freshly grated nutmeg

Pre-heat the oven to 180°C/350°F/Gas mark 4. Butter a gratin dish.

Cut the potatoes into quarters and cook in boiling salted water until soft. Drain well and return to the saucepan.

Add the milk and butter and mash the potatoes really well, keeping them on the heat. Check the seasoning.

Transfer the potatoes to the prepared dish and use a fork to score the top. Sprinkle with the grated Parmigiano Reggiano, freshly ground black pepper and a grating of fresh nutmeg. Add 2–3 more knobs of butter (I remember Nonna always did!) and bake in the oven for 15 minutes or so, until the top is lightly browned and crusty.

Spring vegetables with butter and thyme

verdure di primavera con burro e timo

200 g young turnips, trimmed
200 g young carrots, trimmed
100 g green beans, cut lengthways
200 g sprue asparagus tips
100 g fresh peas, podded weight
knob of unsalted butter
6–8 small wild garlic cloves or 2–3 new-season garlic cloves
200 g young spinach
sea salt
squeeze of lemon juice
leaves from a few sprigs fresh thyme

Place the turnips and carrots in a saucepan of boiling salted water and simmer until just starting to soften. Add the beans and the asparagus and simmer for 5 minutes more. Add the peas and cook for a couple of minutes. Drain and refresh in cold water to keep all the colours bright.

Heat the butter, add the garlic and sauté for a minute to release the flavour. Add the spinach with some salt, then cook for 5 minutes, until the spinach wilts.

Add the mixed spring vegetables to the spinach and toss well. Sprinkle with a squeeze of lemon juice and the thyme leaves and serve warm.

Baked aubergines

melanzane al forno

The marriage of aubergine and mozzarella is really good. The *bocconcini* used here are delicious, bite-sized mozzarella, particularly juicy and sweet when fresh. Buffalo mozzarella is always tastier than the cows' milk type and gives a more authentic flavour to Italian food.

2 violet aubergines
extra virgin olive oil, preferably from Puglia, for frying and drizzling
1 egg
2 tbsp dry breadcrumbs
12 bocconcini di mozzarella
300 g very ripe Pachino cherry tomatoes
2–3 tbsp freshly grated Parmigiano Reggiano
12 or more fresh basil leaves
sea salt and freshly ground black pepper

Discard the spiky aubergine tops and cut the flesh into 3-cm cubes.

Heat some oil in a shallow frying pan, enough to fill it about a quarter full. Meanwhile, beat the egg and season it well. Dip the aubergine cubes in the mixture, then roll them in the breadcrumbs. Fry the cubes in the hot oil, turning them so that all the sides are nice and crispy.

Pre-heat the oven to 190°C/375°F/Gas mark 5.

Transfer the crispy aubergine to an ovenproof dish. Scatter the bocconcini over them, slicing some of the cheese open to release their milky juices.

Squash the tomatoes in your hands and spread them in the dish. Drizzle with olive oil, then scatter a good handful of breadcrumbs and the Parmigiano Reggiano over them. Season with a sprinkling of sea salt, plenty of grated black pepper and at least a dozen fresh basil leaves. Bake for 20–25 minutes, until the vegetables are juicy and crisp.

Serve warm, either as an accompaniment to grilled meat, or just on its own with crusty bread or Bruschette (see page 173).

Pecorino in the springtime

May and June herald the arrival of pecorino – fresh sheep's cheeses (not to be confused with the matured sheep's cheeses that are at their best in autumn (see page 294). Our Italian supplier, Giancarlo Russo, is a professor at Polenzo Slow Food University and also a cheese *affinatore*, so he has the enviable task of selecting and maturing pecorino for us.

Our passion for pecorino is natural, given that our forebears survived for generations as shepherds in the Abruzzi mountains. In June Giancarlo holds a tasting in the shop and we are treated to several styles and ages of the best sheep's and goats' cheeses from all over Italy.

In the later spring months by far our favourite pecorino is Marzolino Rosso, a 40-day-old cheese made from unpasteurised ewe's milk. This is shaped into 750 g rounds and rubbed with tomato to create a red blush, making it instantly recognisable in the market. At its best it is white, creamy and soft inside, full flavoured and perfect eaten with fresh berries.

From nearer home at this time we also get the new-season Lanark Blue cheese from southwest Scotland. Developed about 25 years ago by Humphrey Errington, it was the first blue cheese produced in Scotland for over 300 years. Hand-made with vegetable rennet and matured for two months, the cheese has a tartness and depth of flavour reminiscent of Roquefort.

If any time of the year is the best in which to end a meal with some fresh cheese, it has to be spring. Served with a glass of chilled Pinot Grigio, the pleasure is exquisite.

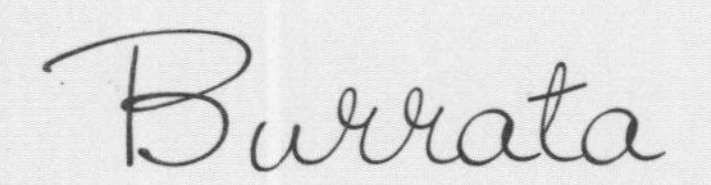

Burrata

Burrata is a specialist buffalo milk cheese, first produced during the 1920s in the then-inaccessible heel of Italy. Production of it begins with rennet curdling warm buffalo milk. Then, unlike other cheese-making, the curds are plunged into hot whey and skilfully pulled into stretchy strings, *pasta filata*, before being shaped as required.

When making burrata, the *pasta filata* are shaped into pouches, small scraps of mozzarella are stuffed into them and these are topped with fresh cream before being closed off in a 'cheese' knot. The finished burrata was traditionally wrapped in leaves of asphodel, a type of leek, and sometimes still comes wrapped in these. While the leaves were green, the cheese was considered still good to eat – an early version of the 'use by' date!

When fresh burrata is sliced open the creamy, buttery centre flows out, an experience you no longer have to travel to the heel of Italy to enjoy. Thanks to better transport systems, we now get deliveries in Edinburgh, the cheese chilled and packed in small plastic bags full of whey. To enjoy at its best, it should be eaten as soon as possible, definitely within a few days. It has an exquisite flavour, creamy and indulgent, sweet without a hint of sour. Its wow factor is its green-striped attire. We open it and spoon out the middle, serving it with prosciutto and bread, or with fresh tomatoes, extra virgin olive oil and cracked black pepper.

Burrata is in season all year round, but is best in springtime, when it is perfect with asparagus.

Asparagus, burrata and culatello

asparagi, burrata e culatello

Culatello is perhaps one of the best cured ham products made in northern Italy. Produced from the rump of the pig, it has long been matured in the foggy lowlands of the Po valley. The pigs are fed almost exclusively on the whey from Parmigiano Reggiano production, lucky beasts!

The *culatello*, or rump, is made from a fillet taken from the hind end, salt-cured then sewn into membrane sheaths and trussed. It is then hung for eight months in damp, naturally aired cellars, allowing natural maturing to do its magic. In the process, the whole leg is cannibalised, the opportunity of producing an entire prosciutto discarded, hence the quality of the finished product – lean, sweet with a halo of meltingly satisfying white fat around its edge – and the price. Burton Anderson in *Pleasures of the Italian Table* (Viking, 1994) calls it the 'fugitive king of foggy bottoms', rare and exclusive, and long may it remain so.

Alternatively, another cured ham you could try is the prosciutto from San Daniele. It is made from a smaller breed of pig which is allowed to roam free and is fed on acorns. The resulting ham is leaner than the *culatello*, with a stronger flavour. Either way, the combination in this recipe is fit for a king – at least one with a good appetite!

500 g plump-stemmed 'jumbo' asparagus
24 thin slices freshly cut culatello or prosciutto di San Daniele
1 fresh burrata cheese or buffalo mozzarella
extra virgin olive oil
freshly ground black pepper
knob of Italian butter

Prepare the asparagus by breaking the stems near the bottom, where they snap naturally. Discard the woody parts. Use a potato peeler to trim off the spikes on the stalks.

Place the asparagus upright in a saucepan of boiling salted water and steam for 10 minutes, until just tender.

Place 6 slices of culatello or 3 of prosciutto on each of 4 plates. Spoon some burrata on to each and dress with olive oil and black pepper.

Drain the asparagus, arrange on a platter and toss generously with the butter. Serve with the culatello.

Burrata with warm roasted asparagus and wild rocket

burrata con asparagi arrosto e rucola

500 g plump-stemmed 'jumbo' asparagus
extra virgin olive oil
100 g wild rocket leaves
200 g fresh burrata
sea salt and freshly ground black pepper

Pre-heat a ridged griddle pan until very hot.

Prepare the asparagus by breaking the stems near the bottom, where they snap naturally. Discard the woody parts. Use a potato peeler to trim off the spikes on the stalks.

Rinse the asparagus, then brush it with oil and season with salt and pepper. Place on the griddle and cook for 4–6 minutes, turning halfway through to cook the other side. Insert a skewer, and when almost tender, remove from the pan.

Toss the rocket in olive oil and salt, then place a small mound on each of 4 serving plates.

Lay the warm asparagus spears on top and put 4–5 generous teaspoons of burrata on the asparagus. Drizzle with a little more oil and finish with a grating of black pepper before serving.

East Lothian: the garden of Scotland

The organic fruit and vegetable movement came as a surprise to me, even though I'd grown up in East Lothian, the 'Garden of Scotland', and been immersed in food all my life. I had noticed, though, what wonderful vegetables and fruit were available in Italy and that we had trouble sourcing items of similar quality in Scotland. For a long time, all we could buy in the local markets was Dutch – bland and tasteless compared to what we saw and ate in Italy.

It was with some suspicion that I started trading with Patricia Stephen. A charming, eccentric and long-time customer, she told me she was growing organic produce in East Lothian and would have some to sell. When I asked her to give me a product list with prices every week, she said she couldn't because she didn't know what would grow! I wasn't filled with confidence, but Patricia, on her small farm, became one of the first to improve locally grown produce – and to change the public attitude towards it. Since her first enquiry at the shop, over ten years ago, she has gone from strength to strength and now grows Italian produce for us from Italian seeds that we source. Now, with a product list and prices every week, she supplies us with wonderful organic *cimi di rapa* (turnip tops), *cavolo nero* (black cabbage) and *scarola* (frisée), all grown just a few miles down the road from the shop. She also supplies us with fabulous organic beetroots, chard and root vegetables, potatoes and wonderful free-range organic eggs.

Although we still import fruit and vegetables from Italy and France ourselves, with the help of Patricia we can also enjoy seasonal luxuries that don't survive the journey from Italy so well, such as courgette flowers, asparagus and fresh herbs, all organically grown and just on our doorstep.

Spaghettini with white sprouting broccoli and Luganega sausage

spaghettini con broccoli bianchi e luganega

Purple sprouting broccoli arrives from the organic farms around March. Later on, some farms harvest a delicate, sweet white sprouting broccoli that has tender flower buds and is especially good with the fresh pork sausage from Luganega, in northern Italy. This sausage is traditionally made with the finer cuts of pork and flavoured with a combination of nutmeg, coriander, pepper and cinnamon.

250 g white sprouting broccoli, trimmed
6–8 tbsp extra virgin olive oil
2 new-season garlic cloves, chopped
1 small piece peperoncino (dried chilli), crushed
2 anchovy fillets in oil, chopped
200 g Luganega sausage, cut into bite-sized pieces
400 g spaghettini
sea salt
1 tbsp finely chopped flatleaf parsley

Place the broccoli in boiling salted water and cook for 5 minutes or so, until al dente. Drain and refresh in cold water. Set aside.

Fill the saucepan with water again and boil in readiness for cooking the pasta.

Heat the oil in a wide frying pan and sauté the garlic and peperoncino for a minute or so to release the flavours. Add the anchovies and stir until melted.

Add the sausage and cook until lightly brown and crisp. Stir in the broccoli.

Meanwhile, cook the spaghettini in boiling salted water until al dente. Using tongs, lift the pasta from the water and add it to the frying pan. (The water that clings to the pasta will moisten the sugo.) Toss thoroughly, then sprinkle with parsley and serve.

Taglierini with asparagus, crab and cream

taglierini con asparagi, granchio e panna

This is an unusual pasta dish because of the rich combination of crab with cream. By the way, Italians don't serve grated Parmigiano Reggiano with seafood dishes – or chips with lasagne, or cappuccino with their lunch...Sorry!

100 g asparagus tips
25 g unsalted butter
200 g white crab meat
1 tsp brandy
1 tsp tomato purée
250 ml double cream
pinch of cayenne pepper
320 g fine Campofilone taglierini (see page 28)
2 tsp finely chopped flatleaf parsley
sea salt

Trim the asparagus and cut into fine slivers. Place in boiling salted water and simmer until tender, but still with a bite. Drain and refresh in cold water. Set aside.

Melt the butter in a saucepan, add the crab meat and warm through. Stir in the brandy, then add the tomato purée. After a few minutes add the cream and asparagus. Season with a pinch of cayenne and simmer gently to thicken the sugo.

Meanwhile, cook the taglierini in boiling salted water; this should take no more than 4 minutes.

Taste the sugo, adjust the seasoning and stir in the parsley.

Using tongs, transfer the pasta straight from the boiling water to the crab mixture; the water clinging to it will moisten the sugo. Toss well and serve.

Linguine with fresh crab

linguine al granchio

We have wonderful crab in Scotland. It comes from fisheries on the east coast, but also from the islands of Skye, Orkney and Shetland. The crab season lasts from March through to October, so we keep it on the menu a lot.

I have cooked and picked crab at home on a couple of occasions because it's the only way to ensure it's really fresh, but it is a 'faff'. To learn how best to do it yourself I'd recommend reading Rick Stein's *Taste of the Sea* (BBC Books, 1995), or Simon Hopkinson's *Roast Chicken and Other Stories* (Ebury Press, 1999).

We get our crab boiled and picked daily by our fish supplier. It is locally caught and is as fresh as a daisy. We now check the crab for bits of shell before cooking because a 'very nice' customer once broke his crown on some shell and charged us for his dentist's bill. We now put a warning on the menu to save further mishaps.

All the fish and crab needed for this recipe can be found in any good fishmonger's. You can also buy crab meat from supermarket fish counters and it's really very good.

This is fast food. The sequence of adding the ingredients is important in achieving the

authentic flavour of this dish. In Naples, when I cooked with Philip's uncle Vicenzo, he always added the wine and parsley and boiled off the alcohol before adding any fish. This alters the garlic, making it a gentle background flavour instead of a pungent fried one.

360 g fine linguine or spaghettini
sea salt
6–8 tbsp extra virgin olive oil
2 garlic cloves, finely chopped
2 small pieces peperoncino (dried chilli), crushed
75 ml dry white wine
2 tbsp finely chopped flatleaf parsley
100 g fresh brown crab meat (optional)
200 g fresh white crab meat (or 300 g if you prefer to use all white crab meat)
handful of flatleaf parsley, very finely chopped

Cook the linguine or spaghettini in a large saucepan of boiling salted water until al dente, about 6–8 minutes.

Meanwhile, heat the oil in a wide frying pan, add the garlic and peperoncino and cook for 1 minute to release their flavours.

Raise the heat to high and add the wine and the 2 tablespoons of parsley. Boil until the alcohol has evaporated. This takes 4–5 minutes, and you can tell by sniffing the vapours: the alcohol will no longer catch the back of your throat.

Lower the heat and stir in the brown crab meat, if using, to create the sugo.

As soon as the pasta is al dente, add the white crab meat to the sugo and warm it through.

Using tongs, transfer the pasta straight from the boiling water to the frying pan; the water clinging to it will moisten the sugo. Toss well over a high heat. Add the final quantity of parsley, toss through and serve piping hot.

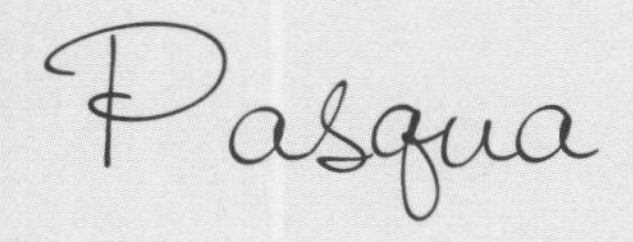

Years ago our shop was a focal point at Easter (*Pasqua*) for Italian families all over the east coast of Scotland. In the days when they had large families and followed the strict feasting and fasting rules of the Catholic Church, Holy Week was as busy as Christmas, with whole families converging on the shop to stock up with Easter necessities. The shelves were laden with fresh ricotta, *salsicce* and pancetta to make *pastone* (Neapolitan Easter pie); fresh pecorino, which arrives just in time for Easter; *baccalà* (salt cod) for all the delicious Good Friday recipes; and *grano cotto* (cooked wheat) for Neapolitan Easter cake. Motta, Alemagne and Bauli *colomba* cakes, shaped like doves of peace and decorated with candied sugar and almonds, were arranged in tempting displays, and cases of Asti Spumante were piled high.

At the same time we sold ice-cream mix, raspberry flavourings, vanilla extract and chocolate vermicelli by the ton, plus ice-cream scoops and sticks for toffee apples and candyfloss – all essential tools of the ice-cream trade that was about to start up again in earnest. There was a sense of relief and renewal: winter was over and business in the caffès and fish and chip shops across the country was ready to boom.

We used to buy five or six 10-kg bags of *baccalà* for the Easter celebrations. Massive sides of it would hang from meat hooks above the counter, infusing the whole shop with an obscene fishy smell that was as traditional as incense in the church on Good Friday.

Italians would converge on the shop all week, from Palm Sunday until Holy Thursday, arriving in carloads, greeting Victor and Dominic and Carlo with genuine fondness, and sharing news and gossip, gesticulating and arguing and getting all hot under the collar over the *baccalà*. The state of last year's purchase

was complained about; it was too thick, too thin, too dry, too salty, too dear! It was better last year, at Christmas, in Sicily! The best cut, the juicy fat slice from the middle, was the only part they would accept; the fins, the tail, the head were all discarded to keep them happy.

On Good Friday the mayhem reached its peak. No time to close for lunch (yes, we used to close for an hour and a half), no time to go to church (3 p.m. at the cathedral), no time to eat (it was a day of fasting and abstinence anyway). But, ever aware of her family's needs, Philip's mother, Olivia, would bring along a steaming bowl of *baccalà* with prunes, which would sit up in the office, on everybody's mind all day, ready to be devoured as soon as the hoards of customers disappeared!

These days Olivia still delivers the *baccalà* with prunes for Philip's lunch, but the Italians have virtually disappeared. Most of the first-generation immigrants have passed away, and their families, now all grown up and earning a living as doctors, lawyers or in businesses of their own, import their Italian produce direct. Their grandchildren may never experience the rituals of buying and cooking *baccalà* because the traditions have been diluted and the religious ritual is disappearing.

The *baccalà* has disappeared as well, as if it knew that it was no longer required. Demand simply dried up, but cod stocks have also fallen anyway because of quotas and overfishing, and brought the processor (Cawood, in Grimsby) almost to closure. Thankfully, the business was rescued at the last minute and is fighting to preserve a dying trade. One glimmer of hope is that the growing Spanish community in Scotland has a fierce love of *baccalà*, so we have started to sell more, but now it comes ready cut and nicely packaged, and is sold to make completely different recipes. Never mind, at least we still sell it!

Frittata with potatoes and salt cod

frittata con patate e baccalà

You need to soak the salt cod at least 48 hours in advance. We leave it in a bowl in the sink with the tap dripping to keep the water moving and wash away the salt. At home you can simply change the water three or four times instead.

250 g salt cod, soaked for 48 hours
250 g waxy potatoes, such as Charlotte or Jersey Royals
2 tbsp extra virgin olive oil
knob of unsalted butter
1 large onion, thinly sliced
100 g smoked pancetta, cubed
6 extra large eggs
2 tbsp finely chopped flatleaf parsley
freshly ground black pepper

Rinse the salt cod and check that it is no longer salty. Place it in a saucepan of boiling water and poach until it is just cooked, about 5–6 minutes. Set aside and leave to cool.

Once the fish is cold, remove the skin. Flake the cod into a bowl, pressing it to find any hidden bones.

Par-boil the potatoes in slightly salted water until just cooked. Drain and set aside. When cool, cut them into cubes.

Heat the oil and butter in a heavy-based frying pan. Add the onion and pancetta and cook slowly for 10 minutes, or until the onions are soft and caramelised.

Add the potatoes and turn them in the soffritto, allowing them to crisp a little and brown at the edges.

Beat the eggs together with the parsley and plenty of freshly ground black pepper. Don't add salt – there is enough in the fish and pancetta to flavour the dish.

Add the egg mixture to the frying pan and dot with the flaked fish. Cook for about 10 minutes, tilting the pan now and again to let the liquid egg run underneath. When the bottom is firm, place a large plate over the pan and invert to turn out the frittata. Slip it back into the pan upside down to finish cooking. The frittata should be quite dry and the egg cooked right through.

Serve hot with Warm french bean salad (see page 91).

Broad bean, spinach and mint frittata

frittata di fave, spinaci e menta

3–4 tbsp extra virgin olive oil
1 garlic clove, finely chopped
1 small piece peperoncino (dried chilli), crushed
250 g fresh spinach
100 g broad beans (podded weight)
6 large eggs
generous handful of fresh mint, finely chopped
50–75 g pecorino, freshly grated
knob of butter
sea salt and freshly ground black pepper

Heat the oil in a saucepan. Add the garlic and peperoncino and sauté for 1 minute to release their flavours. Add the spinach and sauté until wilted. Season it with salt and allow to cool.

Once cooled, drain the spinach in a colander and squeeze out any excess liquid. Discard the garlic and chop the spinach roughly.

Blanch the broad beans in boiling salted water to soften them. Refresh in cold water to keep their bright colour.

Beat the eggs. Add the spinach, broad beans, mint and pecorino, mix well and add seasoning.

Heat the remaining tablespoon of olive oil and the butter in a small frying pan. Add the egg mixture and cook slowly until almost set. Place a plate over the frying pan and invert to turn out the frittata. Slip it back into the pan upside down to finish cooking. The frittata should be quite dry and the egg cooked right through.

The frittata can be made a day in advance, but refrigerating makes it dull and rubbery. If you want to store it, keep it in a cool place covered with foil. I prefer to serve it warm with boiled potatoes and a Spring leaf salad (see page 89).

Spring lamb

Abbacchio, the name for young, milk-fed spring lamb, beloved of the Romans, is a real favourite of mine. If I could, I would go to Italy every Easter just to enjoy it. Its delicious sweet flavour when roasted is just a joy. It is bizarrely very difficult to find in the UK. If you look on the internet, you'll see lots of sites from Australia and America singing its praises, but hardly anything from Scotland (or the rest of the UK). Strange, as we are a major producer of excellent lamb. Could it have something to do with the squeamishness that some people feel about eating certain types of young animals, even though they are happy to eat badly-reared beef that make burgers and cheap sausages?

In years gone by our friend Humphry Errington, whose family has farmed sheep for generations in Lanarkshire, used to arrange for us to have a very young milk-fed lamb for Easter. This was as eagerly anticipated as Humphry's now-famous Lanark Blue sheep's milk cheese, which he produces from his flock's milk.

If you would like to enjoy *abbacchio* at its best, I can only suggest that you visit the Vatican during Easter week and follow the priests as they make their way to lunch after Mass. In unassuming *trattorie* tucked away in the back streets you will get a chance to share in this delicious Roman tradition.

The youngest lamb we get in the shop now comes just in time for Easter, from farms across the border in Northumbria. They are grass-fed but are young and as near to milk-fed as we can source. Wait a few weeks after Easter and the price comes down. That's also when our local, more naturally raised Borders' spring lamb comes on to the market. Look out too for Welsh salt-marsh lamb, which appears in the shops from July; Manx lamb from the Isle of Man in August; and, best of all to my mind, Shetland lamb, which is available for about six weeks at the end of September.

New-season rack of lamb

abbacchio al forno

French-trimmed chops have all the fat cut away from the bones and cook very elegantly and easily. (I prefer the fat still on the bone – very tasty to nibble clean!) The lamb is lovely served with the spring vegetable treat on page 121.

4 racks of lamb, 3 or 4 chops on each, French-trimmed
extra virgin olive oil, for griddling and drizzling
sea salt
3–4 new-season garlic cloves, cut into thin slivers
2–3 sprigs fresh rosemary
2–3 sprigs fresh thyme
3–4 anchovy fillets, cut into thin slivers
2 fennel bulbs, trimmed and thinly sliced, fronds reserved

Remove the lamb from the refrigerator about 30 minutes before cooking.

Pre-heat the oven to 230°C/450°F/Gas mark 8.

Rub the lamb with oil, season it with salt and stud the flesh with the garlic, some of the herbs and all the anchovies.

Heat a frying pan or ridged griddle pan until very hot. Place the lamb in it, fat-side down, to brown the surface and seal the meat.

Heat a heavy roasting tray. Place the fennel and fronds in it, drizzling them with olive oil and sprinkling with salt. Lay the browned lamb on top and drizzle with more oil. Sprinkle with more salt and the remaining sprigs of rosemary and thyme. Roast for about 15 minutes, until the lamb is well browned, but pink juices are released when a skewer is inserted.

Remove from the oven and leave covered in a warm place for up to 15 minutes before serving.

Dreams come true

Venice has one of the most iconic hotels in Europe, perhaps the world. It is a huge treat to visit, a once-in-a-lifetime experience for most people.

We took the taxi-boat to the hotel and were greeted like royalty. On the way into the restaurant we passed a buffet table groaning with food – at least 40 dishes to choose from, including octopus, squid, eel and cockles – sautéd, marinated, *trifolati*, *crudo*, lobsters, langoustines, gamberoni and prawns – cocktailed, with mayo, *fritto*, *farcito*, soup, pasta, artichokes and caviar. You want it, they have it.

On the menu I was drawn to the Easter speciality, *capra arrosto*, roast kid. The menu translated it as 'baby lamb', but I eagerly ordered it. Whatever it was, I anticipated a treat. Only the week before, having heard a Radio 4 report that goat is the most popular meat in the world, I had spent days phoning butchers to order some kid. It was impossible; no one in Scotland could find me some. So if goat is the most popular meat in the world, why are we not eating it?

The dish duly came, stunningly simple, small pieces of rib, chop and shoulder, roasted to perfection and served only with the light juices that it had released during cooking. I decided it must actually be *abbacchio*, baby lamb, and enjoyed every mouthful.

When the charming waiter cleared our plates Philip asked in English for an explanation. Had his wife eaten *abbacchio* or *capra* – lamb or kid?

'Lamb,' the waiter declared without hesitation.

'Oh,' Philip replied, switching to his perfect Italian, 'we were confused. The menu said *capra* but translated it as "lamb". It was very delicious. Compliments to the chef.'

This seemed to alert the waiter, and a comic succession of waiters in more and more important uniforms, each older and more charming than the last, came to discuss with us the origins of my lunch. Eventually, after three gentle interrogations, the restaurant manager approached the huddle of concerned waiters and, shoulders back, came towards our table. The truth came in a torrent of Italian and as a bit of a shock.

'*Signore*, it was *capra*, of course. It is Easter and that is our speciality.' He lowered his voice and bent towards us, looking around at our fellow guests, many of them well-heeled American and British septuagenarians. 'You see,' he said, shrugging his shoulders and smiling conspiratorially, 'if we told them it was goat, they would never order it; and they do enjoy it so much.' With that he bowed, turned around and glided away.

It was the most delicious kid I have ever tasted – and the most expensive.

I can understand the restaurant manager's point of view. I have checked my vast collection of cookbooks and found barely a couple of references to kid. Elizabeth David's *Italian Food* (Penguin, 1954) and Patience Gray's *Honey from a Weed* (Prospect Books, 1986) both extol its virtues, but these esteemed cookery writers were writing before modern squeamishness and Disney cuddly animals altered our perception of the source of food.

Nonetheless, there is an increasing interest in goats' produce – cheeses, milk, yoghurts and ice creams – so goat meat is likely to become more widely available sooner rather than later. Let's hope so.

Roast kid

capretto arrosto

Kid is lean and small, so it is bonier than lamb. A young kid weighing 3 kg or so will be enough for four people. If you are lucky enough to find a source, ask the butcher to prepare it for roasting whole. If you can't get kid, use young lamb instead and don't tell anybody it's not kid!

1 x 3 kg kid
1 garlic clove, thinly sliced
extra virgin olive oil
few sprigs rosemary
few sprigs thyme
2 glasses dry white wine
sea salt and freshly ground black pepper

To serve
500 g pre-boiled Jersey Royal potatoes
mixed green salad
extra virgin olive oil
squeeze of lemon juice
lemon wedges

Pre-heat the oven to 230°C/450°F/Gas mark 8 and heat up a roasting tray.

Using a sharp knife, make small incisions in the kid and stud it with the garlic. Rub it all over with the oil and place in the hot roasting tray. Tuck the sprigs of rosemary and thyme around it. Pour over 1 glass of the wine.

Place the tray in the oven and immediately lower the heat to 190°C/375°F/Gas mark 5. Roast for 15 minutes per 500 g.

Check the kid 10 minutes before the end of the cooking time. As soon as the juices run clear when a skewer is inserted, transfer the meat to a warm serving platter and leave it to rest in a warm spot, covered with two layers of foil.

There will be very little fat from the roasting, but skim it off and place in another roasting tray. Add the potatoes and roast in the hot oven until brown and crisp.

Make a light gravy by pouring the remaining glass of wine into the first roasting tray and scraping up the sediment and tasty morsels. Boil for a minute or so to evaporate the alcohol. This takes 4–5 minutes, and you can tell by sniffing the vapours: the alcohol will no longer catch the back of your throat. Check the seasoning.

The roasted kid is small, so cut it as best you can, jointing it and giving people some of each cut. Serve with the roasted potatoes and the mixed green salad dressed with salt, olive oil and lemon juice. Serve with the lemon wedges.

Wilted bitter greens

verdure in umido

A dish such as kid (see opposite) cries out for bitter greens. Goat meat is quite a strong flavour but it is balanced out by the simplicity of the greens.

500 g green chicory or friorelli (Neapolitan bitter broccoli)
extra virgin olive oil
lemon wedges, to serve

Pick over the greens, discarding any yellow or damaged leaves. Place in a saucepan of boiling salted water and cook until tender.

Drain the greens, transfer to a serving dish and drizzle with a little olive oil. Offer the lemon wedges separately so that they can be squeezed over just before eating, otherwise the acid in the juice will discolour the greens.

Sautéd Swiss chard

bietole saltate

This should be served at room temperature and not refrigerated. Phantassie Farm grows fantastic rainbow chard, which looks beautiful when cooked like this.

500 g Swiss chard
2–3 tbsp extra virgin olive oil
1 garlic clove, thinly sliced
juice of 1 lemon
sea salt

Place the chard in boiling salted water and cook until tender – about 15 minutes.

Drain the cooked chard and refresh in cold water.

Gently heat the oil and add the garlic to infuse its flavour. Add the chard and sauté for 15 minutes.

Serve warm with fresh lemon juice squeezed over at the last minute (lemon juice makes the leaves go black so don't add too soon).

Grilled vegetables with goats' cheese

verdure alla griglia con caprini

The new-season goats' cheeses arrive in March, much anticipated and a real herald of spring. From Italy we buy *caprini*, individual soft white cheeses with a mild tang of grassy herbs. They're also available with black truffles infused in them, an added luxury. They are wonderful with just a drizzle of Tuscan honey, but are also delicious crumbled over roasted Mediterranean vegetables and grilled.

2 peperoni rossi (red peppers)
1 peperone giallo (yellow peppers)
1 violet aubergine
1 fennel bulb
1 head chicory
extra virgin olive oil
3–4 new-season garlic cloves, unpeeled
fresh thyme
fresh oregano
2 tbsp finely chopped flatleaf parsley, plus extra to serve
3 tbsp breadcrumbs
4 caprini cheeses or 200 g fresh goats' cheese
sea salt and freshly ground black pepper

Pre-heat the oven to 230°C/450°F/Gas mark 8.

Deseed the peperoni and cut into long slices 4 cm wide. Trim the aubergine and cut into similar-sized slices. Slice the fennel a little thinner. Trim the base of the chicory and cut into 8 lengthways pieces.

Rub olive oil and salt over the vegetables and arrange in a roasting tray in a single layer. Do not crowd them.

Dot the garlic, thyme and oregano among the vegetables. Roast in the oven for 20–25 minutes, until the vegetables are soft and just starting to brown at the edges.

Pre-heat the grill to high. Meanwhile, mix the parsley and breadcrumbs together with some seasoning.

Pile a selection of the roast vegetables on to 4 heatproof plates. Sprinkle a caprini over each one and about a quarter of the breadcrumbs. Grill until the cheese melts and bubbles. Sprinkle with parsley and serve.

Goats' cheese and anchovy soufflé

soufflé di caprini e acciughe

Ideal as a starter or light supper dish, this recipe is adapted from *Sally Clarke's Book* (Macmillan, 1999). We use it when we have extra stock of goats' cheese. Cleverly, Sally cooks it in a wide soup plate, which is far less risky than a soufflé dish. We cook it in the pizza oven.

Per person

1 large egg, separated
50 g hard goats' cheese, grated or crumbled
1 anchovy fillet, chopped
1 tbsp fresh thyme leaves
25 ml single cream
knob of unsalted butter
25 g grated Parmigiano Reggiano
sea salt and freshly ground black pepper

Pre-heat the oven to 180°C/350°F/Gas mark 4.

Beat the egg yolk, then add the cheese, anchovy, half the thyme leaves and seasoning. Fold in the cream.

Butter a soup plate and sprinkle with half the Parmigiano Reggiano.

Whip the egg white until it stands in stiff peaks. Fold into the yolk mixture, then pour into the prepared plate. Sprinkle with the remaining Parmigiano Reggiano and thyme. Bake for 10 minutes, until brown. Serve immediately.

Glorious garlic

We use seasonal garlic in the shop, sourcing directly from growers to make sure it is of the best quality. The Scottish garlic season begins in late April when wild garlic appears in the local hedgerows. At about the same time, the first new-season garlic arrives from Italy, pearly white, with soft sweet cloves.

By the end of May we get deliveries of the new-season 'wet' garlic from Brittany. Hand-picked, these large, moist bulbs with a purple tinge open to reveal huge, juicy white cloves that give a creamy, aromatic flavour, far different from dried garlic. The cloves have not fully formed, so the whole head can be cut in half and used for flavouring. Even better is to roast the whole head with olive oil and eat the creamy, sweet garlic spread on bruschette or mixed with butter to serve with grilled fish.

Competition comes from the Really Garlicky Company in the north of Scotland. As the French wet garlic is arriving, Heidi is harvesting the first of the 'scapes', garlic shoots – these resemble wild garlic leaves, and give a mild background flavour to spring soups and pastas.

Our main garlic purchase is from France. About 100 km west of Toulouse, lying in rolling countryside within sight of the snowy Pyrenees, lies the sleepy village of Cadours. It is distinguished from thousands of other French villages in that it is the home of the world-renowned violet garlic. Every week from June to the end of November gourmets, chefs and buyers from all over France flock to the market hall, built like a miniature Parthenon in the village square, to bid for what is considered to be the most subtly flavoured of all French garlic.

We take delivery of our consignment at the end of July, hanging huge chandeliers of up to 100 heads from the ceiling, ready to greet the Edinburgh Festival visitors. This garlic will take us right through to the following spring, when the wild garlic shoots again.

Devil's chicken

pollo al diavolo

So called because it is very hot and spicy, you'll achieve the best result with this recipe if you use a free-range corn-fed chicken. It has sweet-tasting, yellow flesh from the corn, and the extra fat it carries under the skin will moisten the meat as it cooks. If you're not up to spatchcocking the bird, ask the butcher to do it for you.

Wild fennel pollen is a typical Tuscan flavouring, harvested in spring and traditionally used to season sausages and salami. It is magical in effect, having hints of aniseed, liquorice and flowers. With lemon juice and extra virgin olive oil, it transforms the flavour of this dish.

1 x 3 kg chicken
2 tbsp black peppercorns
sea salt
1 tsp wild fennel pollen or the fronds from 1 fennel bulb
leaves from 2 sprigs fresh rosemary
3 tbsp extra virgin olive oil
2 Amalfi or unwaxed lemons

To spatchcock the chicken, put it breast-side up on a chopping board and use a sharp knife or poultry scissors to cut down the middle. You can then pull the bird open so that it lies flat on the board. Trim off any excess fat, then cut off the parson's nose and break off the ankle bones. (Don't be squeamish!)

Alternatively, you can cut the bird into pieces, keeping some of the carcass attached. Cut through the skin between the leg and the carcass to remove each leg. Use a sharp knife to remove the breast from the breastbone, leaving some of the ribcage attached if you can. Cut off the wings. Save the carcass to make chicken stock (see page 115).

Wash the chicken quickly in cold running water and pat dry with kitchen paper.

Put the peppercorns in a pestle and crush with the mortar. Mix in some salt, fennel pollen or fronds, the rosemary leaves and olive oil. Rub this mixture over the chicken, making sure the skin is well coated.

Squeeze the juice of 1 lemon over the chicken. Cover the bird and squeezed lemon halves with foil and refrigerate until needed. Remove from the fridge 30 minutes before cooking.

Pre-heat a ridged griddle pan until very hot. Place the chicken and lemon halves on it skin-side down. Cover with a heavy lid, or something to flatten the chicken on to the griddle. Turn the heat down to medium and leave for 20 minutes or so, before turning the chicken to cook the underside. The skin will be blackened and crispy, the flesh inside moist and juicy. Griddle for a further 10 minutes or so.

To make sure the chicken is cooked, check that there is no blood near the bone. Remember that free-range chicken meat is dark in colour and might look uncooked.

Drizzle with a little more olive oil and the juice of the remaining lemon. Serve with boiled new potatoes, Sautéd spinach (see below) and the griddled lemon pieces, which are also good to eat.

Sautéd spinach

Spinaci saltati

Spinach can be gritty, so make sure you rinse it well. I wash it in a sinkful of cold water, then shake it in a colander to get rid of excess water.

3–4 tbsp extra virgin olive oil
2–3 new-season Italian garlic cloves
750 g–1 kg young spinach leaves
sea salt
freshly squeezed lemon juice

Heat the olive oil in a wide frying pan and gently warm the garlic to release its flavour.

Add the spinach to the frying pan, pressing it into the oil. Cook for 4–5 minutes, then add some salt and a good squeeze of lemon juice. Serve immediately.

Valpolicella

Part of Valvona & Crolla's role over the years has been to act as a catalyst between producer and consumer. Sometimes the prejudices against a product have made it a bit of a challenge, not least with Valpolicella wine.

During the 1960s the British market was flooded with cheap 'Val Pol', the tipple of choice for countless Edinburgh University students. They used to queue outside the shop to buy 2-litre bottles, rubbing shoulders with the Morningside ladies queueing up for a refill of Cyprus sherry from the barrels at the front of the shop. Eventually, those students of the 60s became the MDs and politicians of the 'noughties', and along the way gained a taste for classy Valpolicella and its older sibling Amarone (although many deny ever drinking the former because of its association with cheap plonk).

The Allegrini family is the foremost producer of Valpolicella and Amarone in Verona. Made predominantly from the Corvina grape, the wines are traditionally made in several styles to suit all occasions and palates. Fresh, young Valpolicella, with the strong aroma and taste of crushed cherries, is drunk six months after vintage. It is a heady, vibrant drink, ideal at cool cellar temperature. After a year in wood the Valpolicella takes on depth and complexity, and is ideally drunk with first courses and salami. The next stage is *ripasso*, where the wine is refermented with the concentrated dried skins of the Amarone harvest. This second fermentation adds more complexity, but also freshness, more perfume and alcohol. This style is rich and intensely fruity, wonderful with game and rich saucy birds.

Finally, there is Amarone. The same Corvina grapes are dried for three months, so the juice becomes very concentrated and after fermentation the wine is very rich and alcoholic – it's the flagship red wine of Verona.

Sautéd scallops

cape sante in padella

We use hand-dived scallops from the west coast of Scotland. They usually arrive already shucked from their shells as they remain fresher this way. However, we do serve them in their shells as they look so pretty.

16 shelled fresh scallops (ask the fishmonger for 8 shells too)
2 tbsp extra virgin olive oil, plus extra for drizzling
knob of unsalted butter
2 garlic cloves, finely sliced
splash of dry white wine
sea salt
4 tsp salted capers, soaked for 30 minutes in water, then rinsed and drained
1 tbsp chopped parsley
1 tbsp chopped mint
1 tbsp chopped coriander
juice from 1 lemon
100g fresh rocket

Wash the scallops, keeping the pink coral attached, but remove any dark vein running along the side. Pat dry with kitchen paper.

Heat the oil and butter in a large sauté pan that can accommodate the scallops in a single layer. Add the garlic, sauté gently for 1 minute to release its flavour, then discard.

Turn up the heat and add the scallops, wine and a sprinkling of salt. Cook the scallops for 2 minutes on each side until they change from translucent to opaque. Be careful not to overcook them. Transfer to the shells (2 scallops per shell) and keep warm.

Quickly add the capers, herbs and half the lemon juice to the empty sauté pan and cook until the juice concentrates.

Toss the rocket with some of the oil, sea salt and a squeeze of lemon juice.

To serve, sit 2 scallop shells on each plate and spoon over the juices from the sauté pan. Drizzle with a little oil and lemon juice. Serve with the dressed rocket salad.

Grilled red mullet with Taggiasche olive salsa

triglie rosse grigliate con salsa d'olive

Red mullet is a cheap, tasty fish, perfect for cooking on the griddle. Small but full of flavour, it is well matched with tapenade – a blend of olives, capers, anchovies and olive oil. Taggiasche olives are grown in Liguria, the northwestern part of Italy next door to Monaco and Provence, and the tapenade below, which is made from them, is deliberately rough so that all the ingredients can be tasted. Originally grown by Benedictine monks, the olives are black, small and particularly sweet. When harvested, they are traditionally soaked in brine and herbs, changed regularly over 40 days, assuring a fragrant, juicy olive. The light, fruity olive oil that is pressed from them is the natural choice for true pesto.

Fillets of red snapper with the skin on also work well in this recipe.

150 g pitted Taggiasche olives, preserved in olive oil
1 garlic clove, chopped
4 anchovies in oil
2 tbsp caperberries, preserved in vinegar
lemon juice, to taste
2 tbsp freshly chopped parsley
6–8 red mullet or red snapper, depending on size, filleted and scaled, but skin on
extra virgin olive oil, for griddling and drizzling
sea salt

Put the olives, garlic and anchovies into a pestle and use the mortar to crush them to a chunky paste. Add the caperberries and crush again. Squeeze in a little lemon juice to taste, then stir in the parsley.

Pre-heat a ridged griddle pan until very hot. Meanwhile, wash the fish and pat dry with kitchen paper. Season with salt.

Lightly brush the griddle with olive oil, then place the fish in it, skin-side down. Cook for 3–4 minutes, until the skin crisps underneath and the flesh becomes opaque. These fish can usually be cooked from the bottom up, so you might need to turn them only for the last minute to finish the cooking.

Transfer the fish to 4 warm plates, 3–4 fillets per person. Drizzle with olive oil and lemon juice. Add a sprinkling of sea salt and a generous tablespoon of the olive salsa. Serve with Fennel, radish and Camone tomato salad (see page 38).

Puntarelle
produce of Italy
£7.40 kilo

A Neapolitan abroad

We started importing fruit and vegetables direct from the Milan market in 1995 in a desperate attempt to offer more authentic fresh produce in the shop. Visiting the vast market, shed upon shed filled to the brim with the freshest, best-quality produce from all over Italy, was a revelation. Why was no one importing these foods already? Even as recently as 15 years ago, Dutch producers and supermarket buyers had such a stranglehold on the market that uniform, tasteless, out-of-season fruit and veg were the norm. It's no wonder that so many Brits didn't eat them – who would?

Walking around the market, we were overwhelmed by the sheer scale of the business. Whole sheds were dedicated to Sicilian Tarocco oranges, Amalfi lemons and glorious white bulbs of fennel, while whole aisles were individually devoted to ten varieties of artichoke. We also discovered tomatoes we had never seen before – Sardinian Camone and Sicilian Pachino – well before the usual tomato season starts. What amazed us even more was the incredible quality of everything.

As we wandered up and down the aisles we began to lose hope. This idea would never work. We were too small. These guys were dealing in lorryloads, not the one or two mixed pallets we could sell. The salesmen were shouting and gesticulating at us. Any buyer was a potential customer. They didn't know we were small fry!

Out of the blue, among the mixture of northern Italian accents Philip heard the familiar lilt of a Neapolitan. He looked across. An enthusiastic young man in a white shirt with rolled-up sleeves was calling across to his wrinkled old father, a man of about seventy, who was trimming damaged leaves from artichokes, making sure the produce was at its best. Philip introduced himself to the young man, the first person we talked to after an hour wandering around, and within ten minutes the deal was done. A Neapolitan family working out of Milan was going to collect together all the produce we needed from around the market and ship it to the son of a Neapolitan in Edinburgh!

There was huge excitement the day the first delivery arrived. Word had got round, and all the local Italian women converged on the shop to see. They arrived early, one by one, and waited, traditional black handbags hooked over folded arms. As soon as word reached them that the lorry had arrived, they moved forward, spilled down the stairs to the loading bay and out into the lane at the back of the shop. There, dumped unceremoniously, were stacks of tomatoes, oranges and lemons, artichokes and greens, herbs and salads. Without one word of a lie, I tell you some of them wept with joy! They kissed us with gratitude. At last, after years in culinary exile, they could buy and cook the food they knew and really understood.

From 2000 to 2007 Dr Enio Troili was director of the Italian Institute in Edinburgh. Because of our wonderful fruit and veg, Enio became a loyal customer and a great friend. He would arrive religiously at 5 p.m. on a Monday evening to get the pick of the Italian produce that had just arrived. He would share recipes and stories of food, and was relieved that in a country so far away from Sicily he could still enjoy the best of Italian food and wine in his adopted home town. He is in Bahrain now to celebrate the Italian community there. The area in which he lives is famous for its cherries, which are served with two bowls – one of whipped cream and another of melted chocolate – consolation, I'm sure, for the absence of Valvona & Crolla!

Fresh cherries, chocolate and cream

ciliege, cioccolata e panna

Good cherries are still a truly seasonal product, arriving in the markets during the spring, but often elusive because they disappear as soon as they arrive! They are ridiculously expensive at the start of their short season, so wait...the price goes down. Bing cherries from America are spectacular, as are the cherries we get from Italy in May. I have to hide them from staff and customers, as who can resist popping one into their mouth!

125 ml double cream
125 ml mascarpone
icing sugar, to taste
120 ml Fabri Amarena cherries
200 g Valrhona chocolate (70% cocoa solids)
500 g Bing cherries, or the biggest you can find

Whip the cream and fold in the mascarpone. Add sifted icing sugar to taste. Stir in the Fabri Amarena cherries and their juices. Transfer to a serving bowl and chill.

Place a sheet of greaseproof paper on a work surface. Melt the chocolate in a bain-marie, then dip the Bing cherries in and place on the greaseproof paper to set.

Serve the chocolate cherries on a platter in the middle of the table, offering the chilled cherry cream alongside it for people to help themselves.

Cooked cream with Limoncello

panna cotta al limoncello

This smooth, creamy dessert is very easy to make. We like to serve ours firm but not rubbery. It lasts up to four days, so can be made ahead of time. The Limoncello liqueur adds a touch of glamour for a dinner party.

4 tbsp cold water
30 g gelatine powder or 2 sheets leaf gelatine
115 g caster sugar
750 ml single cream
½ vanilla pod
zest from 1 unwaxed lemon
Limoncello liqueur, chilled

Put the water in a small bowl. Sprinkle the gelatine over it and allow it to get spongy.

Place the sugar and cream in a saucepan. Split open the vanilla pod and add to the pan. Heat slowly, stirring constantly until the sugar has dissolved, but do not allow to boil. Remove from the heat and stir in the prepared gelatine. Return to the heat and stir to dissolve the gelatine. Remove from the heat again and sieve the mixture into a bowl.

Scrape the seeds from the vanilla pod into the cream. Allow to cool, then divide the mixture between 4 ramekins. Cover with cling film and chill overnight to set.

To serve, slide a sharp knife around the inside edge of each ramekin, put a plate over the top and tip it upside down to unmould it. Serve with a sprinkling of lemon zest and a generous splash of Limoncello.

Or you could try...

Complementing the panna cotta with various syrups and liqueurs. Here are some ideas.

Sugar syrup: Place 125 g sugar and 190 ml of cold water in one saucepan, and put another 125 g sugar and 60 ml cold water in another saucepan. Stir both saucepans over a low heat until the sugar has dissolved. Bring the larger quantity to the boil and allow to boil vigorously for about 2 minutes. Do not stir while it is boiling. Allow the second saucepan to come to the boil and remove it from the heat as soon as it starts to brown. Very carefully pour the larger amount into the smaller one. Place over a low heat and stir gently until the sticky toffee on the bottom melts. Pour into a jug and use as required. It keeps in the fridge for up to 3 days.

Marmalade syrup: Blanch the rind and juice of 1 Seville orange in boiling water for 5 minutes to get rid of some of the bitterness. Place in a saucepan with the orange juice and 4 teaspoons sugar and heat to a simmer, stirring constantly, until it becomes a light jam.

Raspberry and ricotta tart

torta di lamponi e ricotta

Buffalo ricotta is very creamy, light and moreish, and goes particularly well with raspberries. For the simplest of puddings you could serve it with fresh Scottish raspberry jam, but this tart is not to be missed.

200 g Scottish raspberries, plus an extra handful
50 g caster sugar, plus extra if necessary
2 tbsp lemon juice
200 g buffalo ricotta
1 tsp freshly grated lemon rind
1 drop vanilla extract, or to taste
6 small, ready-baked shortcrust pastry cases

To decorate
handful of fresh raspberries
icing sugar, to dust
1 tsp freshly grated lemon rind
6 small sprigs mint

Place 200 g of the raspberries in a saucepan, add the 50 g of caster sugar and all the lemon juice. Bring to a simmer and cook for 5 minutes or so, just long enough for the raspberries to collapse. The mixture should resemble jam.

Meanwhile, put the ricotta into a bowl, add the lemon rind and the extra raspberries and mix lightly. Stir in the vanilla extract. Taste and add more vanilla and caster sugar if you wish.

Place a teaspoonful of the warm raspberry jam in the bottom of each pastry case and put a generous tablespoonful of the ricotta mixture on top. When the remaining raspberry jam has cooled, spoon some over the ricotta.

Decorate each tart with some fresh raspberries. Dust with icing sugar, then sprinkle with grated lemon rind and add a sprig of fresh mint.

Colomba cake with home-made custard

torta di colomba con crema pasticcera

Shaped like a dove of peace and traditionally given as an Easter gift, *colomba* cake is a sweet, yeast-leavened bread flavoured with vanilla, lemon and chopped peel, and covered with an amaretti-style sugar topping. Like panettone, *colomba* cakes are made by specialist bakers in Italy, and the best ones come from artisan firms rather than big brands such as Motta and Alemagne. We buy ours from a small family baker in Milan. The cake is lovely eaten cold, but can also be warmed and served with the divine home-made custard below.

750 g ready-made colomba cake

For the crema pasticcera
425 ml full-fat milk
1 vanilla pod, split
2–3 long strips unwaxed lemon zest
5 egg yolks
100 g caster sugar

Put the milk, vanilla pod and lemon zest in a small saucepan, warm through, then take off the heat and leave to infuse for 30 minutes.

Remove the zest and vanilla pod from the saucepan, but scrape the tiny black seeds back into the milk.

In a heatproof bowl, whisk together the egg yolks and caster sugar until light and fluffy. Place the bowl over a saucepan of simmering water, not letting the water touch the bottom of the bowl. Keep whisking while adding the infused milk and continue until the mixture starts to thicken. This might take 20 minutes or so. The custard is cooked when it coats the back of a wooden spoon.

Serve with a generous slice of warmed colomba cake.

IL GELATO
il gelato è arte
GELART
IL GELATO È

SUMMER

estate

NOTHING COMPARES TO the sheer joy of a summer in the south of Italy: glistening azure seas; waves soporifically lapping against bobbing boats; uninterrupted sunshine from dawn till dusk; long leisurely lunches; afternoon siestas; and, after dark, relaxing with a chilled cocktail, watching groups of gorgeous teenagers wandering up and down with not a care in the world. This is 'La Dolce Vita'.

Mornings bring cool breezes, smells of pungent coffee and irresistible sugary *graffè* – giant sugared doughnuts. Then a swim, a stroll, an espresso and the tempting smells of cooking – ripe tomatoes simmering on stoves, peperoni sizzling on open grills, the unmistakable aroma of wood-fired pizza ovens – thoughts drift to lunch.

Temptation lurks everywhere as the fast-food sales force descends on the beaches. Dismayed that no one will walk to their shops, the salesmen instead have no choice but to go to the customers. So barefoot bakers stride along the waterfront, trays of ricotta-stuffed *sfogliatelli* and crispy *cannoli* balanced on their heads. Bare-chested young boys offer slabs of rosemary-studded *focaccia*, salty and oily, delicious and indulgent. Old ladies dressed head to foot in black, with baskets of huge ripe peaches or mottled orange apricots picked from the laden trees in their gardens, smile their wrinkled faces to cajole you to buy.

The high-pitched call '*Cocco*'! rings out as *scunignizzi*, barefoot skinny kids, run from group to group, competing with each other to sell slices of creamy white coconut lying in fig-leaf-lined baskets of ice or huge slices of crimson watermelon, the ideal guilt-free, thirst-quenching delight.

The *granita* truck trundles along the beach on makeshift tracks. A clanging bell signals its position, the scraping sound of the ice being pared from a giant block an indication that business is brisk. Giant Amalfi lemons are squeezed by hand through an old-fashioned juicer, the fresh sharp liquid then drizzled over the ice to make the most exquisite refreshing drink.

And all this before noon. Then, as the church bells toll the Angelus on the stroke of midday, the beach empties. Glamorous young mothers lift beautiful bronzed children and take them home...for lunch, not church! All is quiet but for the lapping of the waves and the muffled chatter from beach restaurants until 4 p.m., when the whole opera begins again.

Short of being invited into the kitchen of one of the local's houses, the best places to eat lunch are in the busiest beach caffès. Many of these spring up for just twelve weeks in the summer and operate on a no-menu, cash-only basis. To please the taxman there is a printed menu up on the wall outside, but no one uses it, not even the taxman, who is invariably at the bar getting a free drink. The granddaughter of the cook will tell you what there is or, more often than not, just put a bowl of something in front of you: *spaghetti pomodoro e basilico*, *spaghetti alle vongole veraci*, *impepata di cozze*, *polpettine* or *bruschetta al pomodoro*. *Pane, sale e olio* or a bowl of giant cerignola olives are offered as nibbles.

Gioia!

Aperitifs

After a long, lazy day in the sun, a chilled aperitif is the ideal way to relax before dinner. Dressed for the evening ahead, and flaunting a sun-kissed glow, all you need do is seek out a sleek bar and a chilled drink. A fancy glass and a maraschino cherry complete the look!

VinCaffè bloody Maria

The bloody Mary is said to have been invented in 1920 by an American bartender, Fernand Petitot, at Harry's New York Bar in Paris. Apparently, Ernest Hemingway hung out there, just as he did at Harry's Bar in Paris a few years later...he got around.

Per person

25 ml Wyborowa vodka
125 ml tomato juice
good squeeze of lime juice
splash of Tabasco sauce
splash of Worcestershire sauce
celery salt
freshly ground black pepper

Put the vodka into a highball glass. Pour in the tomato juice, then add the lime juice, Tabasco and Worcestershire sauces. Sprinkle celery salt and black pepper on top and stir well.

Serve with a straw and a swizzle stick.

Gamba di legno

It's a mystery why this drink is called 'wooden leg' – but it tastes great and is wonderfully refreshing.

Per person

4 strawberries, plus 1 for serving
6 raspberries
175 ml freshly squeezed orange juice
ice cubes

Put the berries and orange juice into a blender with half a glass of ice. Blend for about 30 seconds, then pour into a tall, ice-filled glass.

Serve with a straw and a strawberry perched on the rim of the glass.

Multrees Walk

The Valvona & Crolla VinCaffè opened in the newest street in Edinburgh – Multrees Walk – in 2004, part of a new state-of-the-art shopping experience. We created this drink to celebrate.

Per person

crushed ice
25 ml elderflower cordial
25 ml freshly squeezed lemon juice
125 ml tonic water
ice cubes

Fill a tall glass with crushed ice. Add the elderflower cordial and lemon juice, then top up with tonic water.

Serve with a straw and a swizzle stick.

Campari arancia

Per person

50 ml Campari
5 ice cubes
200 ml chilled, freshly squeezed orange juice

Put the Campari and ice in a cocktail shaker and shake together.

Pour the orange juice into a long chilled glass, add the Campari and ice, and serve immediately.

Negroni

A classic aperitif (pictured opposite), though not one for the faint-hearted. As Dean Martin said, 'Ain't that a kick in the head?'

Per person

25 ml Plymouth gin
25 ml Campari
scant 20 ml Martini Rosso
ice cubes
1 long strip orange peel

Put all the alcohol and 5–6 cubes of ice in a cocktail shaker. Stir gently and strain into an ice-filled tumbler.

Hold the orange peel over the glass and set it alight; the orange oils will drip into the alcohol. Add the burnt peel to the glass and serve.

Antipasto misto

Perhaps the most popular dish we serve in the Valvona & Crolla Caffè Bar is our *Antipasto misto* – a mixed platter of Italian cured meats, mozzarella cheese and roasted vegetables. It's much favoured because it's for communal eating, offering a taste of everything and an appealing saltiness that whets the appetite for the food to follow.

The best antipasti provide something for every taste and can be put together with minimum fuss. Cured meats are always better freshly sliced and, to my taste, not always paper thin. At the deli counter we slice meats finely and interleave them with sheets of paper so that they can be easily peeled back and laid on the plate. Alternatively, there are countless packs of ready-sliced cured meats on the market, but the quality varies: the best can be very good, but cheap salamis are often highly laced with salt and preservatives.

Serves 4–6

8 slices Prosciutto di Parma
8 slices bresaola
8 slices speck
8 slices Milano salami
8 slices Napoli salami
4 slices finocchio salami
8 slices Fonteluna sausage
8 slices mixed Griddled vegetables (see page 172)
8 bocconcini di mozzarella
4 tbsp marinated tomatoes (see page 173)
2 tbsp mixed olives
extra virgin olive oil
2 handfuls of wild rocket
sea salt and freshly ground black pepper

To serve
few fresh basil leaves
unwaxed Amalfi lemons, cut into quarters
8 slices Bruschette (see page 173)

Arrange all the meats on a large platter or on 4 or 6 individual plates, fanning them out so each type can be seen.

Place the griddled vegetables, all at room temperature, alongside the meat.

Group the drained bocconcini di mozzarella and the marinated tomatoes together. Add the mixed olives.

Drizzle the whole antipasto with olive oil and sprinkle with black pepper.

Place the rocket in a bowl and dress with olive oil and salt. Add to the middle of the antipasto. Finish with some fresh basil leaves and lemon quarters.

Serve at room temperature with warm slices of grilled bruschette.

Griddled vegetables

verdure alla piastra

For those who don't eat meat, here is an alternative to the antipasto on the previous page. *Alla piastra* means 'cooked on a griddle', and this technique is now as commonplace in British homes as it is around the Adriatic. Griddling is the easiest and tastiest way to cook in the summer. The only problem is that it generates a lot of smoke; in our house we simply open the windows and hope for the best.

4 organic zucchini (courgettes), cut into long slices 2–3 mm thick
1 violet aubergine, cut into rounds 4–5 mm thick
1 fennel bulb, cut into long slices 2–3 mm thick
1 peperone rosso (red pepper), deseeded and cut lengthways into 6–8 pieces
1 head Belgian endive, trimmed and cut lengthways into 6–8 pieces
1 head radicchio di Treviso, cut lengthways into 6–8 pieces
extra virgin olive oil
1–2 garlic cloves, finely sliced
3–4 anchovies in oil
1–2 tbsp finely chopped flatleaf parsley
few Italian mint leaves, Roman if possible
1 quantity marinated tomatoes (see page 173)
sea salt and freshly ground black pepper

To serve
bocconcini di mozzarella
few fresh basil leaves
slices of warm Bruschette (see page 173)

Pre-heat a ridged griddle pan until very hot.

Place a batch of the vegetables and salad on the griddle and brush with a little olive oil. Cook them slowly until they soften, turning so that they get charred lines on all sides. Drizzle with a little extra oil to encourage the sugars to caramelise and their individual flavours to develop. Sprinkle with sea salt.

When cooked, transfer them to a wide plate, drizzle with more oil and add a few slivers of garlic. Cook the remaining vegetables and salad in the same way.

Chop the anchovies finely and scatter over the grilled vegetables. Add a good sprinkling of parsley, some torn mint leaves and a generous grating of black pepper.

Add the marinated tomatoes, either scattered or in a heap.

Serve with some juicy bocconcino di mozzarella, a scattering of fresh basil leaves and the warm garlic bruschette.

Roasted peppers

peperoni arrosto

2–3 Italian peperoni rossi or gialli (red or yellow peppers)
extra virgin olive oil, to drizzle
1 garlic clove, thinly sliced
few leaves fresh basil
1 tbsp black olives, preferably Taggiasche
chopped anchovies (optional)
sea salt

Roast the peperoni over a gas flame or under a grill until the skin is completely charred. Peel over a plate, collecting as much of the juices as possible, but discarding the skin, seeds and stalk.

Slice the peperoni thinly. Drizzle with olive oil, scatter with the garlic and add a little salt to taste. Sprinkle some torn basil leaves and a drizzle of olive oil on top.

If you are not using these roast peppers with the seafood salad, you might like to add a few chopped anchovies as well.

Bruschette with marinated tomatoes

bruschette alla napoletana

The secret here is the tomatoes. Fully ripe Neapolitan San Marzano plum tomatoes are sweet, juicy and with an appealing bite. They are at their very best in July and August.

8 slices sourdough bread
1 garlic clove, cut in half
pitted black olives, preferably Taggiasche, chopped
fresh basil leaves
sea salt

For the marinated tomatoes
6–8 ripe San Marzano plum tomatoes
1 tsp dried oregano
8 anchovies in oil
1 tsp capers, preferably preserved in vinegar (if salted, soak for 30 minutes before using)
extra virgin olive oil

Slice the tomatoes lengthways into 6 pieces, then cut into 5-cm chunks. Sprinkle with sea salt and the oregano.

Chop the anchovies and mix with the tomatoes. Rinse the capers and add them too.

Toss everything in extra virgin olive oil, then place in the fridge for 30 minutes to marinate.

Meanwhile, drizzle the bread with olive oil, rub with the garlic and toast on a heated griddle pan. When crispy on each side, place on a plate and pile the marinated tomatoes on top of each slice. Add a few chopped black olives and a final seasoning of sea salt.

Serve drizzled with more olive oil and a few torn basil leaves.

In the pink

As an alternative to aperitifs we have caught the rosé habit. In fact, rosés are now our fastest-selling wines. If well made, they are wonderfully versatile, ideal for sipping before lunch, and through all the courses that follow. New-style rosé wines are often perfect with either fish or meat, so they can solve the age-old 'couple's problem' of who gets to choose red or white!

Our favourite is Chiaretto, the lightest Italian rosé made from the lightest Italian red, Bardolino. From the elegant vineyards around Lake Garda, near Verona, this perfumed, almost dry wine is fresh and simply delicious, just the ticket if well chilled for all summer long.

As the market is growing, a lot of our red-wine producers are now making rosé too. Paolo de Marchi, one of Tuscany's most respected wine-makers and creator of the legendary Isole e Olena Chianti, decided to go home to Piemonte and create the most 'serious' *rosato*. And he did! His Rosé Sperino is made from 100 per cent Nebbiolo grapes – the same as those used to make Barolo and Barbaresco. This rosé has weight and intensity, and is the serious wine imbiber's pink. You could call it the drinking man's pink.

Prosciutto di Parma with mozzarella and figs

prosciutto di Parma, mozzarella e fichi

Stroll on a summer's evening in the south of Italy and you will be enchanted by the smell of figs. Even though there has already been an early summer harvest, trees still laden with plump, sweet fruits grow on almost every spare patch of ground. For me it is the late summer figs that are the most intense and delicious.

Per person

1 mozzarella di bufala
3 ripe green figs
4 slices Prosciutto di Parma
extra virgin olive oil
freshly ground black pepper

Slice the mozzarella thickly and arrange on a plate.

Peel the figs and cut into quarters, leaving the sweet, juicy flesh nestling in the opened skin. Add to the plate.

Drape the prosciutto slices over the figs. Drizzle with the oil and grind some black pepper on top.

Salad of speck, artichokes and rocket

insalata di speck, carciofi e rucola

Speck is cured ham prepared from the back of the pig rather than the leg, so is less expensive than prosciutto. Good producers create a product that is more flavoursome and salty than prosciutto, with a sweet edge of lard that adds a creaminess in the mouth. The best speck is cured with juniper and herbs to add extra flavour.

Artichokes preserved in olive oil or *olio di semi* (sunflower oil) are produced in countless artisan businesses in the south of Italy. They are wonderfully flavoursome with the saltiness of the speck. This combination of flavours is even tastier with artichokes prepared at home (see page 68).

Per person

handful of wild rocket
2 tbsp extra virgin olive oil
freshly squeezed lemon juice
6–8 thin slices speck
2 artichokes in oil, quartered
Parmigiano Reggiano
sea salt and freshly ground black pepper

Place the rocket in a bowl and dress with the olive oil, lemon juice and salt. Transfer to a plate and cover with the speck and artichokes. Drizzle with a little more olive oil.

Season with freshly grated black pepper and finish with generous shavings of Parmigiano Reggiano.

Seafood salad

insalata di mare

Of all the dishes we serve, I find this one most reminiscent of holidays in the south of Italy. We are so lucky in Scotland to have wonderful seafood available, of equal quality to that in Italy...you just have to try harder to find it! Although it involves quite a lot of preparation, it is simple and pleasurable work, and the end result is spectacular. Use any combination of shellfish and molluscs you find in your fish market, but I suggest you always add the squid.

2–3 squid or small octopus
1 small carrot
1 stick celery
2 tbsp white wine vinegar
10 live langoustines
4–6 handfuls of mussels
4–6 handfuls of tiny clams
10 queenie scallops
1 peperone rosso (red pepper)
handful of pitted black olives
1 garlic clove, finely chopped
extra virgin olive oil
freshly squeezed lemon juice
sea salt

To serve
finely chopped flatleaf parsley
lemon wedges

All the seafood needs to be prepared separately.

Squid/*Calamari*: Ask your fishmonger to prepare the squid for you – it is far less bother! Peel off the fine outer membrane, pull out the eye sack, which is full of black ink, and pull out the guts and clear central spine, which can all be discarded. When you get the squid home, rinse it well in cold water and cut the body into 2-cm rings. Chop the tentacles and slice the fins into fine slivers.

Bring a saucepan of water to a simmer, then add the carrot, celery, vinegar and some salt. Add all the squid pieces and simmer steadily for about 15 minutes. They are cooked when easily pierced with a skewer.

Take off the heat, drain and discard the vegetables. Set aside to cool.

Octopus/*Polpo*: Peel off the skin and discard the eyes and ink sac – or get your fishmonger to do it. Cut the tentacles and flesh into 4–5-cm pieces. Prepare the water as for the squid, and simmer for about 30 minutes, until tender.

Langoustines/*Scampi*: I buy langoustines only if they are alive and kicking. Cook them as soon as you get them home.

Taking care you don't get nipped, squash the backbone with the thumb and two fingers of both hands, then twist the tail, pulling out the black vein along the back in one piece. Wash in cold water.

Bring a saucepan of water to the boil, add the langoustines and cook for 4–5 minutes, just until the shell changes colour from red to opaque pink. Drain, rinse in cold water to stop them cooking and set aside to cool.

Mussels/*Cozze*: Clean and de-beard the mussels, discarding any that don't close when tapped.

Place in a saucepan with the lid on and cook over a high heat for 4–5 minutes, until the shells open. Shake the pan from time to time so that they cook evenly and release their natural juices. Allow to cool, discarding any that have not opened.

Clams/*Vongole*: Rinse the clams in cold water, then place in a saucepan over a high heat for a few minutes until the shells open. Clams can contain sand, so lift them carefully from their juices with a slotted spoon and discard any that have not opened.

Scallops/*Capesante*: Rinse the scallops in cold water, handling them as little as possible because they are very delicate.

Bring a saucepan of water to the boil, adding the vinegar but nothing else. Reduce to a simmer, add the scallops and cook for 4–5 minutes. Drain and allow to cool, then remove from the shell.

Once all the seafood is cooked, it is easy to assemble the salad. Mix all the seafood, except the langoustines, in a bowl. Add the peperone, olives and garlic. Dress with olive oil, lemon juice and parsley. Add salt to taste, but the natural saltiness of the seafood should be enough. Place the langoustines on top and serve with wedges of lemon.

Or you could try...

We sometimes use roasted peppers (see page 173) instead of raw.

Griddled squid salad

insalata di calamari grigliati

There is something uniquely alluring about the charred, sweet flavour of griddled squid. Even better is when it is marinated with herbs and a splash of lemon juice and married with sweet roasted peppers and fennel.

500 g small squid, cleaned
extra virgin olive oil
1 unwaxed lemon
2 peperoni rossi (red peppers)
1 fennel bulb
2–3 tbsp finely chopped flatleaf parsley
1 tbsp pitted black olives, preferably Taggiasche
sea salt
Cos lettuce, to serve

Pre-heat a ridged griddle pan.

Lightly rub the squid with the oil, place on the hot griddle and cook until the squid is well seared with black ridges and is tender when pierced with a skewer.

Lay the squid on a warm plate and sprinkle with salt and a squeeze of lemon juice.

Cut the peppers and fennel into thin slices and griddle as well, turning until they are softened and slightly charred.

Toss the squid, peppers and fennel together, adding any pan juices, plus a generous drizzle of oil, some salt, parsley and a squeeze of lemon juice to taste. Scatter with the olives and serve while still warm on a bed of crisp salad leaves.

Octopus and potato antipasto

antipasto di polpo e patate

The fish markets all over Italy are full of grotesque species of octopus and squid, each one more ugly than the next. They are hugely popular and appear on menus all over the country, particularly in Naples. In Edinburgh the best place to find a good supply of live, ugly octopus is at Eddie's Seafood Market, where the Chinese community congregate to buy their fish. Eddie always has a fabulous selection of octopus, squid and all manner of live fish, including scallops, clams and mussels.

1 octopus, about 750 g–1 kg
1 carrot
1 stick celery
1 tsp black peppercorns
1 kg waxy potatoes, such as Charlottes
3–4 tbsp extra virgin olive oil
2 unwaxed lemons, 1 cut in half, 1 cut into wedges
2 garlic cloves, finely chopped
2 tbsp chopped flatleaf parsley

Make it easy on yourself and ask your fishmonger to prepare the octopus. Wash it well in cold water, then place it between two clean tea towels and beat with a meat mallet or heavy-based saucepan to tenderise the flesh.

Put the octopus in a saucepan of salted water with the carrot, celery and peppercorns. Bring to a simmer and cook for 1 hour or so, until the thickest part is tender when pierced with a skewer. Allow to cool in the water.

Meanwhile, boil the potatoes until tender. Drain and allow to cool.

To prepare the salad, use a sharp knife to cut the octopus into thin slices. Roughly chop the potatoes. Arrange both on a platter and dress with the oil and a generous squeeze of juice from the lemon halves. Scatter with the garlic and parsley, and serve with wedges of lemon.

Sautéd mussels and clams

cozze e vongole veraci in umido

For an alternative starter to pasta, Neapolitans enjoy a plate of shellfish, scooping up fresh mussels and clams lightly steamed and served in their own juices. Halfway through they will reach for some crusty sourdough bread to soak up the flavours, thus replacing the carbohydrate and calories from the missing pasta.

In Scotland the best mussels are rope-farmed on the west coast and are available pretty much all year round. Unfortunately, it is almost impossible to get a supply of tiny *vongole veraci* (carpet clams) outside Italy, bar in the best London fishmongers. Nothing compares to the morsel of clam found nestling in the tiny, almond-shaped shell, still basking in the salty, sweet juices straight from the Mediterranean. Each shell is sucked to release the clam and its delicate flavour. The process takes the eater into a delectable solitude, head down, fingers working, distractions of fellow diners and conversation obliterated. These are the clams that make the real *spaghetti alla vongole* that appears on every menu in the south of Italy. Over here, larger local clams can be used, though they're never as delicate.

Per person

500 g fresh mussels
250 g vongole veraci (carpet clams) or small local clams
2–3 tbsp extra virgin olive oil
1 garlic clove, finely chopped
1 small piece peperoncino (dried chilli), crushed
handful of flatleaf parsley, finely chopped

To serve
unwaxed lemon wedges
crusty bread

Wash and de-beard the mussels, and rinse in cold water, discarding any that don't open when tapped.

Rinse the clams, making sure they are free of grit.

Heat the olive oil in a shallow saucepan. Add the garlic and peperoncino and sauté gently to flavour the oil without burning.

Add half the parsley, then the mussels, shaking them to get rid of any excess water. Cover with a lid and steam for 2–3 minutes, then add the clams, shaking them together with the mussels. Cook for a couple of minutes until all the shells open.

Add the rest of the parsley and serve in a deep bowl with all the juices plus wedges of lemon and plenty of crusty bread.

Chilled tomato soup

zuppa fredda di pomodoro

This is delicious as a light lunch when the weather is hot and sunny.

12 ripe vine tomatoes
2 cucumbers, peeled and deseeded
3 sticks celery
2 peperoni rossi (red peppers), deseeded
2 peperoni verdi (green peppers), deseeded
1 red onion
1 medium red chilli, deseeded, or to taste
2 garlic cloves, or to taste
100 ml extra virgin olive oil
1 tbsp freshly squeezed lemon juice
sea salt and freshly ground black pepper
2–3 tbsp sour cream, to finish
Tabasco sauce (optional)

Chop all the vegetables and garlic. Set aside some tomatoes, cucumber and celery to garnish. Place the remainder of the chopped ingredients in a blender with the oil and lemon juice and liquidise until smooth. Pass through a sieve to get rid of any skins and seeds. Season to taste.

Serve the soup well chilled with a swirl of sour cream and some chopped tomato, cucumber and celery on top. If you like an extra kick, add a splash of Tabasco sauce.

Freschezza e Qualità
Freschezza e Qualità
Freschezza e Qualità
Freschezza e Qualità
Freschezza e Qualità

Spaghettini with chilled tomato sugo

spaghettini al sugo di pomodoro freddo

This recipe, from Philip's great-grandmother, Bis-Nonna Annunziata, is perfect for hot clammy days. She made it when the San Marzano tomatoes were deep garnet-red and so sweet that you could eat them like pieces of fruit. Living in Naples all her life, she had the advantage of a constant supply of the very best San Marzano tomatoes, but we have to make do with what we can get. To ripen them, leave in the fruit bowl or on the window ledge for a couple of days.

750 g ripened plum tomatoes
3–4 tbsp extra virgin olive oil
1 new-season garlic clove, finely sliced
large handful of fresh basil leaves
sea salt
80 g spaghettini per person

Chop the tomatoes roughly into eighths. Place them in a sterile Kilner jar with the oil and garlic. Tear the basil leaves and add to the jar. Season with salt and store in the fridge. They will keep for 4–5 days.

Serve this sugo just warmed through to take the chill off it, or leave it out of the fridge for an hour before using.

Cook the spaghettini in salted boiling water until al dente. Drain, then toss in the sugo and serve. The heat of the pasta releases the aromas of the sugo. Don't add Parmigiano to this dish.

Pasta with tomato, aubergine and pecorino

pasta alla Norma

It is amazing the classic recipes that have been inspired by great music in Italy. Norma is the high priestess in Bellini's opera of the same name, and the song she sings, 'Casta Diva', was made famous by Maria Callas. This pasta dish named after her is equally exquisite. Recently this Neapolitan version has been cropping up on menus in Naples using, you've guessed it, mozzarella di bufala instead of pecorino.

6–8 tbsp extra virgin olive oil, plus extra for drizzling
1 garlic clove, finely sliced
1 small peperoncino (dried chilli), crushed
1 x 425 g can plum tomatoes, sieved or whizzed in a blender
1 violet aubergine
pinch dried oregano
360 g spaghettini
1 mozzarella di bufala, torn into pieces
handful of fresh basil leaves
sea salt and freshly ground black pepper
freshly grated pecorino, to serve

Heat 4–5 tablespoons of the oil in a saucepan. Add the garlic and peperoncino and sauté for a minute or so to release the flavours. Add the tomatoes and cook for 30 minutes, or until the oil starts to separate from the tomatoes. Check the seasoning, but go easy on the salt as more will be added later.

Pre-heat the oven to 230°C/450°F/Gas mark 8.

Chop the aubergine into bite-sized cubes. Toss in 2–3 tablespoons of the oil, then sprinkle with the oregano and some salt. Place on a baking sheet and roast in the hottest part of the oven for 15–20 minutes, until juicy.

About 10 minutes before the aubergine is ready, cook the pasta in boiling water until al dente. Drain and toss it in the hot sugo. Add the mozzarella and basil leaves, then stir in the roasted aubergine. Serve with grated pecorino.

Seafood spaghettini

spaghettini ai frutti di mare

Make sure that all the fish is spanking fresh and cleaned. I always rinse it at the last minute so that there are no stale flavours. You can vary the types of fish and the quantities of each, but steer clear of oily fish.

3 tbsp extra virgin olive oil
1 garlic clove, finely chopped
1 small piece peperoncino (dried chilli)
100 g squid, cleaned and sliced into rings
2 tbsp finely chopped flatleaf parsley
80 ml dry white wine
200 g baby plum tomatoes, quartered, or 1 x 425 g can chopped plum tomatoes
20 small clams, cleaned (see page 177)
12 walnut-sized cubes monkfish
8 live langoustines, cleaned (see page 177)
16 mussels, cleaned (see page 177)
400 g spaghettini
sea salt and freshly ground black pepper

Heat the oil in a wide, flat saucepan. Add the garlic and peperoncino, and as soon as the aromas are released, add the squid and half the parsley. Cook, turning, for a few minutes, then increase the heat and add the wine. Boil to evaporate the alcohol. This takes 4–5 minutes, and you can tell by sniffing the vapours: the alcohol will no longer catch the back of your throat.

As soon as the alcohol has gone, add the tomatoes and allow to cook slowly for about 15–20 minutes, until the tomatoes start to soften.

Meanwhile, place the clams in a saucepan, cover with a lid and heat for 4–5 minutes, until the shells open. Strain them and gently remove the clams from the shells, making sure they contain no grit.

Start adding the fish and seafood to the tomato sugo according to how long they take to cook: 10 minutes for the monkfish, 5 minutes for the langoustines, 4–5 minutes for mussels. Add the pre-cooked clams last, just for long enough to warm them through. Check the seasoning.

Meanwhile, boil the pasta in salted water until al dente. Drain and toss it in the sugo over the heat, adding the rest of the chopped parsley. Serve steaming hot.

Spaghetti with tuna

spaghetti al tonno

5–6 tbsp extra virgin olive oil
1 garlic clove, finely chopped
1 peperoncino (dried chilli), crushed
3 tbsp finely chopped flatleaf parsley
75 ml dry white wine
2–3 ripe plum tomatoes
200 g fresh tuna fish or swordfish
1 tbsp pitted black olives, preferably Taggiasche, chopped
400 g spaghettini
sea salt

Heat the oil in a wide frying pan. Add the garlic, peperoncino and about half the parsley. Stir the mixture, then add the wine and cook over a high heat for 4–5 minutes, just long enough to evaporate the alcohol. You can tell this by sniffing the vapours: the alcohol will no longer catch the back of your throat.

Add the tomatoes, crushing them in your hands to squeeze out the juices. Season with a little salt and cook for 15 minutes or so.

Rinse and chop the tuna fish or swordfish, then add to the frying pan. Stir in the olives and cook for 5–6 minutes. Overcooked tuna is most unappetising, so take it easy.

Meanwhile, cook the spaghettini in boiling salted water until al dente. Drain, reserving a little of the cooking water.

Stir the remaining parsley into the sugo, then toss the pasta in it, adding a little of the cooking water to moisten it if necessary.

Gnocchi with tomato and mozzarella sugo

gnocchi alla sorrentina

The sugo in this recipe is very similar to the one on page 185, but contains no aubergine. The mozzarella makes it wonderfully gooey and decadent. Here it is served with gnocchi. If you don't want to make your own, I suggest using De Cecco gnocchi for a fast, filling supper.

4–5 tbsp extra virgin olive oil, plus extra for drizzling
1 garlic clove, finely sliced
1 small piece peperoncino (dried chilli), crushed
500 g ripe San Marzano tomatoes or ripe vine tomatoes
1 x 450 g can San Marzano tomatoes, sieved or whizzed in a blender
fresh basil leaves
1 quantity Gnocchi (see page 23)
1 mozzarella di bufala, torn into pieces
sea salt and freshly ground black pepper
freshly grated Parmigiano Reggiano, to serve

Heat the oil in a saucepan. Add the garlic and peperoncino and sauté for a minute or so to release the flavours.

Score the tomatoes, place in hot water for 5 minutes to loosen their skin, then peel off and discard. Slice the flesh roughly and add to the flavoured oil.

Stir in the sieved or whizzed tomatoes, then add some salt and an extra drizzle of olive oil. Tear up the basil and add to the sugo. Cook slowly for about 30 minutes, then check the seasoning.

Boil the gnocchi for 4–5 minutes or as required. Drain and toss in the tomato sugo. Add the torn mozzarella and mix gently over the heat until soft and gooey. Stir in the basil and some black pepper.

Serve with plenty of freshly grated Parmigiano Reggiano.

Pasta with courgette flowers, cream and saffron

penne ai fiori di zucchine e zafferano

Zucchini (courgette) flowers are abundant in the summer, even in Scotland. They are wonderful stuffed, deep-fried or used in risottos or pasta, and are particularly good with prawns. Don't wash them, but check inside that they are not housing any hidden livestock!

4–5 tbsp extra virgin olive oil
1 garlic clove, finely chopped
pinch of fresh saffron powder, or pinch of saffron stamens soaked in 2 tbsp warm water
knob of unsalted butter
2 organic zucchini (courgettes), cut into thin batons
2–3 tbsp Chicken stock (see page 115)
2–3 tbsp double cream
4–5 zucchini (courgette) flowers, roughly chopped
400 g penne lisce (smooth)

To serve
freshly grated pecorino
few fresh basil leaves
freshly ground black pepper

Heat the oil in a wide saucepan. Add the garlic, sauté for a few minutes, then add the saffron powder or the strained liquid the saffron stamens have soaked in.

Add the butter and, when melted, stir in the zucchini. Cook gently for about 5 minutes, until softened.

Add the chicken stock, cream and zucchini flowers. Cook gently until the cream has warmed and starts to thicken into a sauce.

Meanwhile, cook the penne in boiling salted water until al dente. Drain and toss in the sauce. Finish with a generous grating of pecorino, some fresh basil leaves and a grinding of black pepper.

Neapolitan seafood risotto

risotto ai frutti di mare

Ask in a Neapolitan restaurant for a *risotto ai frutti di mare* and they look at you as if you're mad. They try to put you off...They prepare it only for two. Fine. You'll have to wait. Fine. Why do they do this? Because no one in Naples waits for food or eats the same thing as anyone else!

I think a well-made Neapolitan seafood risotto is a triumph. The trick is to prepare the *soffritto* well and then add the fish in batches, depending on how long they need to cook.

There are several types of risotto rice. The most popular is Arborio, a nutty, plump rice that cooks easily. Carnaroli is larger grained and, to my mind, most easily spoilt by overcooking. I prefer the Venetian favourite, Vialone Nano. *Nano* means 'dwarf', a reference to the small grain, which is nutty, translucent on the outside, and with a white core that helps to hold the bite. Stirring the grain during cooking releases the outer starches, thickening the stock and coating the more resistant white centre of the grain. In Naples they use Avorio rice, which has a nuttier texture and maintains a bite rather than going fluffy and soft.

This recipe is made with a light shellfish stock, but I often use chicken stock instead (see page 115). You could also use vegetable stock if you prefer (see page 109).

250 g squid
6–8 live langoustines
2 large handfuls of mussels
2–3 tbsp extra virgin olive oil
1 garlic clove, finely chopped
1 small piece peperoncino (dried chilli), crushed
2 tbsp chopped flatleaf parsley
125 ml dry white wine
400 g Avorio rice
2 plum tomatoes, chopped
1 tbsp chopped flatleaf parsley

For the shellfish stock
2–3 tbsp extra virgin olive oil
1 carrot, chopped
1 small onion, chopped
1 stick celery, chopped
500 g shellfish shells or langoustine heads, veins, eyes and dirt removed, rinsed
splash of white wine
1 tomato, chopped
parsley stalks
a few peppercorns

First make the shellfish stock. Heat the oil in a saucepan. Add the carrot, onion and celery and cook until softened.

Add the shells and turn in the soffritto, squashing the shells to release their flavour.

Pour in the wine and cook until the alcohol has evaporated. This takes 4–5 minutes, and you can tell by sniffing the vapours: the alcohol will no longer catch the back of your throat.

Add the tomato parsley, peppercorns and 1 litre of hot water. Simmer for 20 minutes and allow to cool before straining.

To make the risotto, prepare all the seafood as described on pages 176–7. Set aside.

Reheat the shellfish stock to a simmer.

Meanwhile, heat the oil in a shallow saucepan. Add the garlic and peperoncino and sauté for a minute or so to release the flavours. Add the parsley, then the wine and boil to evaporate the alcohol. This takes 4–5 minutes. You can tell this by sniffing the vapours: the alcohol will no longer catch the back of your throat.

Add the rice, stir, and add the tomatoes. Cook until they break down into the rice, then add a ladleful of hot stock. Stir in the squid rings and wing pieces and simmer until the liquid has been absorbed. Repeat this step until most of the stock has been used, stirring regularly to stop the rice sticking. This rice takes about 20 minutes to cook.

The langoustines and squid tentacles can be added for the last 6–7 minutes of cooking time, and the mussels for the final 3–4 minutes.

Sprinkle with the parsley and serve while still moist.

Venetian risotto with langoustines and courgette flowers

risotto veneziano con scampi e fiori di zucchine

This is a luxurious risotto, worth splashing out for as a special treat. I prefer to serve risotto *all'onda* (in waves), with enough liquid to hold the al dente grains in a creamy sauce. Regard risotto as a *primo piatto* – a light first course – and follow with grilled fish and salad to make an easy but spectacular meal.

12–16 fresh langoustines or Dublin Bay prawns

For the risotto

100 g unsalted Italian butter, plus extra to finish
2–3 tbsp extra virgin olive oil
2 shallots, finely chopped
1.25 litres Chicken, Fresh vegetable or Fish Stock (see page 115, 109 or 191)
250 g Vialone Nano rice
100 ml Prosecco or dry white wine

Bring a saucepan of water to the boil.

Meanwhile, prepare the langoustines. Holding them under cold running water, twist off the tail and pull out the black vein that runs along the back. Rinse well to remove any other dirt.

Once they have all been cleaned, add the langoustines to the boiling water, cover with a lid and bring back to the boil. Drain immediately and allow to cool. When comfortable to handle, press the back of the shell to crack it. Turn belly-side up and pull apart the shell, revealing the cooked langoustine inside. You can retain the shells to make fish stock (see page 191).

6 small organic zucchini (courgettes), with flowers (look inside to check they're clean)
1 tbsp finely chopped flatleaf parsley
few fresh basil leaves

To make the risotto, heat the butter and oil in a wide, shallow, heavy-based pan. Add the shallots and cook gently until soft and translucent, taking care not to burn them.

Meanwhile, pour the stock into a large saucepan and heat to a simmer. Check it is full-flavoured as this will provide most of the taste in the risotto.

Increase the heat under the shallots and add the rice, turning it in the soffritto to toast a little. Add the Prosecco and stir – the rice will jump. Cook until the wine is absorbed and the alcohol has evaporated. This takes 4–5 minutes, and you can tell by sniffing the vapours: the alcohol will no longer catch the back of your throat. This is important as the finished dish should not have a background taste of alcohol.

Add a ladleful of hot stock, stir into the rice and simmer until the liquid has been absorbed. Repeat this step until most of the stock has been used. As you do this, the starchy outer coating of the rice gradually breaks down, thickening the liquid.

Meanwhile, coarsely grate the zucchini and finely shred the flowers, keeping them separate.

Add the grated zucchini and the rest of the stock to the rice. Taste the rice to check that it is cooked but still with a bite.

Stir in the zucchini flowers and the reserved langoustines, then the parsley and a few torn basil leaves. The risotto should be very moist.

Take the rice off the heat and stir in a knob of chilled butter to finish. Serve immediately.

Chillies preserved in oil

peperoncini sott'olio

The signature flavour of Neapolitan cooking is peperoncino rather than garlic. Although the smell of sautéd garlic may be one that pervades the air in Naples, it is in fact used sparingly, often as a whole clove to flavour olive oil and then discarded. Fresh parsley is used as a foil to the pungent flavour, making for a more subtle taste.

Peperoncini, on the other hand, have a far more strident flavour. From early summer the first crops of the local red chilli appear in the markets and are strung outside every kitchen window to dry in the sun, ready for the whole year ahead. They are rarely used in the raw state; Neapolitan cooks understand the power of their own dried chillies and break off just as much as their dishes require. Every summer I dry three or four bunches by hanging them above my cooker then use them as I need them.

This recipe is adapted from Patience Gray's *Honey from a Weed*, a longtime favourite book of mine. You really have to make sure you prepare these properly as they can go mouldy and spoil. If you are not a pickle-maker, or are worried about the risk, it might be best to buy a jar of ready-made chillies in oil.

4–5 bunches red peperoncini (dried chillies) or 400 g small, hot round chillies
sea salt
2 fresh bay leaves
2 large garlic cloves
extra virgin olive oil

Wearing rubber gloves, wash the chillies and break off the stalk. Rub them with salt, then cover and set aside for 24 hours.

Sterilise a Kilner jar by boiling it in water for 5 minutes and drying it in a cool oven.

Drain the liquid from the chillies and place them in the sterilised jar. Add the bay leaves and garlic. Cover with olive oil and seal.

Keep refrigerated, and be careful that you keep the jar clean as you use them as they can go mouldy.

La passeggiata, le feste e la notte bianca

Apart from the glamorous villas with private swimming pools and jetties beloved of film stars and crooks, most homes in southern Italy are startlingly modest. The front door from the cobbled street might lead directly into a whitewashed living room with a tiled floor, large wooden table and chairs, a gas canister-powered cooker and a sink in the corner. A toilet and shower room doubles as a laundry room, and a narrow staircase might lead up to bedrooms. What they nearly always have is a balcony from which the woman of the house can hang her washing on a pulley and watch the comings and goings of family, friends and neighbours.

Life is lived in the open – out in the markets, in the piazza or on the beaches. And in the evening, after the heat of the day, the family in its entirety – *nonne*, mother, father, children and babes in buggies – go out for the *passeggiata*, the ritual evening walk that rounds off the day. In virtually every town and village in the south the population descends on to the main street, all gently promenading, chatting, gossiping, looking each other up and down. Music drifts from radios, youngsters gather in groups, old men congregate together on benches outside caffès, young parents and *nonne* push buggies.

Always keen for custom, the fishmongers, butchers, bakers and fruiterers are open for business. There will also be countless small shops selling ready-made food to eat in the street. The aromas are overpowering; resistance is required at every step. *Pizze* dressed with roasted vegetables – sautéd porcini, zucchini and rocket, tomatoes and mozzarella – are displayed in giant trays and sold in slabs by the kilo. Wrapped in brown paper, they are a delicious snack to eat as you stroll around.

Pizze farcite (stuffed pizzas) are even more enticing. Thick wads of dough are filled with various combinations: creamy roasted aubergines, melted mozzarella

PANINI CON
SALAME
€. 2,50 L'UNO

and shreds of fresh basil; slices of spicy pork sausage with softened plum tomatoes, basil and garlic; sautéd *scarola* (frisée), bitter and sweet, powerfully flavoured with anchovies, pine nuts and capers...Oh, why resist?

One shop might specialise in deep-fried treats – not fish and chips as we know them, but more inventive – pastry dough stuffed with salt cod or oozing with melted mozzarella and slivers of speck; potato croquettes, a favourite with Neapolitans, bought warm and revealing stringy mozzarella as you bite into them. No one thinks you're rude or indelicate as you wipe your mouth with the back of your hand, even though you're dressed up in your best summer frock. Nobody minds because everybody is doing it!

Anything that is harvested is cooked and sold. Small portable braziers are set up on street corners roasting whole corn on the cob, or grilled sausages on skewers...imagine! And if that is not enough, there is the constant temptation of *gelato* (ice cream). There is fierce competition among makers of home-made ice cream, their displays and queues of customers vying with each other to be brighter, bigger, fruitier and better. Nearly always family businesses, two or three generations, ashen-faced with exhaustion, will work the crowd, serving glorious flavoured ices, spooned and piled precariously high on narrow cornettos. Customers wantonly lick the melting concoctions as they parade along the street.

As if to prove their stamina, the partying culminates in *la Notte Bianca*, a night in the middle of summer when a town will stay open until dawn. Shops hold sales, caffès continue to ply their trade, bands set up in the streets and give free concerts, museums open their doors and offer free access to exhibitions of priceless artefacts, even the churches keep their doors open and masses are said all night long.

Not to be outdone by the Italians, people in Edinburgh have a chance to strut their stuff in August, when the International Festival hits town. Then the city transforms itself into a fabulous playground, with music, opera and art, street theatre, film festivals, wining and dining from dawn till dusk, a month-long *Notte Bianca*. The city is full to bursting with visitors and performers. People from all over the world come to party. And to keep everyone entertained, the Edinburgh Fringe holds a parallel festival in any space that can become a theatre: church halls, shop windows, graveyards and back rooms.

In 1996 Valvona & Crolla decided to join in and was registered as Fringe Venue 67. Over the years, in what is now a small theatre at the back of the shop, we have staged well over 3000 sell-out performances, celebrating Italian and Scottish music, folklore and comedy. Each year we have 20 different shows, including festival favourite Mike Maran's adaptation of *Captain Corelli's Mandolin*, and another in which Louis de Bernières plays his own mandolin. We have celebrations of Neapolitan and Italian songs and great fun with Philip Contini and his Be Happy Band. It also gives us an opportunity to open our caffè bar for dinner and serve our customers from morning to night – a little part of the Italian *passeggiata* in Edinburgh.

Stuffed courgette flowers with spicy sauce

fiore di zucchine farciti con salsa piccante

For this delicious recipe, choose small zucchini with flowers attached. The male flowers are bigger and better for stuffing. Here they are filled with mozzarella and anchovies. I use sunflower or corn oil for the deep-frying because extra virgin olive oil is too rich and the flavour overpowering. Serve them immediately with the spicy tomato salsa and a crisp green salad to complement the crispy batter and gooey mozzarella.

12 organic zucchini (courgette) flowers, with small zucchini (courgettes) attached
6 bocconcini di mozzarella, cut into quarters
3 anchovy fillets in oil, chopped
handful of fresh basil leaves
seasoned plain flour
750 ml sunflower oil, for frying
lemon wedges, to serve

For the batter
250 ml lukewarm water
25 g fresh yeast
300 g plain flour, sifted
1 tsp fine salt

For the tomato salsa
6 ripe vine tomatoes, peeled, deseeded and chopped
1 fresh green chilli, deseeded and chopped
2 spring onions, finely chopped
1 tbsp chopped coriander
1 tbsp chopped flatleaf parsley
2 tbsp extra virgin olive oil
sea salt

Start by combining all the salsa ingredients. Cover and leave in the fridge for a few hours to infuse the flavours.

Meanwhile, make the batter. Pour the water into a warm, wide bowl. Crumble the yeast into it and mix until dissolved. Gradually add the flour and salt, mixing together to form a thick, gluey dough. Cover and leave in a warm place for about 30 minutes, until it doubles in size.

Check the zucchini for any grit and look inside the flowers for any 'beasties'. Wipe clean, but don't wet the flowers.

Stuff each flower with a quartered bocconcino, some chopped anchovy and a few basil leaves. Twist the ends of the flower to secure the filling, then dust with seasoned flour.

Heat the oil in a deep frying pan until very hot. Test by adding a drop of batter: it should sizzle straight away.

One at a time, dip the zucchini flowers in the batter, shake off any excess and carefully lower into the hot oil. Let it sizzle and float before adding the next one. Don't overcrowd the frying pan as it will lower the temperature and the batter will absorb the oil and become greasy. Work quickly, turning or removing one flower as you add a new one. Drain on kitchen paper and keep warm.

Serve immediately with wedges of lemon. Pretty brilliant!

Roast trio of fish

pesce arrosto

As we have the pizza ovens on in the kitchen all the time, we use them to roast everything – big trays of vegetables, such as peperoni, fennel and zucchini; roast beef and chickens for the counters; large sides of pork stuffed with garlic and herbs. As the temperature is consistently high, over 300°C/570°F, the cooks move things around the ovens with the pizza paddle to get the correct degree of heat. This hot oven is great for roasting fish, either whole or filleted. Cooking briefly at a high temperature produces spectacular results and is so easy to do. For this recipe, ask the fishmonger to fillet the fish and descale it, leaving the skin on.

selection of firm-fleshed fish, such as sea bream, sea bass, cod, monkfish, halibut, wild salmon
extra virgin olive oil, for roasting and drizzling
sea salt

To serve
lemon juice, to taste
finely chopped flatleaf parsley, to taste

Cut the thicker fish (cod, halibut, salmon) into 80 g pieces. Wash all the fish in cold water, dry, rub with olive oil and salt, then cover and refrigerate for 1–2 hours.

About 30 minutes before cooking, pre-heat the oven to its highest setting and heat a roasting tray.

Lay the fish, skin-side down, in the hot roasting tray and roast for 5–6 minutes, until the skin is crispy and the flesh is cooked. If some of the pieces are very thick, put them in to roast a few minutes before adding the thinner fish.

Serve the fish dressed with olive oil, lemon juice and parsley. Sautéd spinach (see page 151) is a good accompaniment, or try Spinach with bottarga, sultanas and pine nuts (see page 211) for a more robust taste.

Or you could try...

Serving the fish with either of the following dressings.

Garlic butter: Melt knob of unsalted butter in a saucepan, add ½ garlic clove and 2 anchovies, in oil, and stir over a low heat for about 2 minutes. Add 2 tablespoons lemon juice and 1 tablespoon very finely chopped flatleaf parsley, warm through and pour over the roasted fish.

Gremolata: Mix together 1 chopped garlic clove, chopped, 2 tablespoons finely grated zest from 1 unwaxed Amalfi lemon, 1 tablespoon finely chopped flatleaf parsley, 1 tablespoon finely chopped fresh mint with a little extra virgin olive oil, in a small saucepan, season with salt and heat gently to release all the flavours. Pour over the roasted fish.

New potatoes

Every year Jimmy Cowan, the shop's builder and general carer and dear friend, brings me some wild salmon and new potatoes freshly lifted from his back garden. Many older folk in East Lothian still grow some vegetables in their gardens or allotments, a habit kept from the war years perhaps. It is now fashionable to grow your own, and allotments are springing up all over cities, but some things really have always been a way of life.

There is a great fuss about Jersey Royals and other new potatoes in the press, but by the time most people get them in the supermarket, they are already past their best. Nothing beats freshly lifted potatoes, especially those from Jimmy's back garden!

I use a pot scourer to scrub my new potatoes so that most of the skin is kept on. They then go in cold water and boil for 15 minutes. I then drain them and serve dripping with unsalted butter and chopped chives and flatleaf parsley.

Poached wild Scottish salmon

Salmone in bianco

My parents were always given a side of smoked salmon as a New Year treat. It was smoked by our local fisherman in Cockenzie, James Dickson, whose family have been fishing and smoking fish at the side of the harbour for generations. He smokes salmon for us still – nowadays eco-friendly farmed salmon – using the original smoke-house, which hasn't changed for over a hundred years. He uses oak chippings and slow-smokes the salmon in a small room whose walls are thick with the build-up of fish oils and smoke.

Sadly, Scottish wild salmon stocks are in short supply, and it is arguable whether we should be eating it at all. We do sell smoked salmon bought from reputable, eco-friendly firms, such as the Hebridean Salmon Company, who smoke with peat. We don't eat or sell much cooked salmon as I think the farmed variety is often dull and uninteresting. Having said that, a wild salmon or trout lightly poached and served cold with fresh mayonnaise is a Scottish treat that everyone should enjoy at least once a year. Ask the fishmonger to gut and scale the fish for you.

1 whole wild salmon or sea trout

For the court bouillon
1 carrot
1 shallot
1 celery stick, destringed and sliced
a few peppercorns
2 fresh bay leaves
1 tsp sea salt
splash of dry white wine

Fill a fish kettle or large shallow saucepan with cold water (make sure the fish will fit first). Add all the ingredients apart from the fish and bring slowly to the boil. Simmer for 15 minutes, then gently lay the fish in the water, making sure it is completely covered. Bring back to the boil, then switch off the heat and leave the fish to cook in the water as it cools down; 30 minutes should do it, depending on the size of the fish. When ready, the flesh is opaque and a skewer will easily pierce the thickest part.

Remove the fish from the cooking water with two fish slices and place on a board. Carefully remove the head, fins and top skin. Lift the top layer of flesh away from the bone. The bone can then be lifted out in one piece, leaving the rest of the fish intact. Ease the flesh away from the lower skin and place on a serving platter. Sit the other half of the fish on top.

Serve with home-made Mayonnaise (see page 73) flavoured with chopped fresh dill or parsley.

Veal chops with sautéd porcini

costolette di vitello con porcini saltati

If you are not lucky enough to find fresh porcini, you can use a combination of chestnut mushrooms and dried porcini instead.

4 x 350–400 g T-bone rosé veal chops
extra virgin olive oil, for drizzling
1 unwaxed lemon
2 sprigs fresh rosemary

For the porcini
300–400 g fresh porcini, or chestnut mushrooms mixed with 50 g dried porcini
5–6 tbsp extra virgin olive oil
2 garlic cloves
1 small peperoncino (dried chilli)
handful flatleaf parsley, finely chopped
sea salt

Prepare and cook the chops as described on page 208.

Brush the porcini clean, trimming the base and slicing them lengthways. Check them all over, cutting away anything you don't fancy eating. (It is worth putting them in a plastic bag for an hour as any infestation will crawl out and stick to the bag.)

If using dried porcini, soak them in a cup of warm water for 20 minutes, then drain through a sieve lined with kitchen paper to remove any grit. Rinse again, then chop finely.

Heat the oil in a wide frying pan. Add the garlic and peperoncino and sauté for a minute or so to flavour the oil.

Add the porcini and cook for 10–15 minutes on a fairly high heat so that they fry rather than sweat. If using dried porcini, add them to the sautéd chestnut mushrooms. When cooked, increase the heat to drive off any excess liquid and concentrate the flavours.

Season the cooked mushrooms with salt and add the parsley. Serve warm, piled on top of the chops.

There is, quite rightly, much debate in Britain around the use of veal. Demand for the meat is currently very low and it is still quite difficult to find in the shops. If we put veal on the menu, however, it sells immediately.

Veal is produced from young male calves, a by-product of the milk industry, to which they cannot contribute. Dairy breeds, such as Ayrshire, Jersey and Friesian, are bred for milk production and are not good for beef, so it became the British habit to send male calves to Holland for the veal market. There, however, bad husbandry produced veal that many consumers considered unacceptable, so the market for Dutch veal collapsed years ago.

This, unfortunately, has left a real problem. Dairy cows still produce male calves, and as these do not make good beef they are, if not kept for breeding, shot at birth. This practice is both distressing for the farmers and a dreadful waste of good resources. Addressing the problem, and the gap in the market, some British farmers are now raising the male calves to six months on grass and feed, producing rosé veal, which is darker than traditional milk-fed veal, but still tender and delicate to eat.

This is an improvement, and it's satisfying to think that Britain is now a nation taking a lead in recreating a healthy and ethical food chain.

Rosé veal chops with rocket and tomatoes

costolette di vitello con rucola e pomodorini

You can make this with pork chops if you can't get veal or are concerned about its provenance.

4 x 350–400 g T-bone rosé veal chops
extra virgin olive oil, for drizzling
1 unwaxed lemon
2 sprigs fresh rosemary
200 g sweet cherry tomatoes, such as Sicilian Pachino
200 g wild rocket
sea salt

Place the veal chops between 2 sheets of greaseproof paper and beat with a meat mallet or heavy-based saucepan to tenderise them.

Rub the meat with some olive oil and a squeeze of lemon juice. Sprinkle with rosemary, then cover and leave in the fridge for up to 24 hours. Remove about 30 minutes before you plan to cook them.

Pre-heat a ridged griddle pan. When very hot, place the chops on it for 4–5 minutes, turning them only when they lift easily and have charred stripes. If turned too soon, they will appear to stick, which just means you should leave them alone. Cook them on the other side for just 1 minute to seal the surface.

Meanwhile, quarter the tomatoes, mix with the rocket and dress with salt, olive oil and lemon juice.

Transfer the chops to a plate, sprinkle with salt and add a further drizzle of olive oil and squeeze of lemon juice. Pile the rocket and tomato salad on top: the flavours together are delicious.

Rosé veal with aubergine and mozzarella

vitello con melanzane e mozzarella

My teenage daughter, Olivia, loves veal and enjoys cooking it for the family. I buy escalopes and ask the butcher to vacuum-pack them so I can keep a stock in the freezer and Olivia can pull them out when she wants to cook tea. They take about 30 minutes to defrost, then she's away! She simply dips them in egg and breadcrumbs and pops them in the frying pan. Free-range pork or even chicken is a good alternative if you don't eat veal.

4 rosé veal escalopes
2 violet aubergines
2–3 tbsp seasoned plain flour
2 eggs
3–4 tbsp dried breadcrumbs
extra virgin olive oil, for frying
30 g unsalted butter
6–8 tbsp Butter tomato sugo (see page 25)
2 mozzarella di bufala, each cut into 8 slices
handful of fresh basil leaves
freshly grated Parmigiano Reggiano
sea salt and freshly ground black pepper

Place the escalopes between 2 sheets of cling film and beat with a rolling pin until thin. Cut each escalope in half.

Slice each aubergine into 4 rounds.

Prepare three shallow dishes – one with the seasoned flour, one with the eggs, beaten and seasoned, and one with the breadcrumbs.

Heat enough oil in a shallow frying pan to fill it a quarter-full.

Season the aubergine slices, then dip them in the seasoned flour, the egg and the breadcrumbs and fry until brown on both sides. Drain on kitchen paper and keep warm.

Add the butter to the oil. This time dip the veal into the seasoned flour, the egg and the breadcrumbs and fry until browned on both sides. Set aside and keep warm.

Heat the tomato sugo in a small saucepan. Meanwhile, pre-heat the grill to high.

Prepare some stacks of veal, aubergine and mozzarella: place a veal slice on a baking sheet, top with a slice of aubergine, a slice of mozzarella, a few basil leaves and a tablespoon of tomato sugo. Repeat with the remaining ingredients, reserving a few basil leaves to garnish – you should end up with 8 stacks in all. Sprinkle with freshly grated Parmigiano Reggiano and some breadcrumbs.

Warm through under the grill until all the mozzarella melts and a tasty crust forms on top. Dress with a few fresh basil leaves before serving.

Spinach with bottarga, sultanas and pine nuts

Spinaci sardi

Bottarga is a Sardinian speciality, consisting of salted, pressed and sun-dried roe of grey mullet or tuna. It has an intense, powerful flavour that, used sparingly, adds a touch of magic to pasta dishes and salads.

extra virgin olive oil
handful of pine nuts
1 garlic clove, sliced
500 g young spinach leaves
handful of sultanas
8–10 bottarga shavings
squeeze of lemon juice
sea salt

Heat the olive oil in a deep frying pan. Add the pine nuts and garlic and sauté to release the flavours. Add the spinach and a sprinkling of salt, then put a lid on the frying pan and sauté the spinach for 5 minutes.

Add the sultanas and mix well to warm through.

Scatter with the bottarga and add the lemon juice just before serving.

King prawn skewers

spiedini di gamberoni

Everyone loves *gamberoni*, and in my book the best way to eat them is straight from the griddle so the sweet juices of the prawn are complemented by the slightly charred flavour of the blackened shell.

Per person

6–8 fresh king prawns
extra virgin olive oil
1 unwaxed lemon
sea salt

If using wooden skewers, soak them in water for 30 minutes before threading them up.

Score the back of each prawn shell with a sharp knife to expose the black vein. Wash this away. Rinse the prawns thoroughly in cold water and thread on to a skewer. Drizzle with some oil and griddle for 5–8 minutes, until the shells have changed from pale to dark pink and have started to blacken.

Serve drizzled with lemon juice, a sprinkling of salt and any juices from the griddle.

King prawns sautéd with wine

gamberoni al vino bianco

If you'd like a more robust flavour to your *gamberoni* than the previous recipe, try this.

Per person

5–6 king prawns
1–2 tbsp extra virgin olive oil
1 garlic clove
1 small peperoncino (dried chilli), crushed
splash of dry white wine
squeeze of lemon
small handful of flatleaf parsley, finely chopped
sea salt

Clean the prawns as in the previous recipe.

Heat the oil in a frying pan and add the garlic and peperoncino. Fry for a minute or so to release the flavours, then add the prawns. As they start to brown, add a good splash of wine and the lemon juice. Cook for 2–3 minutes to boil off the alcohol and reduce the liquid to a sauce. Season with salt and add the parsley to finish.

And to drink...

Fish dishes cry out for a light white wine with a clean taste and no overpowering fruitiness or sweetness. We often opt for local wines on holiday as the *trattorie* in Italian holiday resorts are still careless about the wines they offer. They are more likely to understand their local wine, and a half-carafe of white with some ice cubes in it is often just what you need. Do watch the vintage on offer in restaurants in Italy: they might be tempted to think you don't know what you are talking about and offer vintages that are different from those on the menu or, worse, past their best. As a general rule, light white wines are best drunk within two years of harvest.

A lovely summer white of choice is Verdicchio, made from grapes of the same name in the Marche region on the east coast. The Santa Barbera estate produces a vibrant, dry, creamy ripe Verdicchio that, when well chilled, goes beautifully with any grilled fish.

Another favourite of ours is Fiano from the Mandrarossa label in Sicily. It is lighter in style with a good citrus fruit, so drinks well with white meats and meaty fish, such as tuna and swordfish, and grilled vegetables.

Grilled squid skewers with lemon

spiedini di calamari e limone

8–10 small squid
2–3 tbsp extra virgin olive oil
4 unwaxed lemons, cut into quarters
2 garlic cloves, finely sliced
1 fresh red chilli, deseeded and finely chopped
handful of kaffir lime leaves
1 tbsp flatleaf parsley
few fresh marjoram leaves
sea salt

If using wooden skewers, soak them in water for 30 minutes before threading them up.

Prepare the squid (see page 176), washing it well inside and out. Cut it lengthways into similar-sized pieces.

Put the squid in a bowl with the oil, the juice of ½ lemon, the garlic and chilli and mix together. Add a sprinkling of salt, then cover and marinate in the refrigerator for a few hours.

Pre-heat a ridged griddle pan.

Thread the squid onto skewers, interspersing the pieces with a quarter of lemon and a kaffir lime leaf. Brush with the marinade and griddle for 10–15 minutes, turning and encouraging the squid to blacken and caramelise.

Once cooked, drizzle with a little more oil, sprinkle over the herbs, some salt and a further squeeze of lemon juice.

Griddled Italian sausages

spiedini di salsiccia

Fresh Italian pork sausages are a real luxury. There is a distinctive and unique flavour and texture to pork raised in Italy. We get fresh sausages made for us with our own spices in the UK, as imported ones, being perishable, tend to contain lots of preservatives. Nonetheless, they do taste good.

You will also need four wooden or metal skewers for this recipe.

500 g fresh Italian pork and fennel sausages
2–3 fresh bay leaves
2 peperoni rossi (red peppers), deseeded and quartered lengthways
2 red onions, quartered
extra virgin olive oil

To serve
unwaxed lemon wedges
mixed leaf salad

If using wooden skewers, soak them in water for 30 minutes before using.

Cut each sausage into 4–5 pieces. Thread them onto the skewers, alternating them with a bay leaf, a quarter of peperoni and a quarter of red onion.

Pre-heat a ridged griddle pan. When very hot, place the skewers in it and cook, turning regularly so that everything gets a chance to soften and caramelise.

Drizzle with the oil and serve with lemon wedges and a mixed leaf salad.

Grilled corn on the cob

pannocchia alla griglia

4 corn cobs
extra virgin olive oil, for drizzling
2 garlic cloves, finely chopped
2 tbsp finely chopped flatleaf parsley
75 g unsalted butter, softened
sea salt and freshly ground black pepper
freshly grated Parmigiano Reggiano, to serve

Pre-heat a ridged griddle pan.

Remove the leaves and silks from the corn. Rub the cobs with some of the oil and salt, then place on the hot griddle for 10–15 minutes, turning regularly.

Mix the garlic and parsley with the butter.

Serve the corn with the garlic butter and plenty of grated Parmigiano Reggiano and black pepper.

Roast grouse with mustard fruits of Modena

tetraone arrosto con mostarda di frutta

Such a fuss is made in Scotland on the 'Glorious 12th' of August, when the grouse season opens and the first birds become available for the table. It's actually a bit of a nonsense, as grouse should be hung for 4–5 days before you can eat them.

This recipe is inspired by one from Ruth Rogers and Rose Gray, who run the River Cafe in London. Philip and I admire them greatly, not least because they consistently produce some of our favourite Italian food in Britain.

Mostarda di frutta is a fabulous staple on any table in Emilia-Romagna. Whole fruits, such as small pears, apricots, greengages and cherries, are perfectly preserved in a sugar syrup spiced with mustard. It is a perfect accompaniment to boiled meats (see page 262) and pork products, and adds flavour and sweetness to this grouse.

Per person

few sprigs fresh thyme
2–3 cloves
1–2 tbsp extra virgin olive oil
1 well-hung grouse, plucked and cleaned
25–30 g mostarda di frutta (mustard fruits), plus the syrup, for basting
1 garlic clove, unpeeled and squashed
2 slices smoked pancetta
splash of red wine
sea salt and freshly ground black pepper

Using a pestle and mortar, crush the thyme leaves, cloves and oil to a paste.

Wash the grouse inside and out and rub all over (inside too) with the oil mixture. Cover and refrigerate for at least 24 hours.

Pre-heat the oven to 230°C/450°F/Gas mark 8.

Remove the bird from the fridge, reserving the oil in the dish, and season inside and out, using plenty of pepper. Stuff with the mostarda di frutta, garlic and some more thyme, then cover the breast with the pancetta. Tie in place with string, and tie the legs together to keep the stuffing inside.

Heat some of the reserved oil in a frying pan and brown the bird well. Transfer to a roasting tray and place in the oven for about 20 minutes. If blood is released when you pierce the meat with a skewer, roast for a further 5 minutes or so.

Remove from the oven, take off the pancetta and paint the breast of the bird with the mostarda di frutta syrup. Baste with the frying pan juices, add some wine to the tray and return to the oven for a further 10 minutes to complete the browning.

When cooked, transfer the bird to a plate, cover with foil and set aside to rest in a warm place for 15 minutes.

Deglaze the roasting tray with a little more wine to make a sauce. Serve with the grouse.

Ischian-style wild rabbit

coniglio all'ischitana

There are so many rabbits running wild all over Britain today that I cannot understand why the meat is not on more butchers' counters. A combination of Beatrix Potter and the introduction of myxamatosis to control the rabbit population has frightened off the home cook.

The opposite is true in Ischia, the beautiful island just north of Capri. Apart from the water, which is shipped in from the mainland, Ischia's inhabitants are pretty self-sufficient; rabbit, fish and vegetables making up their basic diet.

We were invited to a friend's home on the island. He proudly showed us around his garden in which he grows everything he needs...He even has his own winery under his house. At the back he showed us his rabbits, about 20 of them, happily bouncing around in a closed-off area. He made us this recipe for lunch but needless to say, Olivia refused to eat it!

I prefer to let the dish cool overnight and then reheat it; the flavours develop. Serve it simply with plenty of rustic bread to soak up the juices. (You can cook chicken like this instead of rabbit.)

3–4 tbsp extra virgin olive oil
2 garlic cloves
1 onion, finely chopped
3 sticks celery, destringed and chopped
2 carrots, very finely chopped
1 fresh bay leaf
100 g smoked pancetta, cubed
1 x 1.5 kg rabbit, jointed and cut into pieces
125 ml Italian white wine
400 g very ripe San Marzano tomatoes or 1 x 425 g can San Marzano tomatoes
leaves from 2–3 sprigs fresh thyme
1 tbsp pitted black olives
sea salt and freshly ground black pepper

Pre-heat the oven to 200°C/400°F/Gas mark 6.

Heat the olive oil in a heavy-based, flameproof casserole and sauté the garlic. Add the onion, soften for a few minutes, then add the celery and carrots. (You need to use a bit more oil than usual in the preparation of this soffritto to make sure the vegetables soften and don't singe at all.)

Add the bay leaf and pancetta and cook for a few minutes.

Use a slotted spoon to remove the soffritto from the oil and set it aside.

Raise the heat and brown a few rabbit pieces at a time, turning them in the oil and setting them aside once they're cooked.

Return all the browned rabbit to the casserole and add the wine. Cook on a high heat to drive off the alcohol, but don't allow all the liquid to reduce.

Discard the garlic and bay leaf from the soffritto, then return the vegetables to the casserole. Stir in the tomatoes and thyme. Add a little hot water so that the liquid just covers the rabbit. Check the seasoning, then cover with a tight-fitting lid and place in the oven for 30–45 minutes, adding the olives for the last 10 minutes. When cooked, the rabbit is tender and falls off the bone. Serve with plenty of rustic bread to soak up the juices.

The Valvona & Crolla Funghi Foray

Our first Funghi Foray took place in 1997, when – as far as I can remember – my Olivia was still in nappies and Professor Roy Watling, the noted mycologist, was still in his prime!

The general interest in wild mushrooms, started by Antonio Carluccio, had reached fever pitch. Every September, as soon as the Italians arrived back in Edinburgh after their extended summer holidays, they would come into the shop and ask us to take a look in the boot of their cars. Invariably, they were stuffed full of wild funghi that they had collected in the woods around the outskirts of Edinburgh, and they wanted us to buy them. We never bought as we were always afraid of getting wrongly identified species and poisoning our customers, but they never gave up trying.

They were all very secretive and obviously didn't want us to know where they found their booty. But, ever opportunistic, my father-in-law Carlo had his own secret supplier. Adalina was a sprightly widow who made a living picking funghi. She came into the shop once a week with baskets full of chanterelles, porcini, puffballs and all manner of delicious species. She was an Italian immigrant from the north of Italy, but had married a Scotsman and lived in Granton on Spey all her life. She spoke broken English and fluent Italian, both with a broad Highland accent.

She constantly wanted us all to visit her and see where she picked her mushrooms. We went only once, four carloads of us, following Adalina's battered old motor. She would drive past a wood and screech to a halt, knowing just by looking at the trees, the terrain and the weather what funghi she would find. We had a ball and drove back to Edinburgh with what must have been 50 or 60 kg of porcini. We all stayed up until the small hours cleaning and drying the porcini,

excited at the sales we were going to make. We locked up, leaving the offices and shop full of trays of sliced porcini, just as Adalina had taught us.

Disaster struck. The next morning, when Carlo went in early, he got the shock of his life. We hadn't realised that some of the mushrooms had been contaminated with maggots. In the heat of the shop they had multiplied and the whole mushroom harvest was ruined. That fixed us!

We decided we had better get educated, so we recruited help and the Funghi Forays were born. Professor Roy Watling, one of our customers, was the chief mycologist at Edinburgh University. Another customer, Guy Cowan, had a mobile kitchen that he used to cook for film crews. We sold tickets for a Secret Foray, hired buses and took a hundred people to pick mushrooms, have their lunch from Guy and then a lecture and identification session with Roy. Happy days!

We still have yearly forays, albeit on a more modest scale, and we also hold free mushroom surgeries in the shop during September, when customers can bring their weekend booty to be identified. Don't underestimate the danger of eating wrongly identified funghi – it is really not worth the risk.

Roger's cream of porcini soup

crema di porcini

My friend Roger, a great author and cook, is in a permanent competition with me to see who can to make the best mushroom soup. This is my latest version of Roger's latest version!

500 g fresh porcini, or 500 g cremini or Paris brown cultivated mushrooms plus 25g dried porcini
50 g unsalted butter
1 onion, finely sliced
½ fennel bulb, finely sliced
500 ml hot Fresh vegetable stock (see page 109) or water
freshly grated nutmeg
extra virgin olive oil, for frying
sea salt and freshly ground black pepper

To serve
3–4 tbsp double cream
small bunch of fennel fronds

Brush the porcini clean, trimming the base and slicing them lengthways. Check them all over, cutting away any contaminated bits. (It is worth putting them in a plastic bag for an hour as any infestation will crawl out and stick to the bag.)

If using dried porcini, soak them in a cup of warm water for 20 minutes, then drain through a sieve lined with kitchen paper, keeping the strained liquid to add to the soup. Rinse the soaked porcini to remove any grit, then trim and wipe them clean. Set aside a few porcini or cremini slices for finishing.

Melt the butter in a saucepan and sauté the onion and fennel until they are soft and transparent. Add the mushrooms and cook for about 10 minutes, turning them in the soffritto. Pour in the hot stock and simmer gently, uncovered, for 20 minutes.

Liquidise the soup and adjust the consistency with water if necessary. Season with salt and plenty of freshly ground black pepper. Grate in some nutmeg.

Heat a little olive oil in a small frying pan and sauté the reserved slices of mushroom until they are slightly crispy. Add seasoning.

Serve the soup piping hot with swirl of double cream, a few crunchy porcini slices and a sprinkling of fennel fronds.

Potato and porcini dauphinoise

patate e porcini al forno

Dishes à la dauphinoise always include cream, and here it makes the porcini taste really luxurious.

175 ml full-fat milk
25 g dried porcini
50 g butter, plus extra for greasing
1 shallot, very finely chopped
700 g floury potatoes, such as Maris Piper or King Edwards, very thinly sliced
75 ml double cream.
55 g freshly grated Parmigiano Reggiano
sea salt and freshly ground black pepper

Pre-heat the oven to 180°C/350°F/Gas mark 4.

Warm the milk and soak the dried porcini in it for 20 minutes. Strain, reserving the milk. Rinse the porcini pieces and chop them finely.

Melt the butter in a frying pan and sauté the shallot until it is very soft.

Put the potatoes in a saucepan and add the strained milk, the shallot and the porcini. Bring slowly to the boil and cook for a few minutes. Add the cream and mix together. Season to taste.

Butter a deep ovenproof dish – one big enough to allow a 4 cm rising space. Pour in the potato mixture and sprinkle with the Parmigiano Reggiano. Place in the oven for 30–40 minutes until the potatoes are cooked and the cheese is golden and deliciously crisp on top.

Soft polenta with porcini sugo

ragù di porcini con polenta

1 quantity hot, soft polenta made without cheese (see page 47)
3 tbsp extra virgin olive oil, plus extra for griddling
1 onion, finely sliced
100 g smoked pancetta, chopped
125 ml glass red wine
10 g dried porcini, soaked in a cup of warm water
300 g mixed fresh mushrooms, such as porcini, cremini, chestnut and chanterelles, brushed clean and roughly sliced
1 x 425 g can tomatoes, liquidised
2 tbsp fresh parsley, chopped
1 tbsp fresh oregano, chopped
sea salt and freshly ground black pepper
freshly grated Parmigiano Reggiano, to serve

Make the polenta as described on page 47, but omit the cheese. Pour it on to a large, flat plate and allow it to cool. Cover it and refrigerate until you have made the sugo.

Heat the oil in a frying pan, add the onion and sauté until softened. Add the pancetta and cook through. Pour in the wine and boil to evaporate the alcohol. This takes 4–5 minutes, and you can tell by sniffing the vapours: the alcohol will no longer catch the back of your throat.

Drain the soaked porcini through a sieve lined with kitchen paper, reserving the liquid. Rinse the porcini pieces, chop them finely and add to the onion mixture.

Add the fresh mushrooms and the tomatoes. Cook slowly for about 30 minutes, adding water if the sugo is too thick. Season well, then stir in the parsley and oregano.

Serve the polenta with the mushroom sugo on top and plenty of freshly grated Parmigiano Reggiano.

Or you could try...

Adding 1 x 125 ml carton of double cream to the sugo at the last minute and serving it with tagliatelle and freshly grated Parmigiano Reggiano.

Grilled puffballs

vesce alla griglia

Puffballs are the easiest wild mushrooms to identify and cook, so they are a favourite.

500 g puffballs
3–4 tbsp extra virgin olive oil
leaves from 3 sprigs fresh thyme
1 garlic clove, chopped
1 small piece peperoncino (dried chilli), crushed
2 tbsp chopped flatleaf parsley
sea salt

Wipe the puffballs clean, trim the base and peel off the skin. Cut into rounds 2 cm thick.

Combine the oil, thyme, garlic and peperoncino in a bowl.

Pre-heat a ridged griddle pan.

Brush each side of the puffball slices with the oil mixture, leaving the garlic in the bowl if you can. Place on the griddle, pouring the leftover garlicky oil into a corner of the pan to warm through, and cook the puffball until lightly browned on both sides.

Transfer to a plate and drizzle with the warmed oil. Add a sprinkling of salt, scatter with the parsley and serve.

Sautéd chanterelles

chanterelles trifolati

Chanterelles are best picked after a warm rainy day – very common in August. Be careful not to pay a lot for very wet mushrooms; they will weigh more and their flavour is less intense.

250 g chanterelles
4–5 tbsp extra virgin olive oil
2 garlic cloves, chopped
1 piece peperoncino (dried chilli), crushed
3 tbsp finely chopped flatleaf parsley

Wipe the chanterelles with a damp cloth and trim off the base.

Heat the oil in a frying pan that holds the mushrooms in one layer. Add the garlic and chilli and fry for a minute to release the flavour. Take care not to let the garlic brown.

Add the chanterelles and 2 tablespoons of the parsley. Sauté slowly, turning the mushrooms in the oil. Allow the juices they release to evaporate a little, then season with the salt and add the remaining tablespoon of parsley.

Pasta frittata

frittata di pasta

When we go on the Funghi Foray we take a picnic that includes flasks of mushroom soup, mushroom quiche from our bakery and this Neapolitan pasta frittata. We transport it wrapped in foil and serve it cut into thick wedges so that it can be eaten with fingers.

200 g spaghettini or bucatini pasta
40 g unsalted butter
2–3 tbsp freshly grated Parmigiano Reggiano
250 g Chanterelle Trifolati (see page 226), or any mushrooms prepared in the same style
6–8 eggs
2–3 tbsp chopped fresh parsley
fresh basil leaves
2–3 tbsp extra virgin olive oil
sea salt and freshly ground black pepper

Break the pasta in half and boil in salted water until it is almost cooked – slightly more al dente than normal.

Drain the pasta and toss it with the butter and 2 tablespoons Parmigiano Reggiano. Add the cooked mushrooms and mix together. Allow to cool.

Beat the eggs and season well. Add the parsley, torn basil leaves and another tablespoon grated Parmigiano Reggiano. Stir in the cold pasta mixture.

Heat the oil in a heavy-based frying pan. Pour in the pasta mixture and cook slowly until almost dry on top.

Put a large plate over the frying pan and tip it upside down so that the frittata sits on the plate. Slide it back into the frying pan to finish cooking the other side. Leave to cool, but don't refrigerate it.

Panzanella salad

panzanella

This salad is perfect for picnics as it tastes better if set aside for a couple of hours before serving. In fact, Philip says all salads should be prepared before the meal to give them a chance to *mescolare* – mix, shuffle or blend.

2 peperoni rossi (red peppers)
2 peperoni gialli (yellow peppers)
1 garlic clove, crushed
5–6 tbsp extra virgin olive oil
2–3 tbsp red wine vinegar
1 tsp salted capers, soaked for 30 minutes and rinsed
100 g cherry or Pachino tomatoes
200 g stale sourdough bread, cut into cubes
½ red onion, very thinly sliced and rinsed well in cold water
handful of pitted black olives
sea salt and freshly ground black pepper
handful of fresh basil leaves, to serve

Pre-heat the oven to 200°C/400°F/Gas mark 6.

Deseed both lots of peperoni and chop them into cubes or, even better, place them on a hot griddle until blackened and softened before peeling and slicing. Allow to cool.

Mix the garlic with the oil, vinegar and capers. Set aside.

Deseed the tomatoes and place on a baking sheet. Cook in the oven for 10 minutes. Meanwhile, toast the cubed bread.

Mix together all the chopped vegetables, the tomatoes and the toasted bread. Pour in the oil mixture, add the olives and toss well. Check the seasoning.

Cover and place in the fridge for at least 2 hours. Dress with the basil leaves just before serving.

Fresh melon and raspberries

melone e lamponi

There is nothing nicer than a big bowl of chilled fresh melon slices and punnets of Scottish raspberries to eat on a picnic. You can eat them standing up with no ceremony.

1 Galia melon
½ watermelon
2 punnets raspberries
1 lemon
2 tsp icing sugar

Peel and seed both melons and cut into cubes.

Mix the raspberries with the melon.

Squeeze over some lemon juice, to taste, and sprinkle with the icing sugar.

Strawberries with aged balsamic vinegar

fragole all'aceto balsamico tradizionale

In the late spring tiny, gnarled alpine strawberries appear in the markets in Italy. They are wonderfully flavoured, delicate and aromatic. Unfortunately, they do not travel well, so we buy our strawberries from local farms.

2 punnets strawberries
1 tsp balsamic vinegar
2 tsp icing sugar

Marinate the strawberries in the vinegar and icing sugar to bring out their flavour. The balsamic acts like magic, enhancing the flavours and aroma.

Refrigerate then remove from the refrigerator 15 minutes before serving.

And to drink...

This is lovely served with glasses of chilled Giosio Fragolino, a lovely strawberry-flavoured sparkling wine from the Veneto.

Blaeberry tart

torta di mirtilli

Blaeberries – Scottish blueberries – work particularly well in this tart but you could use any good summer fruit: strawberries, raspberries, peaches or apricots. The filling is bound together with a delicious custard mixture called *crema pasticcera*.

1 kg blueberries
apricot jam, to glaze

For the pastry
100 g softened butter, plus extra for greasing
50 g caster sugar
120 g plain flour, plus extra for dusting
50 g cornflour

For the crema pasticcera
425 ml full-fat milk
1 vanilla pod, split
2–3 long strips unwaxed lemon zest
5 egg yolks
100 g caster sugar
2 tbsp plain flour
1 tbsp cornflour

Pre-heat the oven to 150ºC/300ºF/Gas mark 2. Grease a 30-cm tart tin.

Start by making the pastry. Beat the butter and sugar until soft and creamy. Sift the flours into the mixture and stir well to make a dough.

Dust a clean work surface with flour and roll out the dough to a thickness of 2–3 cm. Use to line the prepared tin. Bake for 30 minutes, or until the pastry is lightly browned. Set aside to cool.

To make the crema pasticcera, place the milk in a saucepan, add the vanilla pod and lemon zest and bring just to blood heat. Allow the flavours to infuse for 10 minutes.

Remove the vanilla pod but scrape the seeds into the milk for extra flavour. Discard the lemon zest.

Whisk the egg yolks with the sugar until they are light and fluffy. Sift the flours into the mixture and fold together.

Sit the bowl over a saucepan of simmering water and whisk in the hot milk. Cook gently, stirring until the mixture begins to thicken and coat the back of the spoon. Set aside to get cold.

Spread some crema pasticcera into the cold pastry case. Arrange the berries on top in an attractive display.

Melt the apricot jam and brush over the fruit to give a professional glaze.

Summer pudding with orange-flower water cream

tortino di fruta eftiva

During the summer Scotland is awash with wonderful berries, wild and cultivated. Pick-your-own farms are all over the place. As well as fabulous strawberries and raspberries (the best in Britain), there are loganberries, brambles (blackberries), Tayberries (a cross between the blackberry and raspberry), and blaeberries (blueberries). Berries are extremely healthy and Scottish schools are encouraging children to eat them daily. I agree.

We use unsprayed or organic soft fruit and make individual summer puddings. You can use 6–8 individual ramekins or a 1.5 litre pudding bowl.

Serves 6–8

750 g mixed soft fruits: raspberries, blackcurrants, redcurrants, blueberries, loganberries, strawberries
1 vanilla pod, split open
2–3 tbsp caster sugar
½ lemon
1 sourdough or other country-style loaf

For the flower water cream
1 small carton whipping cream
2 tsp orange-flower water
3–4 tsp icing sugar, or to taste

Prepare the fruit, discarding leaves and stalks. Place in a wide saucepan with the vanilla pod and sugar and cook gently until the juices start to run – about 15 minutes.

Remove the vanilla pod and scrape the seeds into the fruit. Taste, adding more sugar as necessary and a squeeze of lemon juice to bring out the flavour.

Cut the bread very thinly (about the thickness of sliced white bread), discarding the crusts. Use to line the base and sides of the ramekins or bowl.

Strain the fruit, collecting the juice in a jug. Pour the juice all over the bread, soaking it well, then pack the ramekins or bowl with the fruit. Cover with more bread to form a lid. Put a plate on top and weigh it down with a tin of beans or something similar. Refrigerate for at least 24 hours.

Lightly whip the cream, then fold in the flower water and sugar to taste.

Tip the pudding(s) upside down to unmould, and serve with fluffy mounds of the flower water cream.

Plum, damson and apple crumble

'crollare' di frutta

Uncle Victor Crolla used to tease us and say that 'Crolla' translated as 'crumble'. Strictly speaking, he is correct, 'crollare' means 'to crumble'! This pudding is in his honour...

I have some small fruit trees in the back garden that we planted for fun. We now have a supply of distorted fruit that is fit only for cooking, but it makes a mean crumble.

900 g (prepared weight) soft ripe plums, damsons and cooking apples
2 tbsp muscovado sugar or caster sugar
1 cinnamon stick

For the crumble
200 g plain flour
55 g porridge oats
100 g soft brown sugar or caster sugar
85 g softened butter

Cut the plums and damsons in half and remove the stones.

Peel and core the apples and cut them into pieces roughly the same size as the plums.

Place all the fruit in a saucepan with the sugar and cinnamon stick and cook gently until softened.

Pre-heat the oven to 200°C/400°F/Gas mark 6.

Mix the flour, oats and sugar in a bowl and rub in the butter to form a mixture that resembles breadcrumbs.

Taste the fruit, adding a little more sugar or water if necessary. Transfer to a shallow heatproof dish and sprinkle over the crumble topping. Bake for about 30 minutes. Serve with vanilla ice cream.

Baked figs with mascarpone whip

fichi al forno con mascarpone

We get Italian figs twice during the summer – once in June and July, then again at the end of August until the end of October. The second crop is always sweeter.

The best figs are those with thin green and purple skin that is soft and almost bursting. They are best peeled and eaten at room temperature, or with fresh goats' cheese or decadently thick slices of Prosciutto di Parma. Lots of recipes call for honey with figs, but I prefer to use sugar that has been flavoured with a vanilla pod. You can also buy little sachets of intense vanilla icing sugar, which can be sprinkled over the figs after they have been cooked.

On late summer evenings in southern Italy the heady smell of ripe figs pervades the air, making me think that this must surely have been where the Garden of Eden was located.

8–12 ripe figs
2 tbsp vanilla sugar
splash of Marsala
1 cinnamon stick or vanilla pod (optional)
peelings from ½ unwaxed lemon (optional)

For the mascarpone whip
250 g mascarpone
2 tbsp caster sugar
2 tbsp Marsala
juice of ½ orange
2 egg whites, lightly whipped

Pre-heat the oven to 200°C/400°F/Gas mark 6 or heat the grill.

Wipe the figs with damp kitchen paper. Put them in a baking sheet, arranged quite tightly together. Sprinkle with the vanilla sugar and add a good splash of Marsala. Add the cinnamon stick and lemon peel, if using.

Bake for 20 minutes, or cook them under the grill for 10 minutes or so, until they are soft and sizzling.

Meanwhile, make the mascarpone whip. Place the mascarpone in a bowl, add the sugar and whisk well.

Fold in the Marsala and orange juice, then fold in the egg whites. Taste, adding more sugar or alcohol if you wish.

Allow the figs to cool before serving them with a little of the juices from the baking sheet and a dollop of the mascarpone whip.

Italian meringues

Spumone

Venice is famous for its *spumone* – giant glorious meringues that adorn bakers' windows and are delicious just eaten in the street as soon as they're purchased. We make them adding chopped almonds, pistachios or raspberries to vary the flavour.

115 g egg whites
225 g caster sugar
30 g flaked almonds or 30 g chopped pistachios or 100 g raspberries (optional)

Pre-heat the oven to 150°C/300°F/Gas mark 2. Line 2 large baking sheets with non-stick baking parchment.

Put the egg whites and sugar in a bowl set over a saucepan of simmering water and stir until the sugar has dissolved and the mixture is quite warm to the touch.

Transfer the mixture to the metal bowl of a heavy-duty electric mixer (I use my Kenwood) and whisk until thick and cool – about 15 minutes. If using pistachios or raspberries, mix in your choice of flavouring now.

Spoon 6 large mounds of meringue on to each tray. If using almonds, lightly sprinkle with the almonds.

Place the meringues in the oven, turn off the heat and leave to dry out overnight.

Whisky-flavoured ice cream

gelato spazzacamino

This *gelato* comes from Marcella Hazan's *Classic Italian Cookbook* (W.H. Allen, 1975), and we have put it on the menu to celebrate the 250th anniversary of the birth of Robert Burns. A rich vanilla ice cream is needed to stand up to the whisky and espresso flavourings.

Per person

2 scoops rich vanilla ice cream
dram of Scotch whisky
1 tsp extra finely ground espresso coffee

Put the ice cream in a bowl. Pour a dram of your favourite Scotch whisky over it and sprinkle with the coffee. Trust me...it's fabulous!

Sicilian profiteroles

profiteroles alla siciliana

In Sicily, more than in any other part of Italy, there is a rich tradition of sweetmeats. These choux buns are filled with a delicious mixture of cream, ricotta and chopped peel.

Makes 10

35 g angelica
35 g candied orange peel
35 g candied citron peel
Marsala, for soaking
120 g whipped cream
225 g fresh ricotta or cream cheese
1 tsp orange-flower water
1 tsp vanilla extract
caster sugar, to taste
squeeze of lemon juice (optional)
icing sugar, to dust

For the choux pastry
65 g strong white flour
150 ml cold water
50 g unsalted butter
1 tsp caster sugar
2 medium eggs, beaten

Finely chop all the candied peel, place in a bowl and add enough Marsala to cover. Leave to soak for 1 hour.

Pre-heat the oven to 200°C/400°F/Gas mark 6.

Grease a baking sheet that has been run under a stream of cold water: the steam produced during cooking will help the pastry to rise.

Weigh out all the pastry ingredients before you start. Sift the flour onto a sheet of greaseproof paper.

Heat the water, butter and sugar in a saucepan until the butter has melted. Take off the heat and slide in all the flour from the greaseproof paper. Stir with a wooden spoon until a soft ball of dough forms. Add the eggs, a little at a time, beating each addition well to make a thick, glossy paste.

Using 2 teaspoons, divide the mixture into 10 portions and place on the prepared baking sheet, spacing them well apart. Bake for 10 minutes, then raise the temperature to 220°C/425°F/Gas mark 7 and bake for a further 15 minutes. When cooked, the choux buns should be crisp and well risen. If they appear to be soggy, cook for a further 5 minutes.

Pierce each bun with a skewer to release any steam trapped inside. This will enable them to dry out and maintain their shape. Cool on a wire rack.

Place the cream, ricotta, orange-flower water and vanilla extract in a bowl. Add the soaked peel and Marsala and mix well with a fork. Add caster sugar to taste and a squeeze of lemon juice if necessary.

Cut the buns open and fill them with spoonfuls of the cream mixture. Dust with the icing sugar and serve immediately.

Lemon sorbet with sparkling wine and vodka

Sgroppino

This is a lovely alternative to a dessert after a summer meal.

Per person

125 ml Prosecco
12.5 ml vodka
2 generous tbsp good-quality lemon sorbet
sprig fresh mint

Add everything except the mint to a blender and whiz until combined. Serve in a chilled champagne glass with the sprig of mint.

Tropical mint milk

latte e menta

In Italy children are often allowed to stay up late with the adults when there's a party...learning how to live La Dolce Vita. This lovely green milk is a favourite among them ensuring they don't feel left out as the adults sip their cocktails.

Per person

3 ice cubes, crushed
35 ml peppermint syrup
125 ml chilled full-fat milk
sprig fresh mint

Put the ice and mint syrup in a tall glass. Top up with the chilled milk and serve with the mint sprig.

ZUCCA
ROSSA
€ 1.00
AL CHILO

AUTUMN

autunno

UNCLE VICTOR CROLLA built up his contacts in the business over many years, but most of them were rooted in the Italian community in London many of whom he built up while he was interned on the Isle of Man during the war. In the camps were British-based Italians from all walks of life: doctors and lawyers, musicians and priests, shop-keepers and chefs. Although some became depressed and languished, Victor used his time to learn. He studied music and language, and made friends with Italians from London, building up business contacts that would be invaluable if he survived the war.

After the war, Victor saw a way forward. Realising that all the boarded-up Italian businesses would need new equipment and people to fit it, he reinvented Valvona & Crolla as suppliers and fitters to the ice-cream and fish and chip shop trade. In this way he helped out his old contacts in Scotland *and* his new contacts in London, saving his own company in the process. Within ten years, all the chip shops and ice-cream shops on the east coast of Scotland, from John O'Groat's to Dunbar, were transformed into Italian caffès, with sparkling windows, shiny tiles and stainless-steel fish-fryers and ranges. Of course, they all needed supplies as well: chip fat, pickled onions and brown sauce; ice-cream mix, wafers, sauces and scoops!

Dominic, the salesman of the two brothers, was sent around the country delivering equipment and stock and taking orders for pasta, cheese and olive oil. Victor was the buyer and took the *Flying Scotsman* to London once a month to visit his new friends in Soho. He dealt with other established family companies, such as Parmigiani & Lawrence, Giardano, R&H Amar and Camissa. He came back with suitcases filled with stock and handwritten orders of goods to be delivered to Edinburgh. The brands being imported were the up-and-coming ones in Italy, and the companies behind them, such as Barilla, De Cecco, Cirio and Negroni, understood brand development and distribution.

Since Philip took over the business, most of the London wholesalers have retired or sold out to larger companies. By the late 1980s nearly all the medium-sized Italian food businesses were being bought out by the giant global players, food conglomerates who traded in food for profit. We witnessed the demise of the independent food shop as the supermarkets started to make their mark. On visits to Italian food fairs we started to see Nestlè and Proctor & Gamble emblazoned over staple food products such as pasta and Parmigiano. We were alarmed. Companies as large as this would surely destroy the authenticity of the product, supply the mass market through the supermarkets and strangle the supply to individual shops.

The inevitable happened, and over the 1990s we saw more and more independent shops close down and leave the high street. Out-of-town shopping centres sprang up, anchored by huge supermarkets and supplemented by free parking. But, miraculously, a resurging interest in honest food has taken place over the last few years, thanks to writers such as Joanna Blythman, Matthew Fort and Rick Stein, who have championed the small producer and exposed bad practice in the food chain.

For many independent food businesses the Slow Food Movement has provided a desperately needed lifeline. A testament to the power of the individual, Carlo Petrini, founder of Slow Food, was also alarmed that food supply was being monopolised by huge corporations. It was witnessing the first McDonald's burger bar opening in Piazza di Spagna in Rome that inspired him to found Slow Food, a movement against the onslaught of fast food. Today it is a worldwide movement that has helped the survival of thousands of artisan producers and small retailers like us. Threatened food traditions and skills have been rescued from extinction and a new benchmark of responsible food production and fair trade has been established. It has also inspired a huge increase in the number of British farmers bringing their produce directly to the market.

For Valvona & Crolla, now in its 75th year of trading, Slow Food has opened up a new route of supply, first from Italy, and then from all over the world. In Scotland particularly the Slow Food movement and farmers' markets have transformed our trade, and the availability of top-quality food has never been greater or more accessible to so many people.

We still have a huge problem to address in educating our youngsters to appreciate good food and eat a healthy diet, but that is now high on the government agenda and, as I see it, the next generation will demand access to the quality of food that our generation have had to fight for. Let's hope so.

Every two years, in October, the Slow Food movement holds its food fair, *Salone del Gusto*, in Torino. This is the most fantastic celebration of artisan producers, mainly from Italy, but also from almost every corner of the globe. Anyone passionate about food will be there, buying and selling and sharing experiences of food production and selling. Apart from that, Torino is a wonderful city to visit, with a stunning fresh food market that vies with the *Salone* for displays of seasonal produce. It also has an abundance of classic caffès, where we enjoy the finesse of a true caffè society. The fair also gives us the opportunity to visit Alba, the centre for white truffles, and spend some time with Gildo Cane, who hangs out in the original Vincaffè, a place that inspired us to open our own in Edinburgh.

Bread, butter and anchovies

pane, burro e acciughe

This snack is often served in Piemonte when you sit down at a restaurant table. It's perfect served with an aperitif of chilled Lambrusco Concerto. In fact, the combination is so good that you might not get round to ordering anything else.

crusty sourdough bread
unsalted butter
anchovies in olive oil

Slice the bread and place in a basket. Place the butter and anchovies in separate bowls. Put everything on the table and allow everyone to help themselves.

And to drink...

Lambrusco is a traditional *frizzante* or fully sparkling red wine from the Emilia-Romagna region in central Italy. It is made from various clones of the Lambrusco grape and can range from medium-sweet to bone dry. During the 1960s and 1970s, in its medium-sweet version, both red and the newly created white, it was produced and sold in vast quantities to eager new wine drinkers in the UK, USA and Germany. In Uncle Victor's Valvona & Crolla of the 1960s, Lambrusco sold in two-litre bottles was the tipple of the masses.

Unfortunately, the domination of this sweet version overshadowed and almost eliminated the dry version, known for its complexity and depth of flavour. It is only now, with the hard work of producers such Ermete Medici that Lambrusco Secco is making a comeback. Their Lambrusco Reggiano doc Concerto is stunning. Fully sparkling, deep purple, smooth, highly perfumed and grapy rich on the palate, it is drunk slightly chilled and can accompany almost any savoury or sweet dish. It is probably the most versatile wine we have ever come across; probably one of the best and most interesting wine buys you will ever make.

Alba truffles

Every year, in a wave of optimism, we buy fresh Alba truffles. They are fabulously expensive (£4000 per kg in 2008), so we don't sell a lot! However, we do enjoy putting them on the menu in the Caffè Bar just for the fun of it. Our best customers for them are Clarissa Dickson Wright and her lunch partner, Isabel Rutherford. We freeze truffles that don't sell as we can shave them from frozen for Clarissa until they are all used up.

We get truffles from the most unusual sources. Summer black truffles have even been found on some of our Funghi Forays in East Lothian, but not often, I have to admit. Elizabeth Luard, whose book *Truffles* is the best on the subject, gave us a secret contact who emails us every year with a price for English black summer truffles, which we receive in the post. These are about a tenth of the price of the white Alba truffle, and are popular, I suspect, for that reason rather than their flavour. However, our main supply of white truffles comes in the autumn directly from our man in Alba.

Cheese fondue

fonduta

Here is a delicious speciality from Piemonte that uses fontina cheese from the Val d'Aosta and white Alba truffles.

300 g fontina cheese
500 ml full-fat milk
4 egg yolks, beaten
unsalted butter
freshly ground black pepper
shavings of white truffle (optional)
crusty bread, toasted and cubed, to serve

Cut the fontina into cubes, place in a heatproof bowl and cover it with the milk. Leave to soak for 3–4 hours.

Place the bowl over a saucepan of simmering water, or put the mixture in a double boiler if you have one. Add the eggs and a knob of butter and cook gently, stirring all the time, until the ingredients combine to form a thick cream.

Serve in a warmed dish with freshly ground black pepper and shavings of fresh truffle (if using). Offer the toasted bread to dip into the fonduta.

Baked Vacherin Mont d'Or

vacherin Mont d'Or al forno

In the Caffè Bar we serve Vacherin Mont d'Or, a cows' milk cheese from France, hot from the oven with toasted bruschette. It's like an easy fonduta – perfect for sharing!

Serves 2

1 x 500 g Vacherin Mont d'Or cheese
1 garlic clove, sliced
1 small sprig rosemary
drizzle of white wine or kirsch
garlic bruschette (see page 173), to serve

Pre-heat the oven to 190°C/375°F/Gas mark 5.

Leave the cheese in its wooden box, but wrap some foil around the outside to prevent it burning.

Make a split in the surface of the cheese and ease in a few slivers of garlic and a sprig of rosemary. Drizzle in the wine.

Bake in the oven for 15–20 minutes, until soft and bubbling. Serve with the crunchy bruschette.

Tagliatelle with truffles

tagliatelle al tartufo

The love of truffles is an obsession and can make a normal, rational man totally irrational. The huge aromatic truffle you are offered in truffle restaurants in Italy is weighed both before and after it is shaved at your table – clever psychology, as the host wants his guests to be conscious of the expense and take as little as possible so he can have loads for himself! The waiter is charming and makes a fuss of the ladies, 'generously' offering them a little extra shaving. Looks like a win-win situation – until the bill comes. Believe me, it is always a shock!

Per person

320 g Campofilone egg tagliatelle (see page 28)
100 g unsalted Italian butter
freshly grated Parmigiano Reggiano
freshly ground black pepper
shavings of fresh white Alba truffle

Cook the pasta in plenty of boiling salted water until al dente, 3–4 minutes. Drain, reserving a cup of the cooking liquid.

Melt the butter in the empty saucepan, add the drained pasta and toss well, adding a little of the cooking liquid if it seems dry.

Take the pasta off the heat and add plenty of freshly grated Parmigiano Reggiano and black pepper. Serve immediately, shaving the truffle onto the pasta at the table.

'Dragged' eggs with white truffles

uova strapazzate al tartufo

Strapazzate – what a delicious word. It means 'dragged', and the trick is to fold the eggs over gently to make a lightly scrambled mixture.

Per person

3 extra large eggs
1 tbsp light extra virgin olive oil, preferably Sicilian or Ligurian
fresh or frozen white Alba truffle
sea salt and freshly ground black pepper

Beat the eggs together. Season well.

Heat the oil in a shallow frying pan. Add the eggs and cook over a medium heat, folding them with a wooden spatula until they resemble ribbons. As soon as there is no raw egg, remove from the heat.

Slide onto a warmed plate and add 6–7 shavings of truffle on top. The heat of the eggs will release the truffle aroma.

Bean soup with mussels

zuppa di fagioli e cozze

This is best eaten the day after it is made, once the flavours have mellowed. If possible, use fresh red and white mottled borlotti beans (in season October–November). Otherwise, use dried beans that have been soaked overnight, or a can of ready-cooked beans, rinsed of their salty juices.

3–4 tbsp extra virgin olive oil, plus extra for drizzling
2 garlic cloves
50 g smoked pancetta, finely chopped
2 small pieces peperoncino (dried chilli), crushed
200 g fresh borlotti beans, podded, or 200 g dried beans, soaked overnight and drained
1 sprig rosemary
30 large fresh mussels
2–3 tbsp finely chopped flatleaf parsley
sea salt

Heat half the oil in a saucepan, add 1 whole garlic clove, the pancetta and 1 piece of peperoncino and fry for a minute or so to release the flavours. Add the beans, cover with cold water (about 1½ litres) and bring to the boil.

Add the rosemary and a drizzle of olive oil, cover with a tightly fitting lid and simmer gently or cook in a low oven (170°C/325°F/Gas mark 3) until the beans are softened. Fresh beans will take about 25 minutes, while dried will take the best part of an hour. Watch that they don't dry out. Add more water if necessary.

Once the beans are soft, remove the rosemary and garlic clove. Take a few spoonfuls of the soup and pass through a sieve or mouli. (A blender or food processor makes the mixture gluey.) Return to the saucepan to thicken the soup. If possible, leave overnight in the fridge.

Warm the soup through.

Clean and de-beard the mussels, discarding any that don't open when tapped. Place them in a saucepan over a high heat, cover with a lid and cook for 4–5 minutes, shaking the pan to release their juices. They are cooked when all the shells are open. Drain off the juices and add to the bean soup.

Remove the mussels from their shells and add them to the soup. Check the seasoning, adding salt to taste. Chop the remaining garlic clove. Heat the remaining oil in a small frying pan, add the garlic and the remaining peperoncino and sauté to release the flavours. Pour onto the soup and serve warm, sprinkled with the chopped parsley.

Or you could try...

Cooking 100 g ditali and adding to the soup at the end, before the flavoured oil.

Cream of cannellini bean soup

zuppa di cannellini

At the end of the summer vegetables from Italy fall in price. We buy extra cannellini and borlotti beans and store them (podded) in the freezer, ready to make soups throughout the winter. This recipe can also be made with dried beans that have been soaked overnight, or cans of beans that have been drained and rinsed.

350 g cannellini beans, soaked overnight if dried
6 tbsp extra virgin olive oil
2 garlic cloves
2 sprigs rosemary
3–4 stalks flatleaf parsley
sea salt
2 tbsp finely chopped flatleaf parsley
Crostini (see page 102), to serve

Put the beans, drained if necessary, in a heavy saucepan and cover with about 5 cm cold water. Add 2 tablespoons of the oil, 1 whole garlic clove, the rosemary and parsley stalks and bring to a simmer. Cook for about 1 hour, or until the beans are soft, either on the stove or in a warm oven (170°C/325°F/Gas mark 3). Be careful not to let the beans dry out. Add more water if necessary.

Once the beans are cooked, discard the garlic and herbs, and add salt to taste. Set aside a few spoonfuls of the beans, then liquidise the remainder.

Put the soup and the reserved whole beans in a saucepan and reheat until piping hot. Traditionally this soup is served thick, but add more water if you prefer it thinner. Season to taste.

Finely chop the remaining garlic clove. Heat 3–4 tablespoons of the oil in a small frying pan and sauté the garlic until sizzling to infuse the flavour. Remove from the heat, add the chopped parsley and pour the hot flavoured oil on to the soup. Serve with the crostini.

Basil from the nuns

Like most of the Italian women in the immigrant community during the war, Maria Crolla was left widowed with a young family to look after and a shop that had been smashed. Her sons were interned. As an alien, her assets and bank accounts were frozen and she was not allowed to run the business. The Scottish bookkeeper, Miss Dennison, took over the running of the shop, and once it was cleaned up, they started trading again. Maria and her three daughters, Olivia, Gloria and Phyllis, had to work for their bookkeeper, getting just a meagre allowance. Maria had no access to the shop's income – not a happy experience.

After the war, when her sons came home and took over, Maria wanted to go back to Italy to visit her family, all of whom had had similar traumatic experiences, though at the hands of the Germans, who suspected they might be spies for the British! Maria and her daughters travelled by train, stopping off to rest and recuperate at a convent in Liguria before completing their journey south. They made friends with the nuns and often returned to holiday there for the rest of their lives.

In those early post-war days Valvona & Crolla needed a source of dry basil, as fresh basil was unheard of in Scotland. But there was a limit on how much money could be taken through the numerous borders and checkpoints across Europe. Ever the entrepreneurs, the family did a deal with the nuns – a deal that we continue to honour to this day. Every autumn we prepare a pack of Twining's Breakfast Tea and send it off to Liguria. In return the nuns send six hand-stitched, white cotton sacks, each filled with fragrant, sun-dried Ligurian basil.

Cream of tomato soup

zuppa di pomodoro con crema

We always have extra tomatoes in the kitchen, so we make this soup regularly. We use the whole tomato, stalk and all, to get maximum flavour.

2 tbsp extra virgin olive oil
knob unsalted butter
1 large onion, finely chopped
1 garlic clove
1 kg fresh ripe tomatoes, stalks included
1 x 450 g can plum tomatoes
1 tsp sugar
1 bunch of fresh basil
sea salt and freshly ground black pepper
double cream (optional), to serve

Heat the oil and butter in a saucepan. Add the onion and garlic and sauté until the onion is softened.

Remove the garlic and add the fresh and canned tomatoes, the sugar and the basil stalks. Cover and cook everything for 45 minutes.

Remove the basil stalks. Liquidise the soup, then pass it through a mouli or sieve and return it to the saucepan. Reheat and season with salt and a generous grinding of black pepper. Just before serving, add the basil leaves and stir in the cream, if using.

Spiced pumpkin soup

zuppa di zucca

The autumn brings fabulous selections of squash and pumpkins, all grown locally. They look brilliant in the shop and are transformed into countless dishes. Pumpkin goes very well with rich cheeses from Piemonte, such as fontina and branzi. It is also enhanced with spices and fresh herbs, such as basil and rosemary. This recipe is based on one by Janet Ross in *Leaves from Our Tuscan Kitchen*, first published in 1899.

75 g unsalted butter
1 large onion, finely chopped
1 garlic clove
2 tsp ground coriander seeds
1 tsp ground cumin
1 tsp paprika
1 kg pumpkin, skinned and diced
sea salt and freshly ground black pepper

To serve
fresh basil leaves
4 Crostini (see page 102)
60 g fontina cheese, grated
pinch of cayenne pepper

Melt the butter in a saucepan and sauté the onion and garlic for 4–5 minutes. Discard the garlic, then add the spices and cook gently to release their flavours.

Add the pumpkin, stir well and cover with boiling water. Put a lid on the pan and cook for 30 minutes, until the pumpkin has softened.

Liquidise the soup, then adjust the consistency with water. Taste and season, adding plenty of freshly ground black pepper. Stir in some torn fresh basil leaves and serve piping hot, with a few crostini sprinkled with some grated fontina and a pinch of cayenne on top.

Pasta with mushrooms, Luganega sausage and cream

tagliatelle con funghi, luganega e panna

Fresh Luganega pork sausages from the north of Italy have the particular sweet flavour of Italian pork. They are mildly spiced with a hint of garlic, and marry well with mushrooms and cream.

2 tbsp extra virgin olive oil
1 garlic clove, finely chopped
1 peperoncino (dried chilli), crushed
1 shallot, chopped
400 g Luganega pork sausage, chopped
300 g chestnut or cremini mushrooms, wiped and sliced
3–4 ripe cherry tomatoes or 2 plum tomatoes, crushed
400 g egg tagliatelle
1 x 250 ml carton double cream
handful of flatleaf parsley, finely chopped
sea salt and freshly ground black pepper
freshly grated Parmigiano Reggiano, to serve

Heat the oil in a shallow saucepan. Add the garlic and peperoncino and sauté for a few minutes to release the flavours. Stir in the shallot and cook it until it is soft and translucent. Add the sausage and fry until brown.

Stir in the mushrooms and tomatoes and cook slowly until the liquid thickens. Check the seasoning; as the sausages are fairly salty, you might not need to add any extra salt.

Meanwhile, cook the tagliatelle in a large saucepan of boiling salted water until al dente.

Stir the cream into the sugo, then add the parsley and freshly ground black pepper.

Drain the tagliatelle, reserving some of the cooking water. Toss the pasta in the sugo, adding a little of the cooking water if it needs more liquid. Serve with freshly grated Parmigiano Reggiano.

Mushroom risotto

risotto con funghi

I like to serve this rich risotto as a small starter rather than a main course – too little makes you want more, too much makes you wish you had eaten less!

25 g dried porcini (optional)
¾ litre Chicken stock (see page 115)
100 g unsalted butter
2 shallots, finely chopped
300 g Carnaroli or Arborio rice
100 ml dry white wine
250 g cremini or porcini mushrooms, cleaned and sliced
2–3 tbsp finely chopped flatleaf parsley
100 g fontina cheese, grated
sea salt and freshly ground black pepper
freshly grated Parmigiano Reggiano, to serve

If using fresh porcini in the recipe, you do not need to use dried porcini as well. The dried mushrooms must be soaked in a cup of warm water for 15 minutes or so. Drain them through a sieve lined with kitchen paper, reserving the liquid. Rinse the mushrooms in cold water to remove any grit.

Place the stock in a saucepan and bring to a simmer.

Meanwhile, heat half the butter in a shallow, heavy-based saucepan. Add the shallots and cook until soft and translucent. Stir in the rice, then add the wine and boil until the alcohol has evaporated. This takes 4–5 minutes, and you can tell by sniffing the vapours: the alcohol will no longer catch the back of your throat.

Add all the mushrooms and the parsley. As the mushrooms start to release their juices, add the strained mushroom liquor (if you have any). Once that is absorbed into the rice, add a ladleful of hot stock, stir into the rice and simmer until the liquid has been absorbed. Repeat this step until most of the stock has been used. I like my risotto moist, so I take it off the heat to add the last bit of stock, which will be absorbed as the rice rests.

Stir in the remaining butter and the fontina. Check the seasoning and serve immediately, piping hot, with freshly grated Parmigiano Reggiano.

Pizza with pumpkin, mozzarella and basil

pizza con zucca, mozzarella e basilico

Makes 4 pizzas

500 g pumpkin
3–4 tbsp extra virgin olive oil, plus extra for greasing and drizzling
1 x 425 g can chopped tomatoes
1 garlic clove, cut into slivers
few pinches of dried oregano
2 x 125g mozzarella di bufala, sliced
sea salt
fresh basil, to finish

For the dough
1 sachet easy-blend yeast
350 g strong white bread flour, plus extra for dusting
1 tsp salt
210 ml hand-hot water

First make the dough. Mix the yeast into the flour with the salt and then add enough hand-hot water to make a dough that leaves the sides of the mixing bowl clean. Knead it in a processor for about 10 minutes, then cover and leave in a warm place until it has doubled in size (about 1 hour).

Knock out the air from the dough by thumping it a bit with your hands, and knead it again for 10 minutes or so. Divide the dough into 4 equal pieces and roll each one into a ball about 10 cm in diameter. Dust with a little flour and place on a baking sheet. Cover with cling film and store in the fridge until needed. They will keep for up to 3 days.

Pre-heat the oven to 180°C/350°F/Gas mark 4.

Cut the pumpkin into slices, scooping out the seeds and fibres. Slice the flesh off the skin. Rub the slices with 1 tablespoon of the oil and add a sprinkling of sea salt. Place in a roasting tray and roast in the oven for about 15–20 minutes, until soft and cooked through, but not browned. Set aside.

Put the tomatoes into a bowl with 2–3 tablespoons of the oil, the garlic, oregano and some salt. Leave to stand.

Increase the oven temperature to 230°C/450°F/Gas mark 8.

To assemble the pizza, knock down the dough again and roll it out on a floured work surface into a circle as thick or thin as you like. Use your hands to stretch it out in the air, and allow the weight of the dough to stretch it out naturally.

Place the pizza base on a greased baking sheet and drizzle with some of the oil. Spread with a little of the tomato topping, taking it right to the edges. Top with 2–3 slices of mozzarella and some pumpkin. Drizzle with some more oil and bake in the top of the oven for 20 minutes, until the base is well cooked and crispy. The extra roasting will caramelise the juices on the pumpkin. Serve with fresh basil leaves wilted on top.

Our Parmigiano Reggiano

It was at the Slow Food Fiera in Torino in 2002 that we first met Giorgio Cravero. The *fiera* has a whole hall dedicated to cheeses from all over Italy, as well as France, Britain, Switzerland...you name it, it's there. Every display is enticing. Every stall-holder calls you over. Every producer wants you to taste.

So in this abundance of choice what draws a buyer to one stall rather than another? Why did we choose Giorgio? Was it the immaculate display? To be honest I think it was the huge smile on Giorgio's face, but once we tasted his rich, creamy Parmigiano Reggiano we were hooked. It was love at first bite!

The Cravero family have been maturing Parmigiano Reggiano since 1855, the last hundred years in Bra, southeast of Torino; they know what they are doing.

The cheese we sell is made from the milk at farm number 1470 in Emilia-Romagna where the herd is fed on specially selected forage. They produce the cheese by hand in the traditional manner; four cheeses a day, each weighing around 30 kg. Each kilo needs 16 litres of milk – that's a lot of goodness in one cheese!

The Parmigiano Reggiano is selected and shipped to the Cravero maturing rooms in Bra, where the cheeses are held at an even temperature and humidity and turned regularly, creating the best product we can buy. It is matured for 26–30 months to produce a rounded, full-flavoured cheese that is still moist and soft when grated, and has a complex, sweet, nutty flavour with a long aftertaste.

Always grate Parmigiano Reggiano fresh, and store it in the bottom of the fridge wrapped in greaseproof paper or aluminium foil. Do enjoy it as an eating cheese as well as grated.

And sorry, Giorgio, no matter how good-looking you are, if your Parmigiano Reggiano wasn't the best quality at the best value for our customers, we wouldn't be buying it! (You are cute, though!)

top left Giorgio Cravero and Philip Contini

SALONE
INTERNAZIONALE DEL
GUSTO
OTTOBRE 2008
www.salonedelgusto.com
TO THE ROOTS OF FOOD
1470
STAGIONATURA - ESPORTAZIONE
FORMAGGIO GRANA
G.CRAVERO
FROM PARTLY SKIMMED MILK
GNOCCHI

Boiled meats with olive oil mashed potatoes

bollito di terza con puré di patate

Bollito misto, mixed meats cooked in their own broth, are eaten with the vegetables that are cooked with them and *salsa verde*. Traditionally, the dish is made with at least five meats – veal, beef, tongue, capon and pork. Included in the choice is usually *cotechino*, a speciality pork sausage made with a mixture of pork rind and lean and fat meat coarsely chopped and flavoured with cloves and cinnamon, stuffed into a pig's intestine casing– almost like an Italian haggis. Very good eating!

An easier way of preparing the same idea is to use only two or three meats – *bollito di seconda* or *bollito di terza*. I like to use lamb shank and a beef brisket or boiling beef and serve it with *cotechino* and *mostarda di frutta* (see page 56). The lamb and beef cook very easily, and the *cotechino* is pre-cooked, so needs only to be warmed through at the end.

2 lamb shanks
500 g beef brisket or well-hung boiling beef
2 sticks celery
2 carrots
2 leeks
2 tomatoes
bunch of flatleaf parsley
1 garlic clove
1 cotechino sausage
sea salt and freshly ground black pepper

For the olive oil mashed potatoes
500 g floury potatoes, such as Maris Piper or King Edwards
2–3 tbsp milk
5–6 tbsp extra virgin olive oil

Wash the lamb and beef. Put them in a saucepan and cover with about 1 litre cold water. Don't be tempted to add more water in the hope of making more stock. The result is diluted flavours and meat with no taste.

Bring the water slowly to the boil, skimming off any scum that rises to the surface. The easiest way is with a small mesh tea strainer or sieve. Simmer gently, skimming regularly until all the scum is away, and use a piece of damp kitchen paper to wipe the inside of the pot.

Add the vegetables, tomatoes, parsley and a teaspoon of salt and simmer gently for 1–2 hours, until the meats are tender. Check the seasoning.

In a separate saucepan of boiling water, cook the cotechino according to the manufacturer's instructions.

Meanwhile, boil the potatoes in salted water. When cooked, drain and mash them with the milk. Add the oil, mixing it in with a fork. Season with freshly ground black pepper.

Serve the bollito in a soup bowl with some shank, some beef, a slice of cotechino and some of each of the boiled vegetables. Add a few generous spoonfuls of mashed potato, and pour over a scant spoonful of the cooking broth to add moisture. Serve with some mostarda di frutta or Salsa verde (see page 263). It's also good with Braised Lentils (see page 263).

Braised lentils

lenticchie in umido

Unless they are very old, the lentils should not need soaking before they are cooked. The finishing touch is Bis-Nonna's trick from Naples, which transforms ordinary lentils to memorable *lenticchie*!

500 g Casteluccio or Puy lentils
¼ x 425 g can plum tomatoes
2–3 tbsp extra virgin olive oil
1 onion, finely chopped
1 garlic clove
1 sprig fresh rosemary
1 fresh bay leaf
few stalks flatleaf parsley
sea salt and freshly ground black pepper

To finish
3–4 tbsp extra virgin olive oil
1 garlic clove, finely chopped
1 peperoncino (dried chilli) or to taste, crushed
2 tbsp flatleaf parsley, finely chopped

Put all the lentil ingredients in a saucepan and add enough cold water to cover. Bring to the boil and simmer for about 45 minutes, until the lentils are cooked and have absorbed all the water. (Add more water if necessary.) Check the seasoning and discard the garlic and herbs.

For the finishing touch, heat the olive oil in a frying pan and sauté the chopped garlic and peperoncino briskly without burning. Take off the heat, throw in the chopped parsley, then stir the mixture into the lentils.

Green sauce

salsa verde

bunch of flatleaf parsley
small bunch of mint
1 tbsp salted capers (soaked)
3–4 small gherkins
2–3 anchovies in oil
1 garlic clove, chopped
extra virgin olive oil
sea salt and freshly ground black pepper

Mix everything together in a food processor, adding the olive oil at the end of the processing. Adjust the seasoning and serve.

Mists of mellow fruitfulness: Nebiolo, Barolo and Barbera

Happy Piemonte, literally the 'foot of the mountains', is the Italian region that lies on the eastern, sunny side of the Alps' borders with France and Switzerland. It is the main wine-growing area of northern Italy. The vineyards around Alba produce Nebbiolo, a noble red grape variety akin to its French counterpart Pinot Noir. In the autumn, when the grape is harvested, a shadowy fog settles over Le Langhe, where most of the vineyards are situated. *Nebbia* is Italian for 'fog', hence the grape's name.

The most famous wine produced in the area is Barolo, 'wine of kings and king of wines', so named after a period of French influence altered it from a sweet wine to a dry, full-flavoured one in the mid-19th century. It then became the favoured wine of the House of Savoy.

The traditional method of making Barolo – long maturation in old oak barrels – produces magnificent wines with mellow tannins and hints of violets, tar, tobacco and cherries. During the 1960s the wine-maker Aldo Conterno began to produce single-estate Barolo, controlling the growing, harvesting and production of the wine himself, and gaining DOCG status for his wines. Denominazione di Origine Garantita is the Italian quality-assurance label for food products and wines (an appelation). Modelled after the French AOC, it was instituted in 1963 and overhauled in 1992 for compliance with the equivalent EU law on Protected Designation of Origin, which came into effect that year. Aldo's Barolos were more fruit-driven with softer tannins, and more popular appeal than his brother Giovanni's versions of the same wines.

Philip met Aldo in the early 1980s when he started visiting VinItaly (see pages 106–8), inviting Aldo to introduce his wines to Scottish customers. Since then they have grown in international appeal, winning awards, and his single-vineyard *cru*, Granbussia, was at one time rated by the critics as the finest Barolo produced.

Do visit the VinCaffè if you are near the small town of Alba. And if you see the octogenarian Gildo Cane, a drinking man's gentleman, sitting in a corner, give him our regards. A wise entrepreneur who has seen and done it all, his passion now is to do nothing but drink great wine and tell tall stories. When you meet him, just tell him you were reading about him in the book written by the wife of the singing Scottish–Neapolitan – and buy him a drink from us! *Salute!*

Less than 10 miles northeast of Alba lies the town of Barbaresco, at the heart of a similar Nebbiolo-producing area that had in the past sold all its grapes to make Barolo wines. Since 1894 the wines have been produced and marketed under the Barbaresco label, in particular by the most famous producer, Gaja. Hotly awaited in the wine world, vintages of Gaja Barbaresco are among the best and most exclusive wines released in Italy. We have held several tastings with Gaja, but also with the lesser-known cooperative Prodotori Barbaresco, whose balanced, well-made wines top the lot for value and flavour.

An even lighter style of wine produced nearby is Barbera, which, when fresh from the vintage, has high acidity and is a very lively, richly fruity, easily drinkable everyday wine. In Piemonte it is sold like beer, on draught, the perfect accompaniment to lunchtime *stuzzichini*, literally 'toothpicks' of food. Valvona & Crolla lists a great range of Barbera wines, from young and fresh right through the spectrum to heavyweight, aged wines of such concentration and depth that they are almost too perfect to drink.

Beef in Barolo or Barbaresco

manzo in Barolo

750g chuck or stewing steak, cut into bite-sized cubes
1–2 tbsp extra virgin olive oil
1 onion, finely chopped
2 sticks celery, destringed and finely chopped
1 garlic clove, chopped
1 carrot, finely chopped
400 ml Barolo or Barbaresco, or any other full-bodied red wine
2–3 canned plum tomatoes
2 fresh bay leaves
small bunch of thyme
sea salt and freshly ground black pepper

Pre-heat the oven to 180°C/350°F/Gas mark 4.

Season the meat well with salt and freshly ground black pepper. Heat the oil in a flameproof casserole. Add the meat, a single layer at a time, and brown it well. Transfer to a warmed plate until it is all browned.

Using a wooden spoon, loosen all the sediment from the saucepan and add the onion and celery, cooking it until softened.

Add the garlic and chopped carrot and stir for a moment. Pour in the wine, turn the heat to high and boil off the alcohol. This takes 4–5 minutes, and you can tell by sniffing the vapours: the alcohol will no longer catch the back of your throat.

Reduce the heat and return the meat and its juices to the saucepan. Add the tomatoes and herbs, then pour in just enough hot water to cover the meat. Bring to the boil, then transfer to the oven and cook until the meat is tender, about 2–3 hours. Check from time to time, adding a little more water if needed. By the time the meat is tender the sauce should have reduced to a nice consistency, but adjust as necessary.

Serve on a bed of Olive oil mashed potatoes and Roasted fennel (see pages 262 and 291).

Sautéd Portobello mushrooms

funghi saltati

Giant Portobello mushrooms are about as meaty as a steak and just as tasty. They are cultivated mushrooms, available all year round.

4 tbsp extra virgin olive oil
1 garlic clove, finely chopped
1 peperoncino (dried chilli), crushed
2–3 anchovies, chopped
8 Portobello mushrooms, sliced
leaves from 2–3 sprigs fresh thyme
sea salt and freshly ground black pepper
finely chopped flatleaf parsley, to finish

Heat the oil in a frying pan. Add the garlic and peperoncino and sauté for 2–3 minutes to release the flavours. Add the anchovies and melt them into the soffritto.

Raise the heat and add the mushrooms, turning them in the flavoured oil so that they cook quickly without losing too many juices. Add the thyme and season with salt and plenty of freshly ground black pepper. Serve sprinkled with the parsley.

Tyrolean potatoes

patate tirolesi

6 floury potatoes, such as Desiree or Maris Piper
6–8 tbsp extra virgin olive oil
2 Spanish onions, quartered, then sliced
sea salt and freshly ground black pepper

Boil the potatoes in salted water for 10–15 minutes until just cooked. Allow to cool, then slice.

Heat the oil in a shallow frying pan and sauté the onions over a fairly high heat so that they brown a little at the edges. Add the sliced potatoes, turn in the oil and fry until crispy at the edges with bits of tasty onion attached.

To get a really crispy result, transfer the potatoes to a small dish and place in a hot oven (200°C/400°F/Gas mark 6) for another 5 minutes or so.

Scotch beef

Good beef is tender, juicy and full flavoured and here in Scotland we have a huge number of wonderful beef producers to choose from. Do find a good butcher and learn from him. The meat will not necessarily be more expensive than in a supermarket, but it is almost guaranteed to be a better product.

For our Caffè Bar and VinCaffè we buy our beef only from local farmers and butchers, who slaughter straight from their own suckler herds, which have been grass-fed where possible. 'Suckler' means that the calves are allowed to drink from their mothers; dairy herds are not allowed to suckle as the milk production is for human consumption only.

Because of its distinctive flavour and cooking quality, I always try to choose Aberdeen Angus-cross beef hung for at least 21 days, producing a full-flavoured, tender beef that cooks well and stays moist.

If you want to buy Aberdeen Angus online, you can't go wrong using www.wellhungandtender.co.uk, who dedicate themselves to raising the best-flavoured Aberdeen Angus. They hang their beef for four weeks. Clarissa Dickson Wright sources her beef from www.Northfieldfarm.co.uk, which I can say is the best I have ever tasted, thanks to a brilliant farmer and a brilliant cook.

Wherever you buy your meat, give the butcher or supermarket feedback, and complain if the meat is not what you expect. Often people say to me they can't cook meat, to which my standard answer is, 'Of course you can, you probably just can't buy it.'

Rib-eye steaks grilled medium rare

tagliata bistecca alla griglia

This simple recipe is made special by including traditional balsamic vinegar, Parmigiano Reggiano and rocket. *Aceto balsamico tradizionale* is made exclusively from crushed Trebbiano grapes, whose unfermented musts are condensed by heating and are aged over a minimum of ten years. Each year the liquid is mixed with a small amount of the new season's must, then decanted through a series of barrels of different woods: oak, cherry, chestnut, mulberry and ash. The ageing vinegar absorbs a subtle hint of each, building up a complex flavour, so when the liquid is added in minute quantities to grilled fish, steak or even ice cream, it imparts one of the most delicious taste experiences. All our traditional balsamic vinegars and blends are sourced from three of the controlled balsamic houses in Emilia-Romagna: Giusti, San Giacomo and Sereni. These three producers make and develop a range of classic, aged balsamic vinegars for us so that we can offer authentic products at affordable prices.

Please don't buy cheap balsamic vinegar. It is usually just a combination of cheap wine vinegar with caramel colouring.

We choose rib-eye steak for this dish as the extra fat in the cut gives a consistently juicy result.

Per person

1 x 350 g rib-eye Aberdeen Angus steak
2–3 tbsp extra virgin olive oil
2 handfuls of wild rocket
squeeze of lemon juice
1 tsp aceto balsamico tradizionale (good-quality balsamic vinegar)
sea salt and freshly ground black pepper
freshly shaved Parmigiano Reggiano, to serve

Take the beef from the fridge 30 minutes before you plan to cook it and rub it with some of the oil and salt and pepper. Pre-heat a ridged griddle pan at least 15 minutes before cooking.

Place the steak on the hot griddle and cook for 4–5 minutes, until well seared and sealed underneath. Don't attempt to turn it or play with it until it is cooked almost one-third of the way through from one side. When the meat lifts easily from the griddle it is ready to turn.

Cook on the second side for 1–2 minutes only, just enough to seal the surface of the steak. Transfer to a warm place to rest.

Place the rocket in a bowl and dress it well with salt, extra virgin olive oil and a good squeeze of lemon juice.

Slice the steak lengthways at an angle into 5–6 slices. Place on a warmed plate with any juices that have escaped. Season well and drizzle with a teaspoonful of aceto balsamico tradizionale. Pile the dressed rocket on top of the steak. Serve with shavings of Parmigiano Reggiano.

Rosé veal chop stuffed with fontina

costoletta di vitello con fontina

Costoletta (chop) is often confused on British menus with *cotoletta* (escalope). A good way to tell them apart is that a *cotoletta* is often served *alla Milanese* (breaded). I trust Anna del Conte when checking out any details for our menus, especially her *Gastronomy of Italy* (Pavilion, 2004). If I don't write the words correctly, Clarissa, a great friend of Anna's, is quick to point it out!

Veal or pork can be used for this recipe; both are very nice! I love to serve this with a 1960s-style Italian salad, the flavours exactly as I remember my mother used to serve...and still does.

Per person

1 x 275–350 g T-bone rosé veal chop or pork chop
1 x 75 g slice fontina cheese
1 fresh sage leaf
1 egg, beaten
2–3 tbsp fresh breadcrumbs
3–4 tbsp extra virgin olive oil
2 knobs of unsalted butter
sea salt and freshly ground black pepper

For the salad

½ red onion, finely sliced
3–4 stem or vine tomatoes
1 head Little Gem lettuce
1 x 8 cm piece cucumber, deseeded and cut into cubes
1 tbsp pitted black olives
2–3 radishes, sliced
3–4 fennel slices
5–6 tbsp extra virgin olive oil
1 tbsp red wine vinegar

Trim most of the fat, but not all, from the chop. Make a horizontal incision in the thickness of the pork and open it out to create a pocket.

Put the chop between 2 sheets of greaseproof paper and beat with a meat mallet or rolling pin to tenderise it.

Season the veal well and slip the fontina and sage leaf into the slit. Press the chop down to seal the pocket, then dip it first in beaten egg and then in breadcrumbs. Leave in the fridge for 1–2 hours.

Pre-heat the oven to 190°C/375°F/Gas mark 5.

Heat the oil and 1 knob of butter in a frying pan and cook the chop until the breadcrumbs are crisp and lightly browned on both sides.

Transfer the chop to a baking sheet and add the remaining knob of butter. Cover with foil and bake in the oven for 15–20 minutes.

Meanwhile, make the salad. Soak the onion in water for 10 minutes or so and drain well.

Cut the tomatoes into eighths. Place in a large bowl with all the other salad ingredients. Season with salt and dress with the oil and vinegar. Leave for 10 minutes before serving so that the flavours can develop.

Veal escalopes with lemon and crispy potatoes

piccatine al limone con patate croccanti

This is easy for a simple supper. You can use chicken breast or pork if you don't eat veal.

400 g veal escalopes
plain flour, for dusting
4–5 tablespoons extra virgin olive oil
knob of unsalted butter
rind and juice of 1 unwaxed lemon
1–2 tbsp chopped flatleaf parsley

For the potatoes
4 large waxy potatoes
extra virgin olive oil, for drizzling
few sprigs rosemary
sea salt

Pre-heat the oven to 200°C/400°F/Gas mark 6.

Boil the potatoes until just cooked and allow to cool. Cut into cubes and place on a baking sheet. Drizzle with plenty of the oil and sprinkle with salt. Add some sprigs of rosemary and roast until crispy, about 20–25 minutes.

About 10 minutes before the potatoes are done, place the escalopes between 2 sheets of greaseproof paper and beat with a meat mallet or rolling pin to tenderise them. Cut the veal pieces in half, season well and dust with flour.

Heat the oil and butter in a wide frying pan and gently cook the veal in a single layer, browning on each side. Transfer to a warmed dish and keep warm.

Add the lemon juice to the frying pan and scrape up all the juices and sediment to make a sauce. Sprinkle in the parsley and lemon rind and pour over the veal before serving.

Veal escalopes with prosciutto and sage

Saltimbocca alla romana

This dish is a brilliant autumn classic that can be easily adapted to make lots of other combinations. *Saltimbocca* means 'jump in the mouth', a tasty morsel that stimulates your appetite. Traditionally, it is made with veal, but you can use free-range chicken breasts or even flash-fry steak. Basically, it is a small piece of quick-cooking meat flavoured with a complementary meat and a fresh herb, held together with a toothpick and fast fried.

Ask for the knuckle end of the prosciutto, which should be cheaper. If sliced thinly, it is perfect for this way of cooking.

4 veal escalopes, about 300 g in total
6 slices Prosciutto di Parma
4 fresh sage leaves
2–3 tbsp extra virgin olive oil
75 ml dry white wine or Marsala
sea salt and freshly ground black pepper

Lay each escalope between 2 sheets of greaseproof paper and beat with a meat mallet or rolling pin to tenderise it.

Cut each piece of veal into small slices, about the size of a playing card. Cut the prosciutto into similar-sized pieces.

Season the veal well, lay some prosciutto on top and then a sage leaf. Pin together with a toothpick.

Heat the oil in a frying pan. Arrange the veal in a single layer and fry quickly on both sides under a lively heat. Once browned, add the wine. Raise the heat to evaporate the alcohol and reduce the liquid to a sauce. This takes 4–5 minutes, and you can tell by sniffing the vapours: the alcohol will no longer catch the back of your throat.

Or you could try...

Any of the following adaptations.

Cocktail nibbles: Make the veal pieces bite-sized and put on long skewers to serve with drinks.

Pork fillet with smoked pancetta and sage: Tenderise the pork, then season and skewer it with smoked pancetta and sage. Fry in extra virgin olive oil and add a splash of balsamic vinegar at the end to coat the pork in some intense sweetness. Serve with some slices of mostarda di frutta (see page 57) added to the skewer.

Melanzane, mozzarella e basilico: Use slices of violet aubergine instead of meat. Drizzle the aubergine with extra virgin olive oil and sea salt and roast in a hot oven (200°C/400°F/Gas mark 6) for 10–15 minutes, until softened and browned. When cool enough to handle, skewer with a bocconcino di mozzarella and a fresh basil leaf.

Slow-cooked peppers

peperonata

2–3 tbsp extra virgin olive oil
2 garlic cloves, sliced
1 piece peperoncino (dried chilli), crushed
1 onion, finely sliced
2 large peperoni rossi (red peppers)
2 large peperoni gialli (yellow peppers)
1 x 425 g can tomatoes, sliced
leaves from 1 sprig fresh thyme
scant amount fresh oregano leaves
handful of fresh basil leaves
sea salt and freshly ground black pepper

Heat the oil in a wide frying pan, add the garlic and peperoncino and sauté for a few minutes to release the flavours. Add the onion and cook slowly.

Deseed the peppers and cut them into long slices. Add to the onion, then stir in the tomatoes and their juices. Season with salt and add the thyme and oregano. Cook for about 30 minutes, until the peperoni are soft. Check the seasoning and add some torn fresh basil leaves to finish.

Creamed celeriac purée

puré di sedano rapa

500 g celeriac, diced
250 ml Fresh vegetable stock (see page 109) or water, salt and a bay leaf
knob of unsalted butter
generous swirl of double cream
2 tbsp finely chopped flatleaf parsley
sea salt and freshly ground black pepper

Place the celeriac in a saucepan, cover with the stock and simmer gently until tender. As it cooks, it will absorb the flavours of the stock, which will gradually all evaporate. Be careful it doesn't boil dry.

Mash well and add the butter, cream and parsley. Check the seasoning and add a generous grinding of black pepper.

Roast pork belly with grilled pear

pancetta di maiale arista con pere grigliate

Pork belly is cheap and tasty. We use free-range pork from Hill Foot Farm in the Scottish Borders.

1 kg thick end of free-range belly pork
leaves from 2–3 sprigs fresh thyme
leaves from 2 sprigs fresh rosemary
2 carrots
2 sticks celery
1 onion, quartered
splash of dry white wine
4 pears
2 tbsp caster sugar
sea salt and freshly ground black pepper

Using a very sharp knife, score the skin of the belly pork, but not right through to the fat (or get the butcher to do it for you). Rub with salt, pepper and the herbs, pushing the seasonings right into the slits. Leave overnight, or at least for a few hours, to absorb the flavours.

Pre-heat the oven to 220°C/425°F/Gas mark 7.

Roughly chop the carrots, celery and onion and place in a heavy roasting tray. Add the wine and a splash of water to make a moist environment. Place the pork on the bed of vegetables and roast for 30 minutes. Lower the temperature to 180°C/350°F/Gas mark 4 and cook for a further hour, or until the juices run clear when a skewer is inserted in the meat. (Like chicken, pork must be cooked right through so that no red blood remains, but avoid overcooking or it can become dry.)

Pre-heat the grill. Cut the pears into quarters, dip in the caster sugar and grill until softened.

Remove the pork from the oven, cover it with foil and allow to rest in a warm place for 10–15 minutes or so. If you need to crisp the skin, cut it off by sliding a sharp knife under it and pop it under the grill for a few minutes.

Carve the pork into thick slices and serve with the grilled pear and roasted vegetables. Sautéd Swiss chard (see page 145) is a lovely accompaniment.

Venison fillet with balsamic vinegar

filetto di cervo all'aceto balsamico

Venison is an undervalued wild meat, which is a pity as it is low in fat but high in vitamins and iron. Wild red deer, from the Highlands, and roe deer, mostly from the lower forest lands and about a quarter of the size of red deer, are both in season from October through to February. Farmed venison is also available and is excellent. As with beef, it is important that venison is hung properly to tenderise it and bring out its full flavour. Fletchers of Auchtermuchty are a world authority on deer, and you can't go wrong sourcing venison from their online site (www.seriouslygoodvenison.co.uk).

Per person

1 x 200 g venison fillet steak
½ garlic clove, finely sliced
extra virgin olive oil, for coating and drizzling
sea salt and freshly ground black pepper

Rub the steak with the garlic, add a generous grinding of black pepper and rub with the oil. Cover and leave to marinate overnight.

Heat a ridged griddle pan for at least 10 minutes. Place the venison in the pan and sear well on both sides. Turn the heat down to medium and cook for 5–6 minutes.

To serve, salt well and drizzle with a little more olive oil. Roasted winter vegetables (see page 61) are a good accompaniment.

Or you could try...

Venison fillet with Stornoway black pudding and apple compote Of all the Scottish products we sell, one of the most popular is black pudding from Charles McLeod in Stornoway on the Isle of Lewis. We get a delivery every week unless the weather is bad and the ferry is cancelled. The delicious spicy but sweet flavour works perfectly with venison fillet and a soft apple compote.

Place 500 g tart cooking apples, peeled, cored and chopped, in a saucepan with 2–3 tablespoons caster sugar and a knob of unsalted butter and stew gently with the lid off to make a soft compote. Grill 4 slices Stornoway black pudding until starting to crisp, then place on a warm plate. Cut the venison fillet into 4 slices and nestle it on the slices of black pudding. Put a spoonful of warm apple compote alongside. Serve with Tyrolean potatoes (see page 272).

Venison stew

stufato di cervo

First open a bottle of Barbaresco! Actually any full-flavoured red wine will do – Montepulciano, or something delicious from the south, such as Primitivo, a fleshy, fruity, dry red from Puglia that is lovely. You will need to prepare the stew the day before you want to serve it.

1 kg venison stewing steak
2 tbsp extra virgin olive oil
200 g smoked pancetta, chopped
2 onions, finely sliced
200 ml fruity red wine
1 x 425 g can plum tomatoes, chopped
sea salt and freshly ground black pepper

For the marinade
2–3 tbsp extra virgin olive oil
1 garlic clove
1 fresh bay leaf
2 sprigs fresh thyme

The day before you plan to cook the venison, place it in a bowl with the marinade ingredients. Mix together, then cover and leave in the fridge for 24 hours.

When you are ready to cook, heat the oil in a heavy-based saucepan and sauté the pancetta for 2–3 minutes, until just starting to brown. Lower the heat, add the onions and cook until softened.

Using a slotted spoon, transfer the venison to the saucepan, turning it in the oil to seal it. Pour in the wine and boil it fiercely to evaporate the alcohol. This takes 4–5 minutes, and you can tell by sniffing the vapours: the alcohol will no longer catch the back of your throat.

Add all the marinade juices and the tomatoes, then cover and cook slowly until the venison is tender, about 2 hours, depending on how well hung the venison was. Add a splash of water if needed. Check the seasoning.

Serve with boiled potatoes or Olive oil mashed potatoes and Creamed celeriac purée (see pages 262 and 271).

Roasted pheasant with apple and prune stuffing

fagiano arosto farcito di mele e prugne

It is a joke in Italy that everything that flies has been shot to eat and there are no birds left. I don't think that is strictly true, but I do know that lots of well-heeled Italians come to Scotland for the shooting season and love shooting our game and drinking good whisky. In our family we don't have a big tradition of eating game, but Eoghan, my Francesca's boyfriend, goes shooting a lot, so no doubt we will have to learn.

The female pheasant is the best and can be identified by her smaller body and shorter tail. The birds need to be hung as long as 15 days before being drawn and plucked, so I would get Eoghan to do it...or the butcher!

150 g new-season Agen prunes, stoned
3–4 tbsp Marsala, for soaking
4 cooking apples, peeled, cored and sliced
2 tbsp medium oatmeal
sugar, to taste
2 hen pheasants, plucked and cleaned
knob of unsalted butter
4 slices smoked pancetta
sea salt and freshly ground black pepper

If the prunes are very dry, soak them overnight in Marsala.

Pre-heat the oven to 190°C/375°F/Gas mark 5.

Put the apples in a saucepan over a gentle heat and cook down to a rough purée. Drain the prunes, reserving the Marsala, and mix with the apples. Stir in enough medium oatmeal to bind the mixture for a stuffing. Check the tartness of the mix, adding a little sugar if necessary.

Wash the birds inside and out. Dry with kitchen paper. Season each bird well inside and fill with the stuffing. Close the opening with cocktail sticks and tie the legs together.

Rub the birds with the butter and cover the breast with the pancetta. Place in a roasting dish and cook in the oven for 15 minutes on each side, then turn them breast up for 20 minutes or so. Baste the birds each time you turn them with the juices from the pan and splash with a little of the reserved Marsala. Remove the pancetta for the last 5 minutes or so to crisp the skin.

Transfer the birds to a serving plate and rest in a warm place for about 10 minutes.

Make a gravy with the juices and crusty scrapings from the bottom of the roasting dish. Serve with the carved birds and the stuffing.

Roast duck breasts with roasted beetroot and mustard fruits

petti d'anatra con barbabietole e mostarda di frutta

Per person

2 beetroots
1 Gressingham or Barbary duck breast
¼ tsp sea salt
¼ tsp freshly ground black pepper
¼ tsp Sichuan pepper
2 tbsp extra virgin olive oil
1 tbsp mostarda di frutta with 1 tbsp syrup

Peel the beetroots and cut into quarters. Boil in salted water until tender, about 10–15 minutes. Drain and reserve.

Score the fat of the duck breast with a sharp knife.

Grind the seasonings together using a pestle and mortar. Rub them over the skin of the duck.

Pre-heat the oven to 180°C/350°F/Gas mark 4.

Heat a heavy-based frying pan until hot. Cook the duck breast, skin-side down, for 4 minutes. Turn and cook for another 4 minutes.

Transfer the duck to an ovenproof dish. Toss the cooked beetroots in a little olive oil and add to the dish. Drizzle some of the syrup from the mostarda di frutta over the duck breast. Place in the oven for 15 minutes or so, then allow to rest for 5 minutes before slicing and serving with the mostarda di frutta.

And to drink...

Rustic recipes call for fruity red wines with a casual price tag. Choose something from southern Italy, where the quality is superb but the cost is far less punishing than on famous wines from the north. Puglia, for example, produces fabulous wines that are largely undiscovered outside Italy, even though it has the highest production in the country – about 15 per cent of the national total. One of the region's indigenous grapes, Primitivo, has evolved to become that most 'indigenous' of Californian grapes – Zinfandel. We, however, love the Negroamaro grape, which is found in Salice Salentino, Copertino and Squinzano, all wonderful-flavoured wines and all less than a tenner. Our V&C label, Brindisi Rosso, is inky black, complex, concentrated, packed with ripe, sweet fruit and so, so smooth.

Roast goose with potato and apple stuffing

oca arrosto farcita con patate e mele

Our Christmas lunch is traditional. A large platter of *antipasto* is on the table – prosciutto, bresaola, roasted peperoni, greens, *scarola* – followed by a huge ashet (serving plate) of home-made tagliatelle with a sugo of *polpettini*, Fonteluna sausage and pork. When it is brought to the table, either in my house or my oldest brother Cesidio's, we all cheer and clap. There are at least 20 of us, four or five generations, everybody with an opinion on the quality of the pasta and the cooking time of the sugo. Then, after we have all had seconds – don't tell a soul, promise – we have roast rib of beef and Yorkshire pudding!

There is abundant wine on the table, good wine, and for Auntie Gloria, lemonade, and for any kids under 15, lemonade with a little bit of red wine added (try it – it's lovely).

We tried goose one year, but although we cooked three, there was so little meat (even though the birds looked very big and meaty), there was nearly a riot! If you are having a Christmas lunch for 4–6, roast goose is a lovely alternative to turkey, or roast beef.

Serves 6

1 x 5–6 kg free-range goose, including the liver
sea salt and freshly ground black pepper

For the stuffing
1–2 tbsp olive oil or goose fat
2 red onions, chopped
1.5 kg potatoes, boiled and roughly mashed
2 cooking apples, peeled, cored and chopped
150 g stoned prunes, soaked in port for 30 minutes, drained and port discarded
handful of flatleaf parsley or lemon thyme, chopped

Prepare the goose by washing it well inside and out and trimming off any excess flaps of fat. Dry it with kitchen paper and prick the skin all over with a fork. Season it well inside and out.

Heat the oil in a frying pan and sauté the onions until softened. Chop the goose liver and add to the onions. Cook for 5 minutes.

Put the mashed potatoes and all the other stuffing ingredients in a bowl, add the onion mixture and stir well. Season generously and allow to cool before stuffing the bird, which should be at room temperature.

Pre-heat the oven to 220°C/425°F/Gas mark 7.

Place the goose on a rack inside a deep roasting tray and cook in the oven for 30 minutes. Lower the temperature to 180°C/350°F/Gas mark 4 and cook for a further 2–2½ hours, until the skin is crispy and brown and a skewer inserted in the fattest part of the thigh releases clear juices. (A lot of fat is released during cooking, so carefully drain the tray from time to time, keeping the fat aside for roasting the potatoes.)

Remove the bird from the oven, cover it and leave to stand in a warm place to rest for at least 15 minutes.

Roast potatoes

patate arrosto

1.5 kg Maris Piper or King Edward potatoes (about 4 pieces per person)
3–4 tbsp goose fat
1 large red onion, unpeeled and cut into 6–8 wedges
2 heads garlic, halved horizontally
few sprigs fresh rosemary or thyme

Pre-heat the oven to 220°C/425°F/Gas mark 7.

Par-boil the potatoes in boiling salted water for 10 minutes or so. Drain, then return them to the saucepan and shake a little to roughen their edges.

Heat the goose fat in a roasting tray and add the potatoes, onion, garlic and herbs. Place in the oven for about 25 minutes, until crispy and browned all over.

Brussels sprouts with lemon and thyme butter

cavolini di Bruxelles al burro e limone

500–750 g very small Brussels sprouts
knob of unsalted butter
1 garlic clove, finely chopped
shaving of lemon rind
few sprigs fresh thyme
1 tbsp finely chopped flatleaf parsley
squeeze of lemon juice

Cook the sprouts in boiling salted water until al dente. Drain and refresh in cold water to keep them bright green.

Melt the butter in a large frying pan and add all the remaining ingredients except the lemon juice. Turn the sprouts in the warm butter and fry gently for 15 minutes or so, until the sprouts are warmed through and starting to brown. Add the parsley and a good squeeze of lemon juice and serve.

Carrots baked with Parmigiano Reggiano

carote al Parmigiano Reggiano

750 g carrots
knobs of unsalted butter
2–3 tbsp fresh breadcrumbs
3–4 tbsp freshly grated Parmigiano Reggiano
freshly ground black pepper

Pre-heat the oven to 200°C/400°F/Gas mark 6.

Roughly chop the carrots and boil them in salted water until soft. Drain, mash well and add a generous knob of butter and some black pepper.

Pour the carrots into an ovenproof dish and sprinkle with the breadcrumbs and a good grating of Parmigiano Reggiano. Add another knob of butter and bake in the oven for 15 minutes, until the topping is browned and crispy.

Roasted squash with fontina and herbs

zucca al forno con fontina e erbe

2 winter squash, preferably boat-shaped
2–3 tbsp extra virgin olive oil, plus extra for drizzling
1–2 tbsp fresh rosemary or thyme leaves
200 g fontina cheese
2 tbsp fresh breadcrumbs
freshly grated Parmigiano Reggiano
sea salt and freshly ground black pepper

Pre-heat the oven to 230°C/450°F/Gas mark 8.

Slice the squash in half lengthways and scoop out the seeds. Cut out the flesh and chop it into cubes. Set aside the empty 'shells'.

Toss the cubes in a bowl with the oil, salt, plenty of black pepper and the herbs. Transfer to a baking sheet and roast until soft and gooey, about 20–25 minutes.

Pile the squash into the scooped-out shells, drizzle with a little olive oil and top with grated fontina. Grate some more black pepper over it, then add a sprinkling of breadcrumbs and some Parmigiano Reggiano. Finish cooking under a hot grill or in the oven for a further 10 minutes to melt the cheese.

The olive harvest

More than any other ingredient imported from Italy, the oil extracted from olives has had the greatest influence on British cooking and eating habits. Encouraged by health officials for its health-giving properties, for once we accept their advice – probably because it just tastes so good!

Grown in the Mediterranean for thousands of years, the ripe fruit of the olive tree is harvested from late autumn through to early winter. The best and most delicious oils are made in single estates pressed from olives picked by hand at their peak. Ladders are balanced against the gnarled trunks, and the farmers, their families and itinerant olive harvesters climb into the silvery, dusty green branches to pick the fruits. Large nets are stretched under the trees to collect any that fall.

The olives are then pressed immediately, either on the farm or at the local mill. Any stray leaves and branches are removed and the olives are squashed between gargantuan stones, just as they have been for hundreds of years. The resulting paste is layered in a press and the 'extra virgin' olive oil is extracted. The water is siphoned off and put back into the soil as natural fertilisation. The olive stones are dried and used as fuel in the winter. Nothing is wasted.

This unadulterated method of extraction results in the highly prized single-estate cold-pressed extra virgin olive oil. If the olives were of the correct ripeness and were undamaged when picked, the resulting acidity of the oil will be less than 1 per cent, which classifies it as extra virgin. The style, flavour, colour and character of the oil, like wine, will depend on the type of olive pressed, the terrain and region – as well as the country – and the weather pattern of the growing season.

The flavour of the oil when first pressed is quite startling, creating a burning sensation at the back of the throat. As the oil matures, the flavour mellows and becomes more balanced and seductive. We recommend you use oil within a year to

VALVONA &
FIOR'
EXTRA VIRGIN
DOP TERRA DI BARI
NET 250 ML

€URO
€URO

18 months of pressing and store it in a cool, dark place. Select oil with a harvest date on it; this that determines how long the oil will be at its best, not the date it was bottled.

We recommend using single-estate oils for drizzling over salads and grilled meats and fish. The big-flavoured, spicy, peppery Tuscan oils are ideal for this purpose.

Ligurian extra virgin oil is light, elegant and fruity, and is ideal for using in spring and summer. It's wonderful for making pesto as the fruity notes perfectly match the full aroma of fresh basil.

In the Caffè Bar kitchen and at home we use Fior Fiore extra virgin olive oil from Puglia for cooking and salads. This is sweet and mellow but with a full flavour. We also select oils from Sicily, which are extremely fruity and light, and from Abruzzo, which are creamy, rich and quite fiery in flavour.

Our best-selling Tuscan oil is made by the Zyw family at Poggio Lamentano, which we have been selling for over 30 years. Indeed, Elizabeth David wrote about it in her first edition of *Italian Food* (Macdonald, 1954), citing it as one of the best extra virgin olive oils she had ever tasted, and even cited Valvona & Crolla as a supplier!

Olive oils, as opposed to extra virgin olive oils, are good for deep-frying. These are produced using chemical extraction from a mixture of olives from more than one producer, and often from more than one country. They do not have the high health benefits that are associated with unprocessed extra virgin oils but are still low in cholesterol and unhealthy fats.

When we were children Mum always put a tumbler of celery sticks on the table and a plate of olive oil to which she had added salt and pepper. We fought to dip the celery in the oil. Known as *pizimonio*, it is a traditional way of tasting the newest pressed olive oil prepared all over Italy and in the south of France. Cut fresh, crisp vegetables, such as celery, fennel, carrot and chicory into finger-sized strips. Pour some single-estate extra virgin olive oil into a shallow bowl and season with sea salt and freshly ground black pepper. Simply dip the vegetables into the oil and eat.

Pan-fried wild halibut with roasted fennel

ippoglosso a taglio con finocchio arrosto

We get wonderful North Sea wild halibut in Scotland, landed from the end of August through to the start of the breeding season in early spring. It is at its best during this time, but the price goes up in January and February when the seas are often rough and the boats may not fish. There are halibut farms, but they don't do us any favours. Our fishmonger, Gavin at Armstrong's in Edinburgh, explained to me that you can tell a farmed halibut as it will have a lot of slime around it, the belly is never pure white as a wild one is, and (absurdly) it stays fresh longer than a wild one, suggesting some preservative in its system.

The wild halibut, the largest of the flat fish, is a predator of crustacea in the sea, resulting in very sweet, 'clean' and full-flavoured flesh. Catfish and monkfish also eat crustacea, and are also firm and sweet-flavoured for the same reason.

We often get the halibut cut into steaks and pan-fry it lightly. With quality extra virgin olive oil and good raw ingredients, you can easily re-create in your own home those Mediterranean flavours that entice you on holiday.

4 x 180 g wild halibut steaks
2–3 tbsp seasoned plain flour
2–3 tbsp extra virgin olive oil
2 unwaxed lemons, preferably Amalfi
2–3 tbsp finely chopped flatleaf parsley

For the roasted fennel
2 large fennel bulbs
extra virgin olive oil, for drizzling
2–3 tbsp finely chopped flatleaf parsley
sea salt

Pre-heat the oven to 220°C/425°F/Gas mark 7.

Cut the fennel in half, discarding the outside leaves and core. Chop the fronds and set aside.

Slice the fennel finely and place on a shallow baking sheet. Drizzle with plenty of the oil and season well with salt. Roast in the oven for 25 minutes. Before serving, drizzle with the warm oil from the roasting tray and sprinkle with the parsley.

Meanwhile, wash the halibut and pat dry with kitchen paper. Dip the pieces in the seasoned flour.

Heat the oil in a frying pan and fry the fish on a lively heat so that it is sealed and crispy on the outside but lightly cooked inside – about 6–8 minutes (don't overcook). Drain on kitchen paper and sprinkle with salt.

Place the halibut on warm plates and squeeze ¼ lemon over each piece. Put some roasted fennel alongside and spoon its juices over the fish. Sprinkle with the fennel fronds and parsley. Serve with wedges of the remaining lemon.

Grilled fish

pesce alla griglia

I can smell the black, charred crispy skin of this moist juicy fish as I write – so easy to make, but brilliant, the essence of good Mediterranean cooking.

500 g whole fish per person (trout, sea bream, red mullet), gutted and scaled.
extra virgin olive oil, to drizzle
sprigs fresh thyme, dill or fennel fronds
1 unwaxed lemon, preferably Amalfi
sea salt

Pre-heat a ridged griddle pan or grill.

Wash and dry the fish, then score the skin with a sharp knife. Rub inside and out with the oil and salt. Stuff the herbs into the cavity of the fish.

Place the fish on the griddle and allow the skin to get crispy before turning it; if you try to turn it too soon, it will stick, so hold your nerve and wait until the skin blackens and lifts naturally from the griddle. Turn and cook the other side until crisp, then lower the heat to allow the fish to cook through without drying out. It is cooked when the flesh becomes opaque: push a knife near the bone to open the flesh and check.

Squeeze lemon juice over the fish and tilt the griddle to flame it. Serve drizzled with some more olive oil.

And to drink...

Big-flavoured, oily fish, such as sardines, bass and bream that are grilled as above, call for a white wine that will stand up to them, but is not so heavily oaked that they 'talk back' and compete for attention. One of our favourites is Bianco di Custoza Amedeo, produced on the Cavalchina estate, west of Lake Garda. The hand-picked grapes are lightly crushed to extract the richest, purest juice. After fermentation, the wine is aged in oak barriques (casks) to amplify and concentrate the fruit. Despite its modest price, its stunning quality gains it frequent accolades, including the top prize, *tre bicchieri* (three glasses), in the Italian Slow Food wine challenge, Gambero Rosso. It vies with Spicogna Pinot Grigio (see page 89) as the favourite white of our most discerning clients.

Another favourite is made by Nino Pieropan, arguably the finest exponent of classic Soave. The Garganega grapes that Pieropan grows in La Rocca vineyard, next to the *castello* in the heart of the village of Soave, are from ancient vines, and under his care produce a fragrant, mouth-filling, rich, concentrated and balanced Soave, a wine for long ageing, certainly drinking well after two or three years.

These wines are also good with autumn treats, such as Roasted squash with fontina and herbs and Mushroom risotto (see pages 286 and 258).

Oven-roasted sardines

sarde al forno

Sardines are cheap and cheerful, but leave a very strong smell all round the house. Best cook them outside on a barbecue, or invest in some strong air freshener!

3–4 fresh sardines per person, gutted, washed and dried
extra virgin olive oil, for drizzling
handful of mixed fresh herbs, such as parsley, bay leaves, lemon thyme and sorrel
sea salt and freshly ground black pepper
2 lemons, cut into wedges, to serve

Pre-heat the oven to 200°C/400°F/Gas mark 6.

Using a sharp knife, score the skin of the sardines 3 or 4 times on both sides. Rub inside and out with plenty of the oil, salt and pepper, then stuff with a mixture of the herbs.

Place the fish in an ovenproof dish and bake for about 20 minutes, until well cooked and the skin is charred and crispy. Serve with lemon wedges.

Roast pumpkin wedges

zucca al forno

In the autumn we decorate the shop with all shapes and sizes of spectacular pumpkins, gourds and squash. We have an ethos that although they look stunning, they must still be good to eat, so the only ones left after Halloween are the plastic ones with candles inside!

1 pumpkin
extra virgin olive oil, for drizzling
sea salt

Pre-heat the oven to 230°C/450°F/Gas mark 8.

Cut the pumpkin into thin, melon-like slices and peel off the skin. Toss the pumpkin in some oil and salt, then place in a roasting tray. Roast in the oven for 25–30 minutes, until soft and caramelised around the edges.

Aged pecorino

In the latter part of the year the pecorino (sheep's milk) cheeses that were made in the spring are reaching their peak. These are classified as 'mature'. Some cheeses are made specifically to be eaten young, like Marzolino or Castegnolo from Tuscany, which are eaten at about 40 days old and taste like delicious creamy butter. These are classified as 'fresh'.

Other pecorinos are made traditionally to survive the winter and are matured for 6–9 months, being at their best from October onwards. These are semi-hard, full flavoured, tasting almost of apricots, and still moist to eat. Our favourite is Tinaio, a cheese produced in the Oristano province of Sardinia from a select Sardinian breed of sheep reared in the wild. Made by traditional methods in limited quantities, the cheese begins life in the form of pasteurised curds, about 2 kg, which are bathed in brine, then aged on wooden boards for about five months.

Our other favourite is Canestrato pecorino from Puglia, which owes its name to the hand-made reed baskets in which it is set to ripen. The reeds lend a sweet taste to the cheese and also produce its signature crinkled rind. Creamy, full flavoured, with the sharp tang of sheep's milk, this is especially good with autumn fruit.

Aged pecorino with honey, pear and pine nuts

pecorino stagionato con mele, pere e pinoli

The combination of cheese and fruit is a classic one. Pears are particularly good with pecorino, but are also delicious with creamy robiola, which arrives at this time of year from the Bergamo area. We also serve either with figs that are dried in vine leaves.

Per person

125 g pecorino stagionato or robiola cheese
2 tsp millefiori honey
2 tsp toasted pine nuts
½ Comice pear, quartered and cored

Cut the pecorino into thick triangles, keeping the skin on. Place on a plate and drizzle the honey over the cheese. Sprinkle with toasted pine nuts and serve with the pear.

LA FRUTTA GUSTOLOSA
VIGNOLA
LA FRUTTA GUSTOLOSA
NERI
VIGNOLA

Sautéd Italian pears in Barbaresco

pere al Barbaresco

Comice pears are so good at this time of year. This recipe is adapted from a dessert of bananas sautéd in butter, sugar and rum which my mother-in-law, Olivia, used to make. It is deadly and delicious!

4 slightly under-ripe Comice pears
knob of unsalted butter
6 tbsp demerara sugar
2 fresh bay leaves
450 ml Barbaresco or other full-bodied red wine

Wash the pears and cut lengthways into eighths, trimming away the core but leaving the stalk.

Heat the butter in a wide, shallow frying pan. Add the pears in a single layer and cook until they brown a little on each side.

Add the sugar and bay leaves, then pour over the wine. Cook for about 20 minutes, until the pears are easily pierced with a skewer but still firm. The wine will have reduced to a gorgeous syrup.

Serve warm with some whipped mascarpone flavoured with orange peel.

Torino; capital of caffès and chocolate

The home of FIAT (Fattoria Italia Automobile Torino) since the late 1890s, Torino has been the industrial powerhouse of Italy and the brand leader in religious artefacts. But long before cars and shrouds, Torino was famous for far more convivial things – its caffès and chocolate. The former were designed and built when Torino was French, so they are exquisite and palatial, dripping with Venetian chandeliers and lined with hand-crafted wood and Carrara marble. The grand caffès of the 18th century were the meeting places of aristocrats, poets and philosophers of the day.

Italy's first prime minister, the Conte di Cavour, was known to hang out in the Caffè al Bicerin in Piazza Consolata, waiting to catch the king on his way out of Mass in the Sanctuary opposite. The rest of the Catholic faithful, having fasted from the night before, would also pour into the caffès and order an espresso with cream – *pur e fiur*, an espresso with hot chocolate – *pur e barba*, or a small heated glass with all three – *n poc de tut*. The famous *bicerin* was the Conte di Cavour's favourite – an exquisite combination of chocolate, coffee and cream.

Years later the *bicerin* habit came under threat when, in 1852, due to economic hardship, the young Italian government put a tax on the importation of cocoa. To stretch his cocoa allowance, an enterprising chocolatier, Pierre Paul Caffarel, developed a new recipe that carefully combined cacao solids, cacao butter and sugar with 50 per cent ground hazelnuts. His brilliance was in his business sense; the added ingredient was free, gathered easily from the abundant hazelnut trees all around Torino. He shaped the chocolates like the pointed hat of Gianduia, a Torinese pantomime character, and a brand was born. Deliciously sensuous, the Gianduia is a chocolate to be savoured and enjoyed, just like time spent in the coffee-houses of Torino.

MARTINI
Caffè Torino
BERGUI
PAISSA
TORINO
FIAT
MAJANI
Cremini Assortiti
FIAT
Cremini Assortiti
FIAT
MAJANI

Bicerin coffee

bicerin

The classic caffès in Torino are famous for this chocolate-coffee drink (see page 298).

1–2 tbsp Baratti & Milano cioccolato (chocolate) flakes, or your own favourite brand
75 ml hot water
1 espresso (see page 309)
sugar, to taste
2 tbsp warmed cream or frothed full-fat milk

Mix the cioccolato with the hot water.

Make an espresso and froth the milk, working quickly to keep the drink piping hot.

Pour the espresso into a short tumbler or an Irish coffee glass. Sweeten to taste, then spread the hot cioccolato on top.

Finish off with a layer of thick cream or frothed milk.

Mochaccino with Nutella

mochaccino con la Nutella

Our Baratti & Milano chocolate supplier, Gianni Borgogna, used to work for the Chocolatier Pietro Ferrero and tells a story that during the war the American soldiers billeted in Piemonte had plenty of chocolate. Pietro Ferrero had no chocolate, but plenty of hazelnuts. He did a deal with the Americans and mixed some of their chocolate with his nuts. He then gave the paste to the American quartermaster to spread on bread or toast. The quartermaster came back for more and Nutella was born.

After the war, Ferrero invented a way of mass-producing chocolate, and with brand development and marketing, created a company that within three generations has become one of the biggest confectionery brands in the world. Who hasn't enjoyed a morning croissant spread with gooey, delicious Nutella or a Ferrero Rocher?

Nutella chocolate spread
1 espresso
75 ml full-fat milk
Baratti & Milano cioccolato (chocolate) flakes, or your own favourite brand

Spread some Nutella around the edge of a small glass that has a handle. Pour in the espresso.

Froth the milk and pour into the glass, spooning the froth on top. Sprinkle with cioccolato flakes and serve.

Crêpes with Nutella

crespelle con la Nutella

Bought in any street in Italy at any time of the day or night, these crêpes can easily be made at home. Olivia makes them for her breakfast every morning! She uses a small hand whisk that fits into the measuring jug and the whole job is done in minutes. Easy peasy!

Makes 2

2 tbsp plain flour
1 tbsp caster sugar
1 medium egg
250 ml semi-skimmed milk
unsalted butter, for greasing
Nutella, to serve

Sift the flour into a bowl and mix in the sugar. Whisk the egg, add the milk, then beat into the flour, using a hand-held whisk, to form a batter.

Warm a heavy-based non-stick frying pan. Rub with a block of butter to lightly grease the bottom.

Pour in half the batter and cook until small bubbles appear on the surface. Flip over and cook the other side for 2 minutes. Transfer to a plate and keep warm. Rub the pan with a block of butter again and make the second pancake. (If you prefer to make just one pancake, the leftover batter will keep in the fridge for the next morning.)

Spread the crêpes with Nutella and serve.

Chocolate-covered coffee beans and hazelnuts

chichi di caffè e nocciole coperti di cioccolato

Fancy bags of chocolate-covered coffee beans, nuts and raisins are popular gifts sold all over Italy at a very expensive price. Making them at home is so easy, and much cheaper.

100 g chocolate (minimum 70% cocoa solids), such as Valrhona or Amadei (or Valrhona chocolate infused with orange or coffee extract)
100 g coffee beans
100 g hazelnuts, lightly toasted
3–4 tbsp bitter cocoa powder, icing sugar or ground cinnamon

Melt the chocolate in a heatproof bowl over a saucepan of boiling water. Add the coffee beans and hazelnuts and stir to coat. Gently lift them out with a fork and lay them on waxed paper to cool for a few minutes.

Dust them with the cocoa powder, then leave until cold. Pack in shiny gift bags or eat them yourself!

Fresh cream brandy truffles

tartufi al cioccolato

If we were staying at his house when we were kids, my grandfather, Hugh Hilley, allowed us one sweet from the dish in the lounge if we ate all our supper. All eight of us lived over my father's sweetie shop, so one sweet was no good to us! However, these truffles are so decadent and delicious, one of them might do the trick...though I suspect not.

150 ml double cream
25 g caster sugar
1 egg yolk
200 g chocolate (minimum 70% cocoa solids)
50 g unsalted butter, softened
1 drop pure orange oil (optional)
2 tbsp cognac
bitter cocoa powder, to dust

Place the cream in a medium saucepan and bring to the boil. Remove from the heat.

Whisk the sugar and egg yolk together and add to the cream. Return the saucepan to the heat and heat through gently. Add the chocolate and stir until it has all melted.

Remove from the heat and beat in the butter, orange oil (if using) and cognac. Transfer to a bowl and refrigerate for about 30 minutes. Before the mixture gets too hard, use 2 teaspoons to shape it into balls. Place on a plate and chill until completely hard. Dust with bitter cocoa powder and serve.

Chocolate hazelnut cake

torta di gianduia

200 g unsalted butter
125 g caster sugar
3 large eggs, beaten
1 tbsp grated orange zest
1 tbsp orange flower water
2 tbsp cognac
165 g plain flour, sifted with 1 tsp baking powder and a pinch of salt
165 g ground hazelnuts
4 tbsp flaked chocolate (minimum 70% cocoa solids)
1 tbsp milk
cocoa powder, for dusting

Pre-heat the oven to 180°C/350°F/Gas mark 4. Line and grease a 30-cm spring-form cake tin.

Cream the butter and sugar until light and fluffy. Add the eggs, orange zest, flower water and cognac. Mix in the flour a spoonful at a time to stop the eggs curdling.

Fold in the hazelnuts and chocolate flakes, then add the milk.

Pour the mixture into the prepared tin. Place a roasting tin in the oven and half-fill it with boiling water. Carefully sit the cake tin in the water and bake for 45–50 minutes, until a skewer inserted in the middle comes out clean.

Cool in the tin for 15 minutes or so, then turn out onto a wire rack. Dust with cocoa powder before serving with a blob of cream flavoured with orange flower water and orange zest.

Sienese fruit and spice cake

panforte

At Christmas time the shop fills up to bursting with all manner of delicious goodies from all over Italy. Gorgeous piles of whole glacé fruits from Sicily; evocative-smelling dried figs wrapped in tobacco leaves; gaudy whole marzipan fruits; French prunes stuffed with prune paste: crunchy *torrone* (nougat) and glamorously packaged panettone (sponge cake).

Long awaited is *panforte* (literally 'spicy bread'), the ancient Christmas cake of Siena, smelling enticingly of dried fruit and vanilla sugar. It comes in huge 20 kg slabs, which we slice to order and wrap in a variety of packaging. You can try to make your own at home.

200 g chopped candied peel
50 g ground almonds
100 g roasted almonds, crushed
150 g glacé fruits (these add moistness to the panforte)
3 tsp ground cinnamon
1 tsp ground mixed spice
pinch of freshly ground white pepper
generous pinch ground mace
90 g plain flour, sifted
100 g clear honey
100 g caster sugar
drop of natural vanilla essence or 1 tsp orange water
icing sugar, for dusting

Pre-heat the oven to 160°C/325°F/Gas mark 3. Grease a 15-cm shallow round tin and line with rice paper.

Mix together the peel, nuts, fruits, spices and flour in a large bowl.

Warm the honey and caster sugar in a medium saucepan over a low heat and, when the sugar has dissolved, bring just to the boil and mix into the bowl. Add the vanilla essence or orange water and mix again.

Spoon the mixture into the prepared tin and flatten down. Bake for 35–40 minutes. Cool on a wire rack and dust with icing sugar.

The cake will keep for a couple of months if wrapped in a double layer of foil and stored in a cool dry place.

White Christmas cake

torta di natale in bianco

This recipe came from a friend of my mother, and lots of people ask me for it. It's lighter than the usual rich Christmas cake because it contains glacé fruits instead of currants and raisins. I like to coat it with a simple vanilla butter icing and decorate it with brightly coloured French glacé fruits and a fine gold ribbon swathed around its sides. It will look so beautiful you might not want to eat it!

100 g mixed peel
100 g glacé angelica
100 g glacé cherries (green or yellow)
100 g chopped crystallised ginger
100 g crystallised pineapple
100 g walnuts (make sure they are not rancid)
100 g almonds
275 g plain flour, sifted, plus a little extra
225 g unsalted butter
225 g unrefined caster sugar
5 large eggs
grated rind of 1 unwaxed lemon
½ tsp almond essence
3–4 drops natural vanilla essence
1 tsp baking powder
pinch of salt
1 tbsp milk

For the icing
50 g unsalted butter, softened
few drops natural vanilla essence
pinch of salt
150–200 g icing sugar, sifted

Roughly chop all the fruit and nuts, then coat them in a little of the flour.

Cream the butter and sugar until light and fluffy. Beat the eggs in a separate bowl and gradually add them to the creamed mixture, adding a tablespoon of flour to stop the mixture splitting. Mix in the fruit, rind and essences, then fold in the sifted flour, baking powder and salt. Mix well, adding the milk to moisten the mixture.

Pout into the prepared tin and bake for 2½–3 hours. The cake is cooked when it starts to shrink from the sides of the tin and a skewer inserted in the middle comes out clean. Transfer to a wire rack once it has cooled in the tin. Keep the paper on until you are ready to ice it.

To make the icing, beat the butter until light and creamy. Add the vanilla and salt to the icing sugar and gradually beat into the butter. Add a little hot water to adjust the consistency of the icing and make it spreadable. Beat it well to make it smooth.

Using a palate knife dipped in boiling water, smooth the icing over the cake, coating the top and sides. Decorate as you wish.

Established 1934
CROLLA

Carlo's blend

If you walked down Elm Row in Edinburgh during the 1950s and 1960s, an exotic, pungent aroma of roasting coffee would assault your nostrils. Carlo Contini, Philip's father, was the man in charge of coffee. Our coffee was developed from a blend of Arabica and Robusta beans from different countries, making a particular flavour unique to Valvona & Crolla. The coffee was roasted in the shop throughout the day. Carlo often over-roasted the beans, but – ever the salesman – sold them as Special High Roast, which is still our best-selling coffee today.

The coffee has to be cooled after it is roasted, and the oils that are thrown off have to be piped and cooled away from the source. This was all very easy unless Carlo went off for an extended break, or talked too long to a pretty lady. In that case, the coffee-roaster occasionally caught fire. The fire brigade didn't mind being called out every so often as they too were addicted to Carlo's high-roast coffee. Eventually, of course, it had to stop, and now we have our coffee freshly roasted for us and prepared to this day to Carlo's original specifications.

If you are hooked on espresso and want to make your own at home, I would suggest investing in a professional machine, preferably an Italian brand...they know what they are doing after all. I have had a Gaggia at home for years and it works a treat.

A cheaper option is a Bialetti coffee-maker. It makes the coffee by pushing the steam from boiling water up through the ground coffee by natural force – pretty ingenious. This produces a good-flavoured coffee but not a true espresso.

An authentic espresso should be short, intense and with a soft *crema* on top, just enough to make you feel the smooth texture. It must be served in the right type of espresso cup – narrower at the bottom and preferably made of thick, old-fashioned porcelain. Oh, and the cup must be warmed! Even better in my book is *caffè stretto*, a very short espresso that will knock your socks off. Your shout!

Baked alaska

gelato e meringa

If anything, this is my favourite dessert to serve on Christmas Day! It's so easy but pretty spectacular: ice cream sits on a sponge base and is coated in a meringue mixture, which is cooked in a hot oven to create a hot, crispy crust enclosing cool, refreshing ice cream. You can make the sponge base yourself, as below, but a ready-made 25-cm flan case is perfectly acceptable.

2 tbsp dry sherry
fresh fruit of your choice to cover the base of the sponge, e.g. mango, banana, mixed berries
1 litre vanilla ice cream, partly frozen
caster sugar, for sprinkling

For the sponge base
2 large eggs
70 g caster sugar
70 g self-raising flour

For the meringue
4 egg whites
225 g caster sugar

Line and grease a 23-cm round baking tin. Pre-heat the oven to 180°C/350°F/Gas mark 4.

To make the sponge base, whisk the eggs and sugar together until they are light and fluffy. Sift the flour into the mixture and fold in lightly, using a large metal spoon.

Spoon into the prepared tin and bake for 20–25 minutes, until the cake is lightly browned and a skewer inserted in the centre comes out clean. Remove from the oven and leave to cool on a wire rack.

When you're ready to assemble the Baked Alaska, pre-heat the oven to 230°C/450°F/Gas mark 8.

To make the meringue, whisk the egg whites in a clean bowl until they are fluffed up and stiff. Gradually add the sugar, whisking until it is all incorporated.

Place the sponge base on a decorative ovenproof dish. Sprinkle with the sherry and layer with the fruit.

Pile the ice cream on top of the fruit, spooning it into a dome shape. Cover the whole thing with the meringue mixture, being very careful to seal the ice cream and all the edges: there must be no holes or gaps.

Sprinkle the meringue with a generous amount of caster sugar. If you wish, it can be frozen at this stage and baked from frozen when required. In this case, leave it at room temperature for 15 minutes or so before baking it.

Bake in the oven for 5–10 minutes, until the meringue is crispy and its peaks slightly browned. Serve immediately.

Polenta cake

torta di polenta

This recipe is gluten-free and, as such, is probably one of our most requested. It is adapted from a recipe by Rose Gray and Ruth Rogers from the River Cafe.

450 g unsalted butter
450 g caster sugar
450 g ground almonds
6 eggs
juice of 1 lemon
zest of 2 lemons
zest of 2 oranges
250 g fine polenta flour
125 g coarse polenta flour
1½ tsp baking powder
good pinch of salt

Pre-heat the oven to 180°C/350°F/Gas mark 4. Line and grease a 30-cm baking tin.

Beat the butter and sugar together until light and fluffy. Stir in the ground almonds. Add the eggs, lemon juice and both types of zest.

Combine the polenta flours, baking powder and salt, then add to the butter mixture a spoonful at a time, mixing slowly so as not to curdle the eggs.

Pour the mixture into the prepared tin and bake in the oven for 40–45 minutes, until a skewer inserted in the middle comes out clean. Allow to cool in the tin for 15 minutes or so before turning out the cake on to a wire rack. Once cold, it can be wrapped in foil and kept for up to 6 days.

Panettone and Asti Spumante

The big nostalgic treat for all our customers at the festive period is a panettone and a bottle of Asti Spumante. A traditional celebratory cake, the panettone dates back to Roman times, but it was a Milanese baker, Angelo Motta, who, in 1919, started its production and packaging that led to it becoming a major Italian brand. Motta changed what had been a traditional leavened bread with candied peel into the dome-shaped cake we know today by raising it three times. For this reason, it takes at least 20 hours to make and is not something we would advise you to do at home!

The Alemagna company followed Motta in 1925, and until the 1990s, when Nestlé bought out both brands, there was a huge market for both. The success of panettone lay in its availability to the Italian immigrant population across the world, and in Britain, North America and South America it became the symbol of Italy on the Christmas tables of hundreds of millions of families.

Today we import our own brand of panettone from a small baker outside Milan, and it has taken over as our customers' panettone of choice. The favoured drink to serve it with is Moscato d'Asti, a light, semi-sparkling wine, slightly honeyed, but clean and fresh with the vanilla-flavoured cake.

To be honest, having eaten so much on Christmas Day, the panettone is often merely tasted and left aside. It is the next day that it is best enjoyed – toasted with warm butter for breakfast or, if it's a late start, as described in the following recipe.

'French toast' panettone

panettone in carrozza

This is a variation of classic French toast dipped in egg and fried in oil. *In carrozza* means 'in a carriage', and refers I suppose to the panettone being carried. You can get all sorts of things *in carrozza* – mozzarella, melanzane – but panettone is the best!

2 eggs, beaten
3–4 tbsp sunflower oil or light olive oil
8 slices panettone, about 3 cm thick
sea salt
icing sugar and cinnamon, for dusting

Beat the eggs in a shallow soup plate and add a pinch of salt.

Heat the oil in a frying pan. Dip the slices of panettone in the egg, coating each side. Place in the frying pan and cook over quite a high heat until crispy on each side. (The high heat cooks the egg quickly and seals the panettone, preventing it from absorbing all the oil.)

Drain on kitchen paper and serve hot, dusted with icing sugar and some cinnamon.

A way of life

DECEMBER IN VALVONA & CROLLA is the most demanding month: manic, busy, stressful and rewarding. Goods come in at the back door and out the front door at great speed and with huge excitement. When it is all over we reflect with gratitude and humility.

In the aftermath of the pandemonium that is Christmas and New Year's Eve, the shop is cloaked in a weary silence. Intense aromas of roasted coffee, ripe cheese and pungent salami linger heavily in the air. Shelves groan with relief, their burden willingly dispatched to countless homes around the country. Uncompleted paperwork flutters in defiance of any accountant, tills flip open, their job completed for another year.

Philip and I have worked in the shop for over thirty years. The satisfaction of the job is not in the elusive profit or accolades that come and go. It is definitely not in the heavy workload and long, exhausting hours. For us the real joy is in the trading – the searching for gems of undiscovered food and wine, the phone call from a supplier with news of a harvest or bottling, the unmarked parcels arriving mysteriously at the back door, and the fun of sharing the enclosed delights enthusiastically and generously with anyone who wants to participate. For more than seventy-five Christmases and Hogmanays, the parcels have been arriving, the excitement has been maintained. And, who can count the hundreds of thousands of customers who have queued in front of the long, narrow counters to be served – many regarding Valvona & Crolla as much a part of their life as it is of ours?

A year's trading is a constant journey of exploration and discovery, and so far, believe me, we have always ended up surprised by the turn of events, which are rarely what we expect or plan for. Never a dull moment is an understatement!

Locking up the shop last thing on New Year's Eve generates a profound sense of achievement. The last customer of the year has gone, happily clutching bags stuffed with last-minute goodies, bottles of Prosecco and half-price Christmas sweeties. Managers and staff, elated but exhausted, have kissed and hugged each other, crumpled aprons tucked into their bags, panettone and Asti Spumante thrust into their arms, doors slammed behind them, relieved it is all over.

Once again, we have survived and, as Uncle Victor would have said, 'we've done the business'. We've seen births, marriages, romances and divorces. We've traded mozzarella from Naples, oranges from Sicily and mushrooms from Perthshire. We've served Alba truffles, Lanarkshire milk-fed lamb and scallops from the west coast. On the menu we've had fish on Fridays, pancakes on Shrove Tuesday and no meat at all on Good Friday! We've had Scots eating polenta and Italians eating haggis! And in our small way, like the grand caffès of Torino, we've seen plotting and planning from all walks of life – prime ministers, archbishops, princesses, authors and stars.

And, just as the party is not over until the fat lady sings, we lock up Elm Row, change into our glad-rags and head off to VinCaffè in Multrees Walk for our Hogmanay dinner and party with 'Philip Contini and his Be Happy Band'. We round off the year in style – counting down to the New Year, popping Champagne corks and joining in with our loyal customers and friends, singing and dancing and partying till dawn!

As the message that pops up on Philip's computer screen every morning says, 'Valvona & Crolla, not so much a deli, more a way of life!'.

Index

Acknowledgements

The Directors of Valvona & Crolla Ltd. would like to thank all those who have contributed to the production of this book: everyone at Ebury Press, especially Imogen Fortes, Carey Smith and Fiona MacIntyre; Vanessa Courtier for her wonderful photography and design; Karolina Sutton, our agent, and Kate Jones, who was so unique.

To all the people who have worked in the kitchens, cafes, bakery and shop with so much tenacity and good humour, thank you.

To all producers, suppliers and customers: you are the inspiration, joy and lifeblood of the company.